I0063998

Advance Praise for

Once Upon A Claim

"Number 1 Best Seller—Non-Fiction" — *Brothers Grimm News*

"CHANTAL ROBERTS IS a genius storyteller with a true talent for making insurance interesting." — *The Enchanted Quill*

"THE ABSOLUTE truth about insurance!"
— *Puppet Masters Quarterly*

"Meet Goldilocks, the new MASTER OF interior design!"
— *Home Intruder Weekly*

"The Genie: GRANTING knowledge on claims!"
— *Magicians Monthly*

"The Pig Brothers are the EXPERT in structural integrity!"
— *Builders Quarterly*

"Despite being about INSURANCE,
this book kept me awake!" — Sleeping Beauty

"Mirror, mirror on the wall, *Once Upon A Claim*
gives the fairest ADVICE of them all!" — *Mirror^2*

Snow White and the Seven Dwarfs
Jack and Jill
Old Woman Who Lived in a Shoe
Three Little Pigs
Little Miss Muffet
Dells
Mama Duck
Chicken Little
Mother Hubbard's House
VA Meeting
NEWS
Little Red Riding Hood's Grandma's Bistro
BISTRO
Cobbler
Hospital
POLICE
The Fallen Sparrow Tavern
Puppet
THEATRE
University
Courthouse
London Bridge
Fairytale Land Map

Queen Mary
Princess and the Pea
Bearskin
King Cole
Lingxiu
Three Bears' Home
Rapunzel's Tower
Sleeping Beauty
Kleinlandje
Rock of Kanamé
The Practical Bride
Ugly Duckling
Mary's Little Lamb
Humpty Dumpty
Kosala
Goldilocks' House
Baa Baa, Black Sheep
Jack and the Beanstalk
Kaukaban
Howling Desert
Three Spinning Women
The Shahzadi in the Suit of Leather

Once Upon a Claim

Fairy Tales to Protect Your Ass(ets)

by Chantal M. Roberts

Tilting at Windmills Press, Overland Park, KS

ISBN
Print: 978-1-7374268-5-1; E-Book: 978-1-7374268-6-8; Audio: 978-1-7374268-7-5

Library of Congress Control Number
2024934157

Disclaimer

I am not an attorney. The information in this book does not convey any legal or professional advice of any kind. This publication is designed to provide accurate and dependable information regarding the subject matter covered and be a source of valuable information for the reader. Each insurer handles their claims differently, and readers should keep in mind this book is intended for informational purposes only. It is sold with the understanding that the publisher and the author assume no responsibility for errors, inaccuracies, omissions, or any other inconsistencies herein.

The opinions expressed in this book are those of the author.

Nothing in this book is intended to recommend a specific course of action. If specific information is needed, please consult with an attorney. The author's opinions may change based on the specific circumstances of the situation. The coverage discussions are based on the standardized ISO policy forms.

The sample scenarios are an amalgamation of real claims. Since all depict combinations of two or more claims, all examples are fictitious. Any similarity to actual persons, living or dead, is coincidental.

Indemnity

You agree to defend, indemnify, and hold harmless the author and the copyright holder(s) from and against all the liabilities, claims, damages, and expenses (including reasonable attorney's fees and costs) arising out of your use of this material; your breach or alleged breach of this agreement; or your breach or alleged breach of the copyright, trademark, proprietary or other rights of the author or copyright holder(s).

For information, please contact:
Chantal M. Roberts, CPCU, AIC, RPA
editor@tiltingatwindmillspress.com

Printed in the United States of America

Book Cover Design by Chantal M. Roberts
Illustrations: Clint Lander De Jose, Chantal M. Roberts, Laura Orsini, and AI text-to-image generators
Interior Design by Laura Orsini, Panoply Publishing LLC

Mr. De Jose can be reached at: Clintlander26@gmail.com, facebook.com/In2kk.illust, Instagram.com/lander2kk.

The Art of Adjusting: Writing Down the Unwritten Rules of Claims Handling

A Love Story:
How the Heartland Fell in Love
With a 400-Year-Old French Comedic Playwright

Acknowledgments

The author would like to thank:

Mary Teodosio

Felicia Londré

Sayanti Puckett

Vampire

Lauren Cella

Clint Lander De Jose

Jason Billington

Virginia Phillips

Aaron Roberts

Table of Contents

Once upon a time, there was an adjuster who, through a series of misfortunes and to keep herself sane during a global pandemic, wrote a book to help mid-career adjusters handle their claims in a more efficient and professional manner.

Because the adjuster was vain and cared what others thought of her, she hired an editor who knew next to nothing about insurance. The editor had many questions and learned a great deal from the adjuster while the adjuster learned a great deal from the editor's suggestions for her first book.

The adjuster realized that the world of insurance can be intimidating and overwhelming to those outside the industry. She made it her mission to demystify the process and provide readers with the knowledge and tools needed to advocate for themselves. The adjuster set out to write a new book and to share it with a wider audience—this time, with laypeople in mind.

So it came to pass through a series of fables and real-world examples, a book that takes readers on a journey through the insurance claims process. With a touch of humor and a healthy dose of practical advice via the Morals of the Stories, readers will gain the confidence needed to navigate the complex and often overwhelming world of insurance claims.

This book is for the insured homeowner dealing with property damage, a businessowner facing liability claims, or simply someone looking to better understand the insurance industry.

But be careful, dear readers, as there are many different insurers, each with their own policies and ways of doing things. Just like the seven dwarfs who each has his own unique personality and quirks, seven different insurers could interject seven different opinions, rules, and methods into insurance policies and claims. Therefore, readers should be aware that the author must speak in general terms. Just as Goldilocks has to choose between three different bowls of porridge, each with their own temperature and texture, the author must provide information that is applicable to a broad range of insurance policies and claims-handling practices—neither too broad nor too narrow.

Please remember that while this book provides valuable insights into the world of insurance claims handling, various insurers may interpret and handle claims differently. The information provided in this book should be used as a general guide, and readers should always refer to their own policy documents and consult with their insurer or legal advisor for specific advice.

This book is divided into several sections, much like the division of the kingdom of Fairytale Land into different provinces.

The first section of the book discusses insurance policies in general, providing readers with a broad overview of the insurance world. Just like the king's advisors who provide counsel on matters of state, this section of the book is full of valuable information to guide readers through the claims-handling process.

The second section of the book focuses on property policies, much like the landowners who tend to their fields and crops. This section delves into the details of property damage claims and how to navigate the complex world of property insurance.

The third section of the book reviews liability or casualty insurance, which is much like the knights who defend the kingdom from harm. This section provides insights into the world of liability claims.

The fourth section of the book concerns auto losses, much like the horses and carriages that travel throughout Fairytale Land. This section covers everything from fender benders to total losses and provides readers with the knowledge needed to navigate the world of auto insurance claims.

Finally, the last section of the book examines miscellaneous things that affect all claims. This section covers a variety of topics, including the claims process, fraud, and settlement negotiations.

Throughout the book, readers will also find fables and rhymes that can illustrate several points. Just like the town crier who announces news and events, these tales and rhymes provide a fun and engaging way to learn about the world of insurance. To help readers find specific topics quickly, the author placed these fables in the section that relates to the primary point. For example, *Patty Cake, Patty Cake* discusses not only adjuster bonuses but also insurers' use of money for investment. The reader is encouraged, therefore, to see the Index of Morals if looking for a specific topic.

Because insurance has a language all its own and some of the stories are set in far off lands with unfamiliar words, bolded words can be found in the glossary.

So, sit back, relax, and let the ***fabulist*** guide the insurance buyer through the twists and turns of insurance and claims handling.

Three Blind Mice

Three blind mice. Three blind mice.
Read all the parts. Read all the parts.
There are five parts in the policy.
It's easy to remember, you'll see.
Just look for the sections which spell
clearly,
Find the DICE. Find the DICE.

Moral of the Story

Insurance policies have 5 main parts:

1. ***D***eclarations Page
2. ***D***efinitions
3. ***I***nsuring Agreement
4. ***C***onditions
5. ***E***xclusions/***E***ndorsements.

There could be more sections, such as "additional coverages" or "additional exclusions," but the policyholder who reads their policy from beginning to end will usually become familiar with all of this.

1. DECLARATIONS

The Declarations Page will detail who, what, where, when, and how much of the policy. It is a summary of the coverages offered to the insured. It is often, but not always, one of the first pages in a policy.

Who

The "Who" of the Declarations Page is the *First Named Insured*, the person or entity who is insured on the policy. The First Named Insured has some rights and obligations granted by the policy which other insureds do not. The First Named Insured(s) is/are responsible for payment of the premiums. They also have the right to cancel coverage. To be perfectly clear, just because Mr. Insured is named first, doesn't mean Mrs. Insured doesn't have the same rights and duties. She, too, is a First Named Insured.

Other people or entities can be insureds.

- **Named Insureds** (also known as **Additional Named Insureds**)**:** These insureds also are listed on the Declarations Page. The Additional Named Insured is usually found in a liability policy. This person does not have the same rights and obligations as the Named Insured, although, unlike the Additional Insured, mentioned below, the policy will cover all of the same actions they take as the insured.
- **Additional Insured:** This person has been added to the insurance policy, usually a liability policy, via endorsement because he has a contract or indemnity agreement with the Named Insured that requires his addition. The agreement states that the First Named Insured must accept the transfer of ***risk*** for the Additional Insured. However, unlike the Additional Named Insured, the policy will only cover the Additional Insured for his acts performed by or on behalf of the First Named Insured.
- **Defined Insured:** This person may not be named on the Declarations or Endorsement but may become an insured based on the definition of ***insured*** in the policy. In property policies, this can be the spouse of the Named Insured, a child, or a resident relative.

It is very important for the blind mice and the adjuster to know who the insured is, since notifying the insured of coverage issues/questions will often involve notifying *all* the insureds. For example, while the three blind mice are insureds, the mouse that ran up the clock may simply be an Additional Insured.

An Additional Named Insured and a Defined Insured are entitled to 100 percent of the benefits and coverage provided by the policy. An Additional Insured is not. Therefore, the insurer may have obligations to the Additional Named Insured and Defined Insured that it does not have to the Additional Insured.

What

The "What" in a policy is a building, its contents (personal property), loss of use, personal liability, and/or medical payments to others.

Where

The "Where" provides the address for the "What" that is insured. In homeowner policies, it is usually referred to as the "residence premises." This is important because the policy has a specific definition of what a residence premises is, such as an "owner-occupied dwelling."

When

The coverage dates are the "When" of the policy, usually called the "policy period." This policy doesn't give an end date—it simply shows the beginning or effective date. Almost all policies are for one year. If they are not, there will be an endorsement—effectively, an addendum—stating how long the policy is. ***Endorsements*** are discussed further below.

How Much

The policy limits, or Limit of Liability, are the "how much" on the Declarations Page.

2. DEFINITIONS

Insurance policies can be confusing because the carrier and adjuster may use words in a different manner from the way that word is normally used. Therefore, that word will be found in the definition section of the policy. If the word is defined, it will have quotes around it or it will be bolded.

Without getting too far into the weeds in insurance theory, if there is a question regarding the meaning of an undefined word in the policy, the normal, everyday meaning applies. This being said, sometimes adjusters, attorneys, and courts look to other sources to define words. This concept is discussed in a bit more depth in *Old Mother Hubbard*.

3. INSURING AGREEMENT

The insuring agreement tells the insured what the carrier will do in the event of a loss. Many ***claimants*** and attorneys read this section and think there is coverage because the policy will state something to the effect of, "The carrier will pay a claim in the event

Basic Cause of Loss		Broad Cause of Loss
• Fire	• Aircraft, Vehicles	• Everything in the Basic Cause of Loss Form
• Lightning	• Sinkhole Collapse	• Falling Objects
• Explosion	• Volcanic Action	• Weight of Snow, Ice, or Sleet
• Smoke	• Sprinkler Leakage	• Water (from appliance leakage)
• Windstorm	• Hail	• Collapse from Specified Causes
• Riot, Civil Commotion	• Vandalism	

of a loss." In actuality, the adjuster must consider the rest of the policy before coverage or liability is accepted.

Property Insurance

For property insurance, which covers the insured's possessions, the policy states the carrier will pay for loss or damage due to a particular ***cause of loss***. Simplifying this to the most basic level, there are three cause-of-loss forms, two of which are Named ***Perils*** and the other which is Open Perils (which many insurance professionals call a "Special Cause of Loss form," though certain others may still refer to it as an "all-risk" coverage form). Policies used to reference coverage for "risk of (damage)" or "All Risk" but this language caused some policyholders to believe the policy covered everything, even if there were things specifically excluded. Therefore, the wording was removed to avoid confusion.

Many carriers use standardized numbering for their forms, easily indicating which type of policy they use.

Named Perils

Under this type of policy, only the risks which are specifically named are covered. Homeowners and businessowners will usually see a 01 or 02 to indicate the named perils. This stands for a basic cause of loss form (01) and a broad cause of loss form (02). For example, a homeowner with a broad cause of loss form will see that their homeowner form is an HO 02, which covers a broad form cause of loss policy.

Open Perils

In the open-perils policy form, all losses are covered except what is excluded. Obviously, this form is preferred, since it offers more coverage than the previous two. It is usually denoted with a 03. Therefore, an open-perils homeowner policy would have an HO 03 cause of loss form.

Finally, the author has chosen to omit some of the form numbers for sake of brevity and ease of understanding. Readers should be aware that they may see forms abbreviated even more with just the relevant numbers which are likely to mean more to insurance professionals than to consumers. For example, the open perils homeowner policy can be referred to simply as the "HO3 policy." More information on the types of policies can be found in *The Magpie's Nest*.

Liability Insurance

The liability insuring agreement states it will pay claims for which the insured becomes legally liable. Liability policies will encompass damages to a person, such as bodily injury or death, and for a person's property. The carrier will also pay the expenses to defend the insured in a lawsuit.

4. CONDITIONS

This part of the policy states the requirements of the insured and insurer and describes how certain situations will be resolved. For example, the policy will describe how the claim will be paid, the duties of the insured, subrogation (also known as reimbursement), and how notice of a claim should be provided to the insurer.

If the insured does not meet the policy conditions, the carrier does not have to pay the claim.

5. EXCLUSIONS/ENDORSEMENTS

Exclusions are often the most discussed aspect of insurance policies when it comes to filing claims. It might seem as though the policy consists solely of exclusions, but this could be due to the insured having purchased the incorrect policy or a misunderstanding of the function and intention of insurance. The three categories of exclusions include: (1) perils, (2) losses, and (3) property.

Perils

Insurance is not a warranty policy. The policyholder must provide continuous maintenance on the insured property. For example, if a roof wears out, the insurer will not pay for a new roof; the damage to the roof must be caused by a covered peril.

Losses

There is a condition of the policy that the insured must protect the property from further damage in the event of a loss. Assuming the aforementioned scenario, suppose that the roof damage was caused by wind, which is a covered peril. However, the insured did not tarp the roof and allowed rain to enter their home which created further damage. This further damage is excluded.

Property

Although vehicles are listed as a covered peril in a property policy, this means damage caused by a vehicle. Vehicles which are damaged as a result of a motor vehicle accident with another vehicle would fall under an automobile policy. In this instance, if a car crashed through the insured's living room due to the fault of a drunk driver, the homeowner policy would pay for the damages to the home, then seek subrogation (reimbursement) from the drunk driver. See *Sleeping Beauty* for more information on subrogation. If, on the other hand, the policyholder's car was hit, while on the road, by the drunk driver, then that automobile carrier would pay for the damage.

There is usually an insurer who will write coverage for something that is excluded. If a policyholder wants to have a specific "thing" (whatever that "thing" may be) covered, the carrier will add an endorsement to the policy. Endorsements are changes to the policy and are often found "outside" the base form of the policy—meaning they are on different sheets of paper with different form numbers.

Exclusions can either be in the base form, meaning the exclusion is located inside the policy, or, like endorsements, they can be on separate sheets of paper with different form numbers.

A final word of warning about exclusions and endorsements: the purpose of the exclusion and endorsement can change based on the language in the particular section of the policy. As mentioned in *The Elves and the Shoemaker*, for businessowners, there is an endorsement which, because of its language, becomes an exclusion. Likewise, in some property policies, there is language known as "***exceptions to the exclusions***." That convoluted name simply means that there is coverage for that one specific scenario.

Again, the policyholder must read the policy front to back, along with any additions, to understand what is and is not covered. In this manner, the insured will be on the same wavelength as the adjuster.

Adjuster, Mend My Shoe

Adjuster, adjuster, mend my shoe.
I'm sorry, but that is not what I do.
What is broken, you must fix.

No, it is not I who picks
A contractor who is the tops
Of all the shops
To repair
That which causes you despair.
For when you have a loss
It is you who are the boss.

You told me to wait
That was my fate
As my claim stagnates
While I try to resuscitate.

Yes, I must inspect
The damaged object.
But that is done,
And I have paid which is my function.
So, I bid you adieu
You should repair your property
without further ado.

Moral of the Story

Everyone in the claim has a duty. For the insured, it is spelled out in the Conditions; a claimant must provide the information they want the adjuster to consider for their claim; the adjuster must adhere to the standards of their profession, colloquially called ***"good-faith" claims handling***.

In *Three Blind Mice*, the condition of protecting the property from further damage was used as an example. There tends to be a hesitancy from insureds and claimants to begin repairs because they've been told not to do anything until the insurer has inspected the damages. It's a fine line, but the overarching idea is not to destroy evidence of the damage so the insurer can write an estimate. Performing temporary repairs is fine. For example, if a windstorm strips shingles from the roof, a homeowner can place a tarp over it in order to avoid the roof from leaking inside the home creating more damage. If a concern arises, capturing photos and presenting them to the adjuster can be a helpful measure.

On a similar note, there is the insured or the claimant who will not begin repairs until a "final" estimate for property damages is received and/or agreed. This is a more difficult concept for some although, again, it deals with the fear that if the property is repaired the carrier will later deny any other possibly related damage.

The issue is proving that the additional damage found is related to the original claim, and neither due to either failing to protect the property from further damage nor an entirely new claim due to a new cause of loss.

The insurance policy is there to restore the insured and the claimant back to pre-loss status. Once an estimate of damages (and hopefully a check) is received, then the insured and the claimant have the insurer's tacit "permission" to begin repairs. Permission is in quotes because it is widely held in insurance circles that an insurer cannot grant permission to begin repairs. The property does not belong to the insurer; it belongs to the insured or the claimant, and, therefore, it is they who must grant permission to begin repairs.

Regardless, the fear is that the claim will be denied unless everything is agreed to prior to beginning repairs. Estimating property or auto repairs is not a science, despite the fact that insurers use computer software which is updated with a pricing codex down to specific zip codes, because things are often missed and costs increase.

The best piece of advice to follow in this situation is to begin repairs when the estimate and check arrive. Prior to this, though, an ***agreed estimate of repairs*** can be obtained to alleviate the fear of a possible denial of damages. An agreed estimate means both the contractor and the carrier have agreed to the amount (scope) of damages and their costs.

If additional damages, called "supplemental" damages, are found, the insured or the claimant should immediately contact the adjuster and ask for another estimate. This is called a "***supplement***." Failing to initiate repairs in the hopes of arriving at a final and agreed estimate may lead to additional damages which would not be covered because the property is not protected from further loss.

Once the first- or third-party has been paid, they can begin repairs immediately.

One final note: in this nursery rhyme the adjuster states it is not her job to choose the contractor to repair the damage—this is the job of the property owner. *Baa, Baa, Black Sheep* discusses the preferred vendor system.

The Three Little Pigs

There were three brothers: Pete Pig, RePete Pig, and ReRun Pig. Pete was the oldest; RePete was the middlest; and ReRun was the youngest pig, but he was also the smartest.

One day, Pete left the farm to go find his fortune. He found a little hill in the grassland, gathered up some of that dry grass, and built a house from the straw on the hill. The next day, RePete left the farm to go find his fortune. He found a little dell where he built a house of wood from the dell. On the third day, ReRun left the farm to go find his fortune. He found a clay pit where he built a house of bricks.

Now the Brothers Pig, despite living in different areas, still lived relatively close to one another and could visit each other every once and again. Pete, RePete, and ReRun were having supper one night at RePete's house when the conversation turned to the weather forecast.

"It's supposed to be windy," claimed Pete.

"Yes, I heard it's wolf whirlwind season," RePete agreed.

"It's true. Big Bad Wolf is coming to town according to *Brothers Grimm News*," confirmed ReRun.

None of the Pigs were worried, because they each had a nice, warm house to shelter them during the storm. But the very next night, there was a howling at Pete's door, and Pete heard, "Little Pig, little Pig, let me in!"

To which Pete replied, "First, I'm not the little Pig. I'm the eldest. Second, not by the hair of my chinny-chin-chin!"

The Big Bad Wolf took a deep breath and said, "Then I'll huff and I'll puff and I'll blow your house down!"

Which is essentially what happened. Fortunately for Pete Pig, he went out the back door and headed over to RePete's house for safety.

The Big Bad Wolf was understandably, upset at not having pork for his dinner that night, so he continued on to the dell where he found the middlest brother Pig.

There he said, "Little Pig, little Pig, let me in!"

To which RePete replied, "Mr. Wolf, I am the middle Pig. I'm afraid you do not want me—I'm not very tender or juicy. And I'm afraid I will not open the door by the hair of my chinny-chin-chin."

The Big Bad Wolf took a deep breath and said, "Then I'll huff and I'll puff and I'll blow your house down!" Which is essentially what happened. Fortunately, Pete and RePete were able to sneak out the back door and make their way to ReRun's house for safety.

The Big Bad Wolf was now quite hangry because he had not eaten all day and was expending a lot of energy blowing all these houses down. He continued on to the clay pit where he found the youngest brother Pig.

There he said, "Little Pig, little Pig, let me in!"

To which ReRun replied, "No! My brothers are here, and they tell me you blew their houses down. I must respectfully decline by the hair of my chinny-chin-chin."

The Big Bad Wolf took a deep breath and said, "Then I'll huff and I'll puff and I'll blow your house down, too!" So he blew and he blew. When he finished, he saw there were only a few shingles missing from the roof. So, he took an even deeper breath, and he huffed and he puffed, but nothing further happened. The wolf tried a third time, also to no avail.

Finally, the Big Bad Wolf gave up and went to Red Riding Hood's Grandma's Bistro in Enchanted Hollow to get a drink, because all that huffing and puffing had made his mouth dry.

Moral of the Story

Everyone with insurance is familiar with ***deductibles*** and ***premiums***, but not everyone is familiar with how they relate to one another. Insurers attempt to control their costs with deductibles. Deductibles can either be monetary or in a time format (also known as a waiting period). Deductibles also prevent small losses which might occur frequently from being filed, since the policyholder's damage would not exceed the deductible amount. When a policyholder has a high deductible, it means that they will pay more out of pocket when a loss occurs; on the other hand, it also means that the carrier will assess a smaller premium for the policy.

With the advent of more frequent catastrophic events, such as wildfires and hurricanes, insurance carriers are placing specific deductibles for these perils; often these deductibles are higher than other risks' deductibles. These higher deductibles may be placed on hurricanes, named storms, and/or tropical storms—all of which have different meanings and are beyond the scope of this tale.

MULTIPLE CLAIMS

The states' departments of insurance have begun to weigh in on insurers assessing multiple deductibles due to multiple claims from the same cause of loss.

For example, Louisiana Revised Statute 22:1337 states that insurers may only apply named-storm, hurricane, and wind and hail deductibles once per calendar year for homeowner policies. However, there is a caveat. If the damage from the first storm is beneath the deductible, the insurer will count the deductible and subtract it from the second loss.

EXAMPLES

ReRun has 3 losses from one event—i.e., the Big Bad Wolf tried three times to destroy his house. This means he will make three separate claims due to wind.

Scenario #1:

ReRun has a windstorm deductible that is 3% of his home policy limit, which is $100,000. Therefore, ReRun's deductible is $3,000.

In the first event, only shingles were disturbed, so the total damage was $1,200. ReRun would not receive any money from his claim because the amount of damage is less than the deductible. However, Begonia Gemforest, ReRun's adjuster, would take the deductible, less the damage, in case there was another claim that year.

Deductible	$3,000
Damage	$1,200
Deductible Left for the Year	$1,800

Scenario #2:

In the second event, there's some damage, but not a lot. ReRun files a second claim. His damage is $500 this time. Adjuster Gemforest would take the remaining deductible and apply the new claim's damage:

Remaining Deductible	$1,800
Damage 2nd Claim	$500
Deductible Left for the Year	$1,300

ReRun wouldn't get paid for this claim either, because it's still beneath his deductible.

Scenario #3:

This time, ReRun sustains $2,500 worth of damage. Again, Adjuster Gemforest would take the outstanding deductible and apply it to the damage.

Outstanding Deductible	$1,300
Damage 3rd Claim	$2,500
Amount Owed to ReRun	$1,200

Begonia would now cut a check to ReRun for $1,200, because he finally breached his deductible. In the new year, the deductible would reset to $3,000.

It would be tempting to say, "OK. Then I won't repair my home so that I finally have 'enough' damage to breach my deductible in the next storm." However, as discussed earlier in *Three Blind Mice*, there is a condition in the policy which states the insured must protect the property from further damage.

WAITING PERIODS

Florida statute Title XXXVII, Chapter 627.4025, has a waiting period for the deductible which begins at the time a hurricane watch or warning is put into effect for "any part of Florida by the National Hurricane Center of the National Weather Service." It ends 72 hours after the last hurricane watch or warning for any part of Florida expires. This is to prevent the insurer from assessing multiple deductibles in a short period of time.

Fortunately for Adjuster Gemforest, ReRun lives in Fairytale Land and does not have to worry about these issues. It's advisable to research whether your state of residence shares similarities with Louisiana or Florida in the case of a claim.

PREMIUMS

Most people have an idea how premiums are determined. The brothers Pig would each pay different premiums for their homes. Premiums are not only based on the claim history (how many claims the insured has had in a year) but also the neighborhood, the type of construction, materials used, and the quality of the materials, to name a few things in the instance of homes. For automobiles, it would be the type of vehicle, driving history, urban or rural neighborhood, etc.

In addition to premiums being based on the insured's history, these premiums also take into consideration other people who are like the insured, which is why teenagers have higher premiums: they are more easily distracted; they don't have a long driving history; they tend not to have the best decision-making skills, etc.

Finally, additions to the policy through endorsements or exclusions will increase or decrease the premium amount. All of these items are taken into consideration when pricing the policy, which is why insureds may not have the same premiums as their neighbor's girlfriend's Aunt Martha, even if they are insured by the same carrier.

Sleeping Beauty

Moral of the Story

Wait. Why does the moral come first?

This fairy tale may be more difficult to read than the rest, but the reader should not be deterred. There are three morals packed into this single story: ***adjuster notes***, ***statute of limitations***, and the concept of ***subrogation***.

This tale is told in the format of an adjuster's notes for illustrative purposes. An insured or claimant (i.e., the person who has filed a claim) will not see the adjuster's notes unless a lawsuit is filed—and maybe not even then, unless their attorney allows it. So, why use notes as a story?

Readers should be aware that the carrier documents everything that occurs throughout a claim. Claimants should do the same as well, noting the time, date, and who the claimant (whether first- or third-party) spoke with. Notes like this will help in the case of a dispute.

Insurance companies are required by the states' departments of insurance to keep notes in the claimant's file with enough detail to recreate the adjuster's thinking. It stands to reason these notes would have copious amounts of abbreviations in them since the adjusters must work quickly and efficiently and keep a good record in the file of what transpires. In the event of a lawsuit or a complaint against the insurance company or adjuster, these notes are reviewed to see if the carrier and adjuster are adhering to the standards, practices, and procedures of claims handling. It behooves the adjuster to enter notes that are as accurate, as precise, and as timely as possible. This by no means infers the notes are 100 percent correct. As the Evil Queen in *Snow White and the Huntsman* has taught youngsters, one bad apple can spoil the whole bunch.

On the other hand, just because there is a missing note or the note was not entered into the system in a reasonably timely manner does not necessarily mean the carrier or adjuster has acted in ***bad faith***. Good faith claim handling is discussed in *Adjuster, Mend My Shoe.*

Notes are kept in real time, and it's not uncommon to see grammar errors, misspellings, and abbreviations, several of which are featured throughout the story. These are mostly known to those in the industry. For example, "s/w" means "spoke with." "R/S" means "***recorded statement***." "Est.," "I/A," or "atty." are all common abbreviations for "estimate," "independent adjuster," and "attorney." As a side note, there are several mentions of a coverage question and a "ROR" which is a reservation of rights. Readers will learn more about this in *Snow White and the Seven Dwarfs.*

The notes in a claim file are organized in reverse chronological order, the oldest being at the bottom, with the most current at the top. This story begins at the ending and ends at the beginning if one were to read it in the order of a normal claim file. Of course, since it is ultimately up to the reader to choose how they read this tale, they might choose to begin at the with beginning the last note and work their way forward in time. Or read it as it's written, starting with the most recent note and working backward. See? A bit difficult.

Toward the bottom (or beginning) of the file notes, the adjuster discusses a possible coverage question regarding when the loss occurred in relation to the policy period (time that the insurance policy would be in effect and pay for covered losses). The ***at-fault*** carrier attempts to deny the loss due to the statute of limitations. Not only do policies have limitations as to when the first- or third-party can file a claim, but the states do as well.

Claimants should be aware of the time limitations in their insurance policies for filing claims and the ***statute of limitations*** that applies to their specific situation. These limitations vary depending on the type of insurance policy and the jurisdiction in which the claim is made.

First-party losses are claims made by the policyholder against their own insurance policy. For first-party claims, the policy specifies the time limit for filing a claim which is sometimes a year after discovering the loss, although it can be shorter or longer depending on the policy. For third-party claims, the statute of limitations typically applies. The statute of limitations is the period of time during which a claimant must file a lawsuit against the responsible party in order to preserve their right to recover damages. If the claimant does not file a lawsuit within the statute of limitations, they may be barred from bringing the claim at all.

It is important for every claimant to be aware of the time limitations in their insurance policy and the statute of limitations that applies to their situation to ensure that they file their claim in a timely manner and do not lose their right to recover damages. Claimants should consult with an attorney if they have questions about the time limitations or statute of limitations that apply to their claim.

Slightly complicating this limitation issue is the idea of an ***occurrence*** or a ***claims-made policy***. Most policies are "occurrence" policies, and for the most part, the majority of people never need this information. This is a type of insurance policy that provides coverage for claims arising from incidents that occurred *during* the policy period, regardless of when the claim is actually made. With an occurrence policy, as long as the incident that led to the claim occurred during the policy period, the claim would be covered, even if the claim is not made until years later.

For example, if the King and Queen (Sleeping Beauty's parents) have an occurrence policy with the policy effective dates of 01/01/1500 to 12/31/1501, and the loss occurred on July 04, 1500, but it was not reported until June 30, 1502, the policy would provide coverage for that claim, even though it was not reported to Mother Goose Insurance Mutual until years later.

Occurrence policies are commonly used in general liability insurance, such as for businesses or individuals, and they typically have no retroactive date. This means that all claims arising from incidents during the policy period will be covered, regardless of when the policy was purchased or when the claim is filed. However, occurrence policies tend to be more expensive than claims-made policies because they provide longer coverage and are therefore riskier for insurers.

Policyholders also rarely need to know about ***retroactive dates***, which are just as they sound; a specified date in an insurance policy that marks the beginning of the coverage period for incidents that occurred *before* the policy was issued.

In many liability insurance policies, such as professional liability insurance, a retroactive date is used to define the scope of the policy's coverage. If an insurance policy includes a retroactive date, that policy will only cover claims arising from incidents occurring on or after the retroactive date. Any claims arising from incidents that occurred before the retroactive date will not be covered.

Let's say the King and Queen have a retroactive date to 1500 and the loss of rents and income occurs between 1500 and now. In their case, the policy will pay for those covered claims; if the loss had occurred in 1499 or earlier, those claims would not be paid, even if the loss was from an insured peril because the loss would have occurred outside the coverage period.

There is another sort of policy: a claims-made policy is a type of insurance policy that covers claims that are made and reported to the insurer during the policy period. With a claims-made policy, coverage is triggered only if the claim is made and reported to the insurer while the policy is in effect. If a claim is made after the policy has expired or been canceled, it would not be covered.

Claims-made policies are often used in professional liability insurance, such as errors and omissions insurance for professionals like doctors, lawyers, and accountants. These policies typically require that the claim be made and reported to the insurer during the policy period, even if the alleged error or omission occurred before the policy period began. As a result, claims-made policies often include a retroactive date.

The tale also discusses the concept of ***subrogation***, which simply means reimbursement.

Subrogation is a legal concept in insurance that allows an insurance company to pursue a third party responsible for causing damage or loss to the insured due to the subrogation clause in the policy. When an insurer pays a claim to its insured, it has the right to step into the insured's shoes and seek reimbursement from the responsible third party. This is done to prevent the insured from being unjustly enriched by receiving compensation for damages caused by the at-fault party and their insurer, and to shift the cost of the loss to the responsible party.

Subrogation can be beneficial to the insured. In this tale, the at-fault insurer denied the King and Queen's claim. Fortunately for the King and Queen, Mother Goose Insurance Mutual paid the claim, and the King and Queen can go on with their lives. Granted, because the King and Queen used their policy, they must pay the deductible, but that is a small price to suffer for the peace of mind of having their loss reimbursed.

Knowing that the deductible has been withheld, adjuster Gemforest will ask for it, as well as any out-of-pocket expenses to be honored by the at-fault insurer (Sorcerer's Insurance Company). If they say no, the two insurance companies can "fight it out" rather than the King and Queen having to deal with the stress and anxiety of a lawsuit against the at-fault party. In this instance, it behooves the insured to use their policy—which is one of the reasons one purchases insurance in the first place!

The final note discusses "inter-co arbitration," which stands for "intercompany arbitration." Insurers have a variety of methods to arrive at settlements without going to court, which is expensive and unpredictable. Three of these methods are: ***arbitration***, ***mediation***, and the ***appraisal*** process.

Arbitration is similar to litigation. A judge is present and it is he or she who will make the final decision, which is binding, meaning no take-backsies. It is a win/lose situation. Attorneys are often present since the process is formal.

Mediation is an informal process in which a mediator—often a retired judge—attempts to bring the two parties to an agreement or resolution by going back and forth between the two to help each other understand the other's point of view. It is less expensive than arbitration and is a win/win situation. Attorneys may be present, but in some cases, it can be the adjusters themselves.

The appraisal process is defined in the property policy when there is a dispute concerning the scope, amount, or cost of the damage. In this process, both sides elect an independent person to estimate the damages. Those two people, prior to inspecting the property together, agree on an umpire. If the appraisers come to an agreement, then payment can be issued for the agreed amount. If the appraisers cannot agree, the matter goes to the umpire who will be the tie breaker.

The appraisal process should not be used to address coverage issues, such as what are and are not covered damages. Independent estimators should be used. This means the carrier should hire a second field adjuster (in other words: the carrier cannot use the initial field adjuster for the appraisal, as that person is seen as biased). Likewise, if the insured has a public adjuster, that public adjuster cannot be the appraiser for the insured again.

There is a concern amongst insureds that using their policies will result in higher premiums. If this is a worry, the policyholder should discuss this possibility with their agent. However, usually if the insured is not at-fault for the loss, their premiums do not increase. Again, this is the prerogative of the insurer.

Finally, it is possible that Sorcerer's Insurance will reimburse Mother Goose a portion of the loss. If this occurs, then depending on the state rules and regulations, Mother Goose will attempt to make the King and Queen "whole." The "***made whole***" concept in subrogation refers to the principle that an insured should not be left in a worse financial position after a loss is reimbursed by the at-fault carrier. In other words, the insured should be fully compensated for their loss before their insurance company can recover any payments made through subrogation. This means that Mother Goose would reimburse the King and Queen their 300 gold-piece deductible before they reimburse themselves.

The story, in the form of an adjuster's notes, begins on the next page.

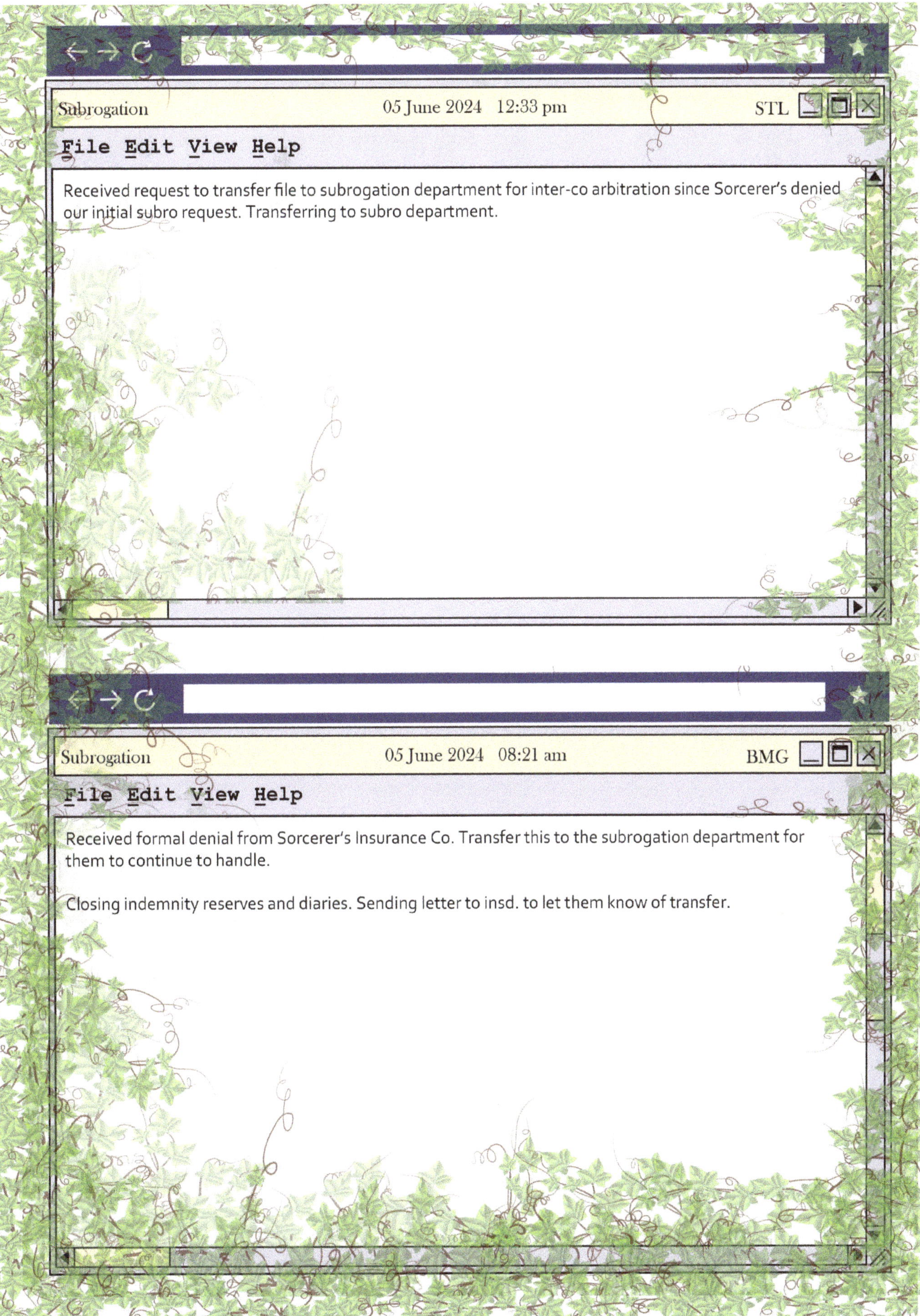

Subrogation 05 June 2024 12:33 pm STL

File Edit View Help

Received request to transfer file to subrogation department for inter-co arbitration since Sorcerer's denied our initial subro request. Transferring to subro department.

Subrogation 05 June 2024 08:21 am BMG

File Edit View Help

Received formal denial from Sorcerer's Insurance Co. Transfer this to the subrogation department for them to continue to handle.

Closing indemnity reserves and diaries. Sending letter to insd. to let them know of transfer.

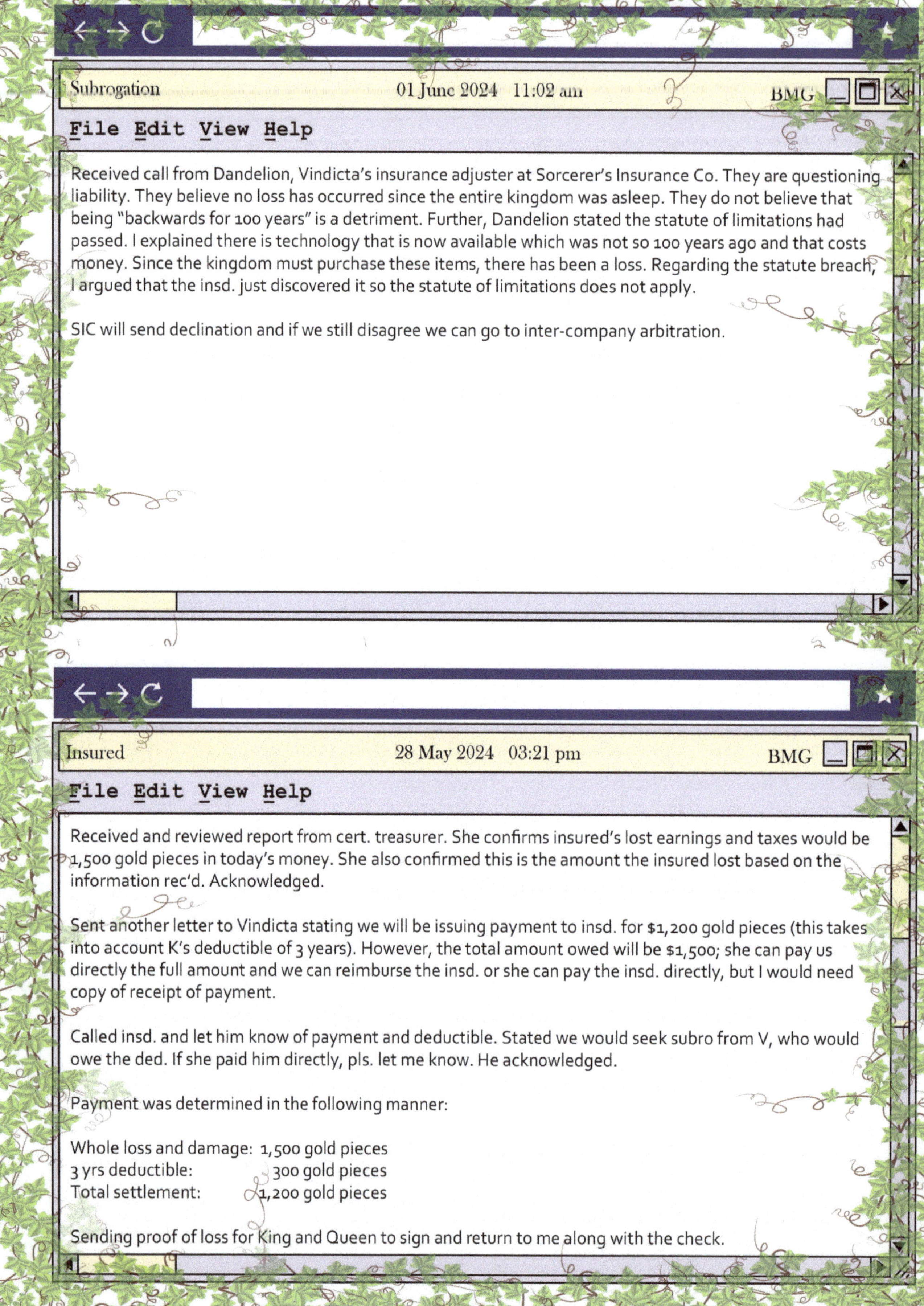

Subrogation 01 June 2024 11:02 am BMG

File Edit View Help

Received call from Dandelion, Vindicta's insurance adjuster at Sorcerer's Insurance Co. They are questioning liability. They believe no loss has occurred since the entire kingdom was asleep. They do not believe that being "backwards for 100 years" is a detriment. Further, Dandelion stated the statute of limitations had passed. I explained there is technology that is now available which was not so 100 years ago and that costs money. Since the kingdom must purchase these items, there has been a loss. Regarding the statute breach, I argued that the insd. just discovered it so the statute of limitations does not apply.

SIC will send declination and if we still disagree we can go to inter-company arbitration.

Insured 28 May 2024 03:21 pm BMG

File Edit View Help

Received and reviewed report from cert. treasurer. She confirms insured's lost earnings and taxes would be 1,500 gold pieces in today's money. She also confirmed this is the amount the insured lost based on the information rec'd. Acknowledged.

Sent another letter to Vindicta stating we will be issuing payment to insd. for $1,200 gold pieces (this takes into account K's deductible of 3 years). However, the total amount owed will be $1,500; she can pay us directly the full amount and we can reimburse the insd. or she can pay the insd. directly, but I would need copy of receipt of payment.

Called insd. and let him know of payment and deductible. Stated we would seek subro from V, who would owe the ded. If she paid him directly, pls. let me know. He acknowledged.

Payment was determined in the following manner:

Whole loss and damage: 1,500 gold pieces
3 yrs deductible: 300 gold pieces
Total settlement: 1,200 gold pieces

Sending proof of loss for King and Queen to sign and return to me along with the check.

Subrogation
21 May 2024 08:13 am
BMG
File Edit View Help
Sent Vindicta subrogation letter stating our intention to reimburse insd. for lost earnings/taxes. Stated I find her to be at fault for this loss and asked her to send the letter to her insurance comp. If she doesn't have one, she should call me.
Diary file for 30 days.
Witness Statement
21 May 2024 07:59 am
BMG
File Edit View Help
Zephyrus called back stating he conferred with his colleagues who confirmed there was a spell on the castle, and the reason he didn't know is that he's also affected. He finds this hard to believe since fairy magic is less powerful than sorcery or wizardry, but if Vindicta is actually a witch and not a fairy this would make sense. He said everyone thought of V as a fairy, but no one really knows her. But now that he knew there was a spell, with the help of other witches and warlocks he broke the spell.
He has notified Talia so she doesn't go exploring again. Acknowledged.

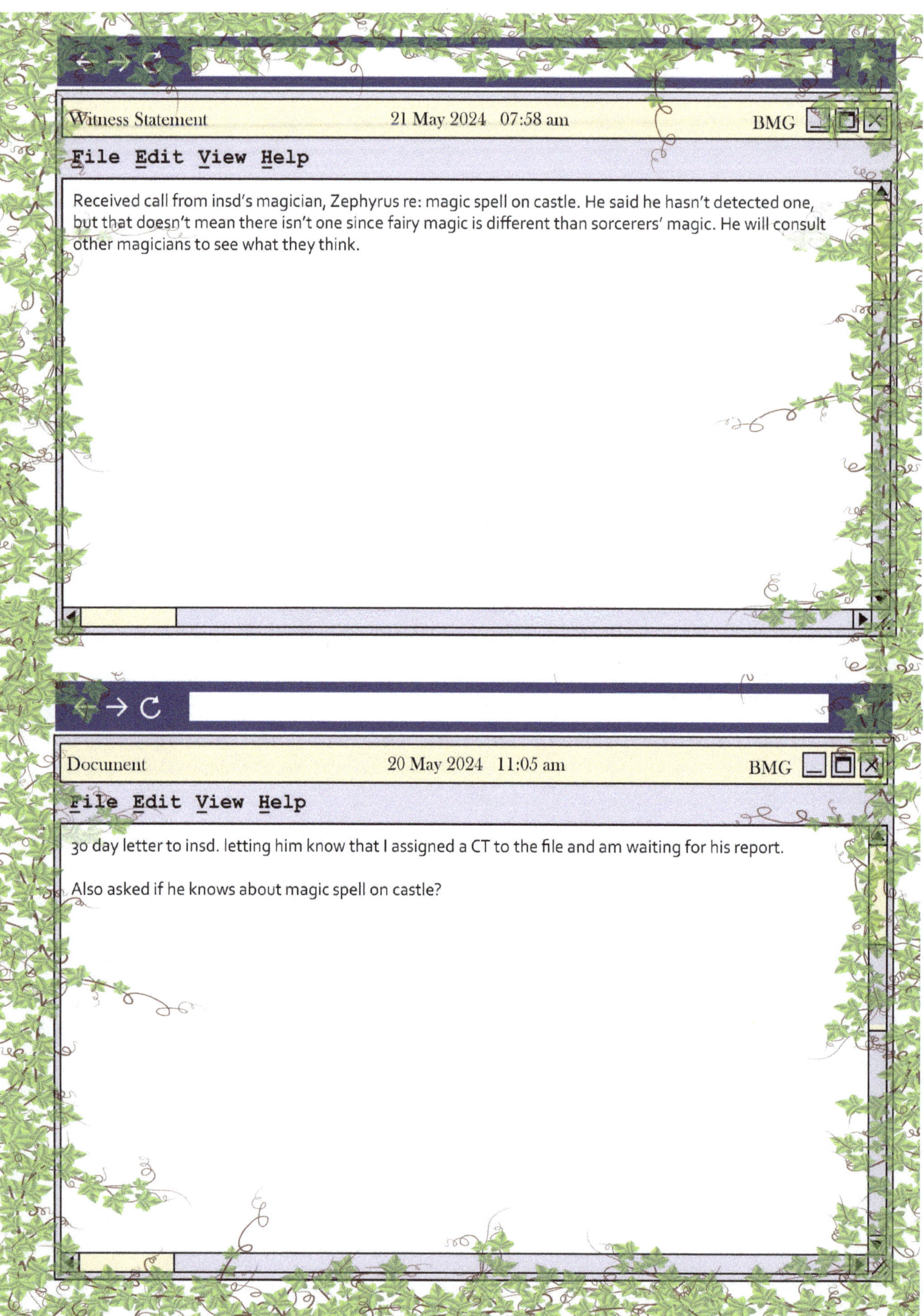

Witness Statement
21 May 2024 07:58 am
BMG
File Edit View Help
Received call from insd's magician, Zephyrus re: magic spell on castle. He said he hasn't detected one, but that doesn't mean there isn't one since fairy magic is different than sorcerers' magic. He will consult other magicians to see what they think.
Document
20 May 2024 11:05 am
BMG
File Edit View Help
30 day letter to insd. letting him know that I assigned a CT to the file and am waiting for his report.
Also asked if he knows about magic spell on castle?

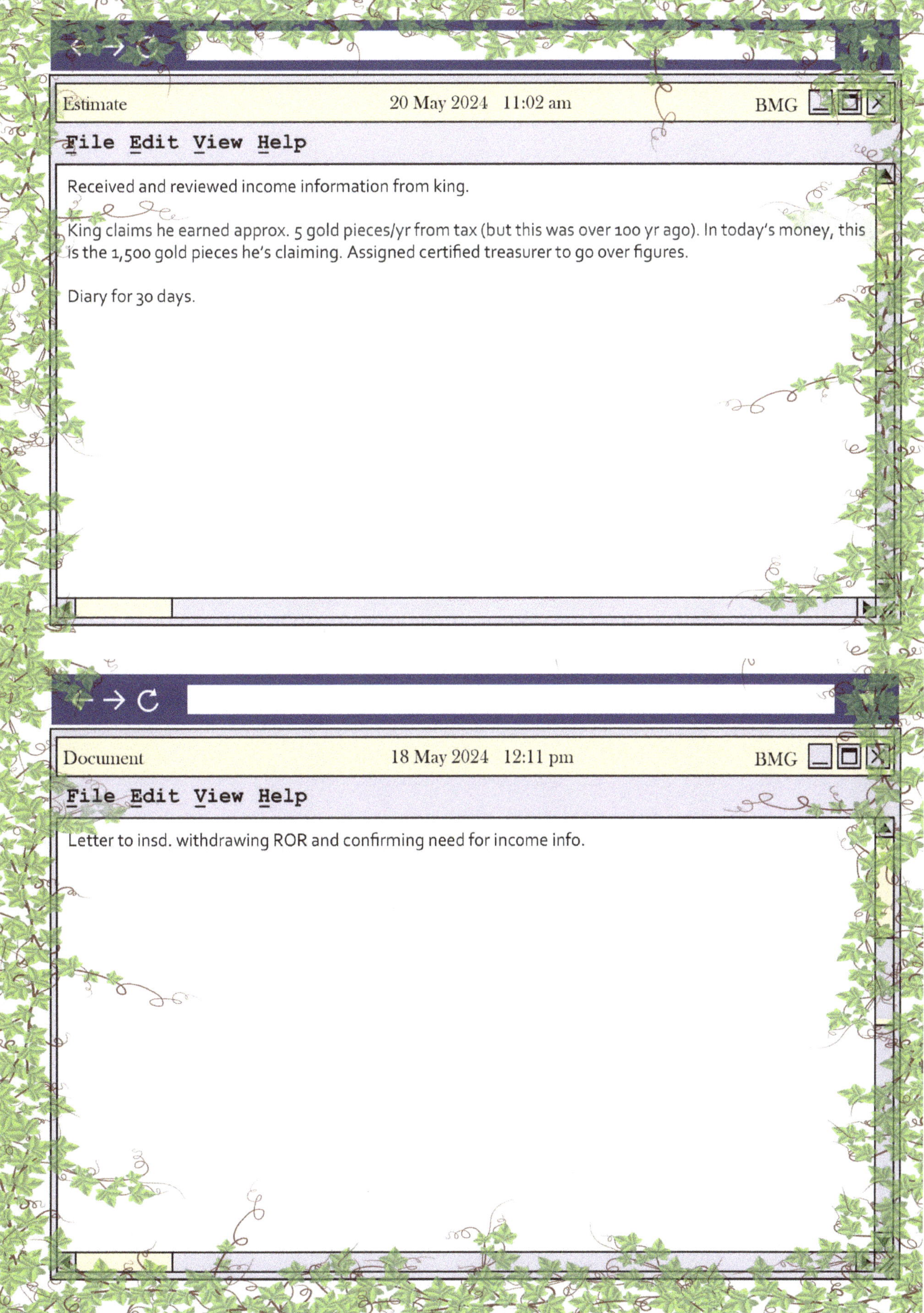
Estimate
20 May 2024 11:02 am
BMG
File Edit View Help
Received and reviewed income information from king.
King claims he earned approx. 5 gold pieces/yr from tax (but this was over 100 yr ago). In today's money, this is the 1,500 gold pieces he's claiming. Assigned certified treasurer to go over figures.
Diary for 30 days.
Document
18 May 2024 12:11 pm
BMG
File Edit View Help
Letter to insd. withdrawing ROR and confirming need for income info.

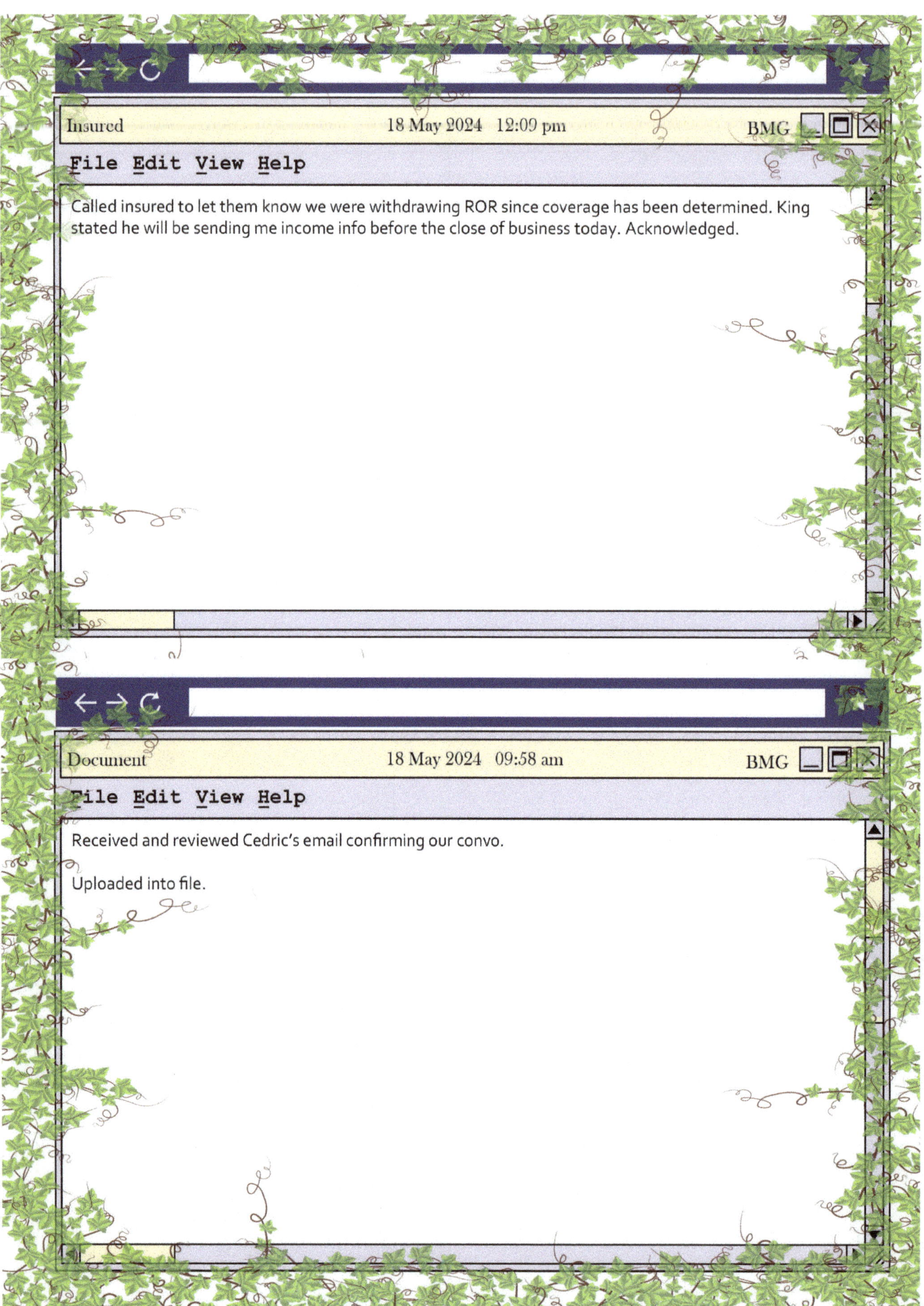

Called insured to let them know we were withdrawing ROR since coverage has been determined. King stated he will be sending me income info before the close of business today. Acknowledged.

Received and reviewed Cedric's email confirming our convo.

Uploaded into file.

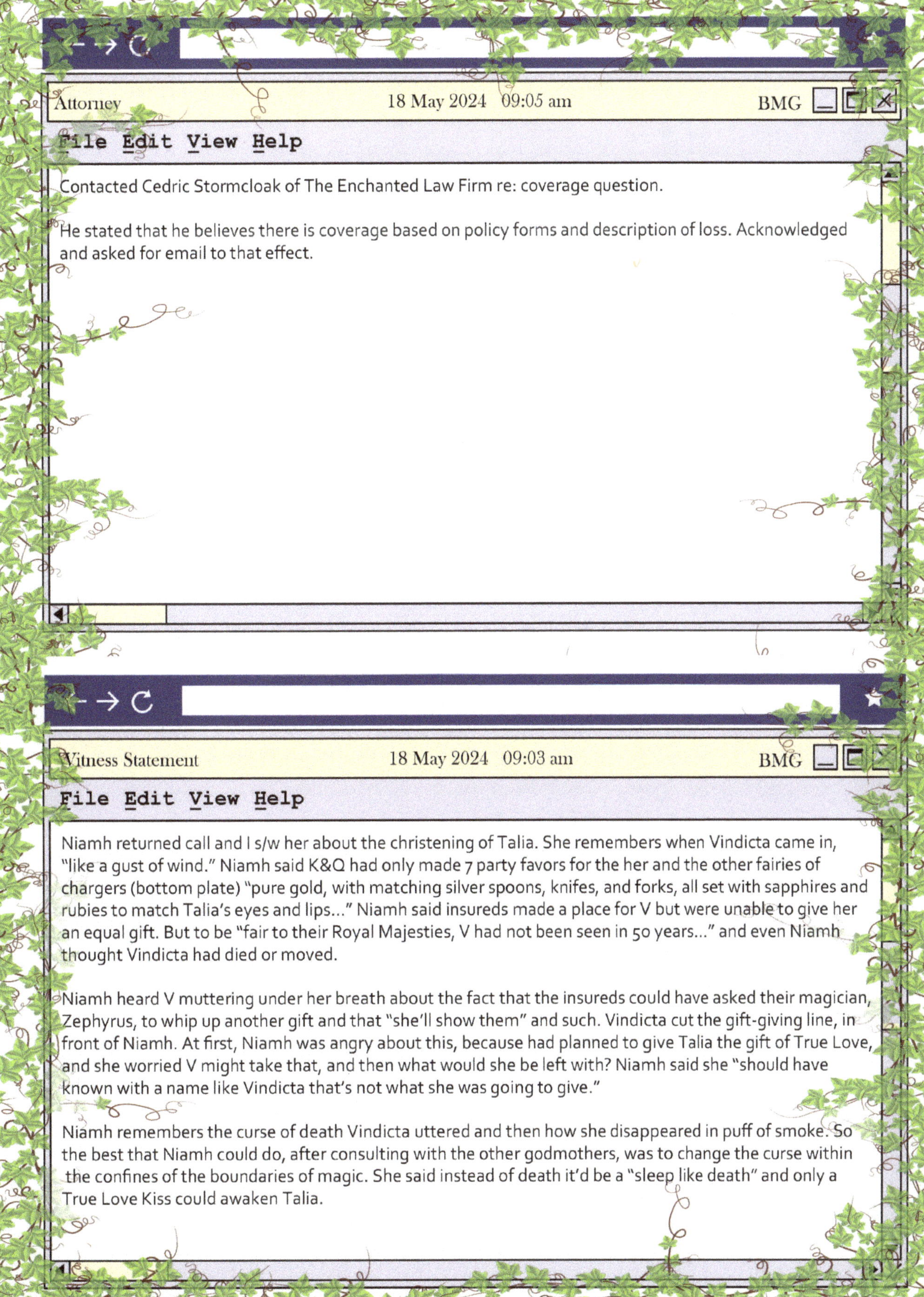

Attorney 18 May 2024 09:05 am BMG

File Edit View Help

Contacted Cedric Stormcloak of The Enchanted Law Firm re: coverage question.

He stated that he believes there is coverage based on policy forms and description of loss. Acknowledged and asked for email to that effect.

Witness Statement 18 May 2024 09:03 am BMG

File Edit View Help

Niamh returned call and I s/w her about the christening of Talia. She remembers when Vindicta came in, "like a gust of wind." Niamh said K&Q had only made 7 party favors for the her and the other fairies of chargers (bottom plate) "pure gold, with matching silver spoons, knifes, and forks, all set with sapphires and rubies to match Talia's eyes and lips..." Niamh said insureds made a place for V but were unable to give her an equal gift. But to be "fair to their Royal Majesties, V had not been seen in 50 years..." and even Niamh thought Vindicta had died or moved.

Niamh heard V muttering under her breath about the fact that the insureds could have asked their magician, Zephyrus, to whip up another gift and that "she'll show them" and such. Vindicta cut the gift-giving line, in front of Niamh. At first, Niamh was angry about this, because had planned to give Talia the gift of True Love, and she worried V might take that, and then what would she be left with? Niamh said she "should have known with a name like Vindicta that's not what she was going to give."

Niamh remembers the curse of death Vindicta uttered and then how she disappeared in puff of smoke. So the best that Niamh could do, after consulting with the other godmothers, was to change the curse within the confines of the boundaries of magic. She said instead of death it'd be a "sleep like death" and only a True Love Kiss could awaken Talia.

Witness Statement cont'd 18 May 2024 09:03 am BMG

File Edit View Help

Niamh said it was godmother Kalina who put the spell on the kingdom where everyone fell asleep and the trees grew around them. Ginevra was the one who spoke to the Prince and led him to the castle.

Asked about a magic spell on the section of castle Talia was describing with old woman. Niamh said she didn't know about that, but it seems like something Vindicta would do and it "stands to reason that's how she's been hidden so long." Niamh will speak with the other g/m and get back with me. Acknowledged. Said I'd need to talk w/them as well to get their version of the story. Asked her to have them call me.

30 Day Review 18 May 2024 08:15 am BMG

File Edit View Help

Received, reviewed, and ack. Supervisor's note.

Sent 2nd request letter for lost rents and income information and documentation.

Called and left message for Niamh.

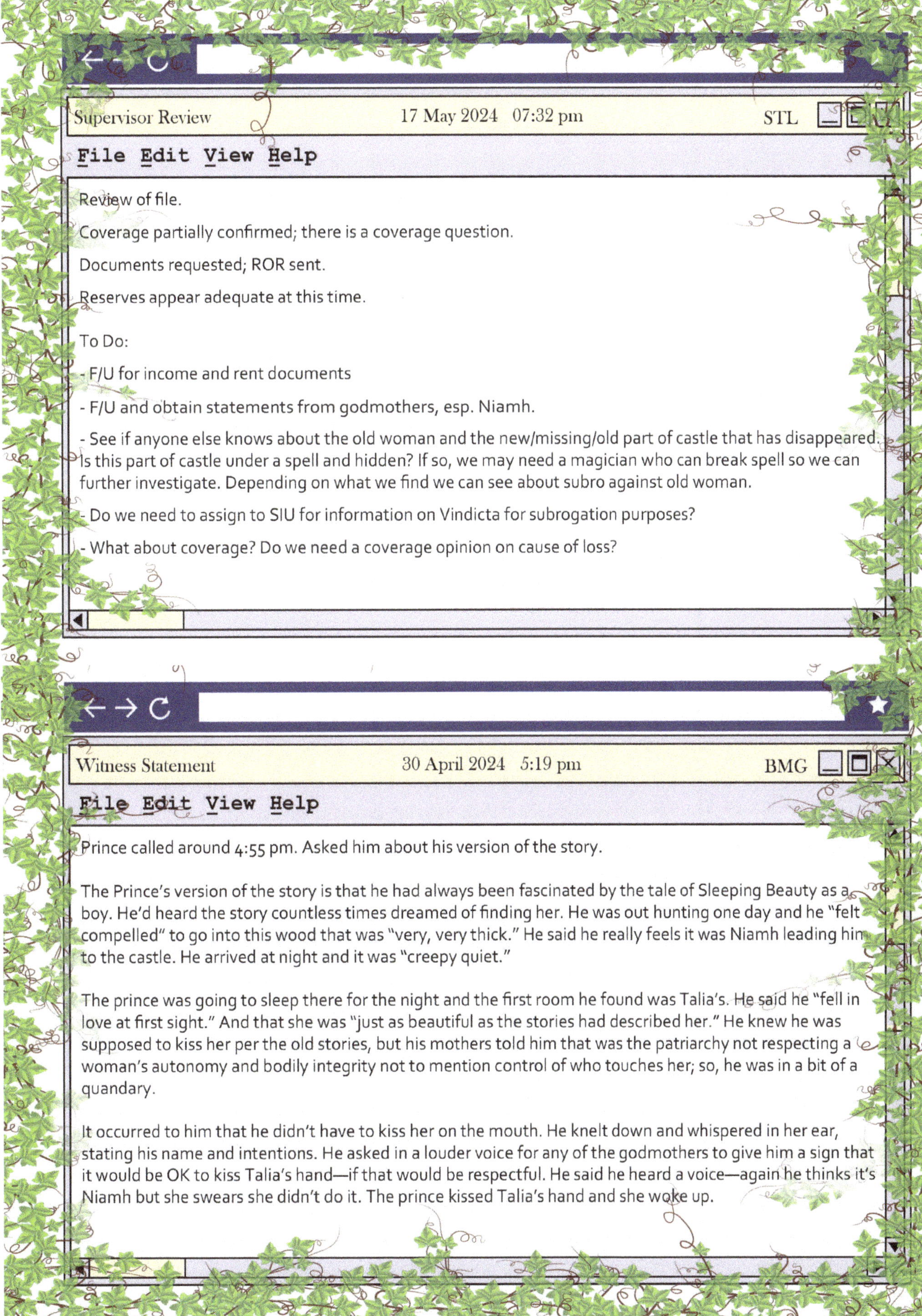

Supervisor Review 17 May 2024 07:32 pm STL

File Edit View Help

Review of file.

Coverage partially confirmed; there is a coverage question.

Documents requested; ROR sent.

Reserves appear adequate at this time.

To Do:

- F/U for income and rent documents
- F/U and obtain statements from godmothers, esp. Niamh.
- See if anyone else knows about the old woman and the new/missing/old part of castle that has disappeared. Is this part of castle under a spell and hidden? If so, we may need a magician who can break spell so we can further investigate. Depending on what we find we can see about subro against old woman.
- Do we need to assign to SIU for information on Vindicta for subrogation purposes?
- What about coverage? Do we need a coverage opinion on cause of loss?

Witness Statement 30 April 2024 5:19 pm BMG

File Edit View Help

Prince called around 4:55 pm. Asked him about his version of the story.

The Prince's version of the story is that he had always been fascinated by the tale of Sleeping Beauty as a boy. He'd heard the story countless times dreamed of finding her. He was out hunting one day and he "felt compelled" to go into this wood that was "very, very thick." He said he really feels it was Niamh leading him to the castle. He arrived at night and it was "creepy quiet."

The prince was going to sleep there for the night and the first room he found was Talia's. He said he "fell in love at first sight." And that she was "just as beautiful as the stories had described her." He knew he was supposed to kiss her per the old stories, but his mothers told him that was the patriarchy not respecting a woman's autonomy and bodily integrity not to mention control of who touches her; so, he was in a bit of a quandary.

It occurred to him that he didn't have to kiss her on the mouth. He knelt down and whispered in her ear, stating his name and intentions. He asked in a louder voice for any of the godmothers to give him a sign that it would be OK to kiss Talia's hand—if that would be respectful. He said he heard a voice—again he thinks it's Niamh but she swears she didn't do it. The prince kissed Talia's hand and she woke up.

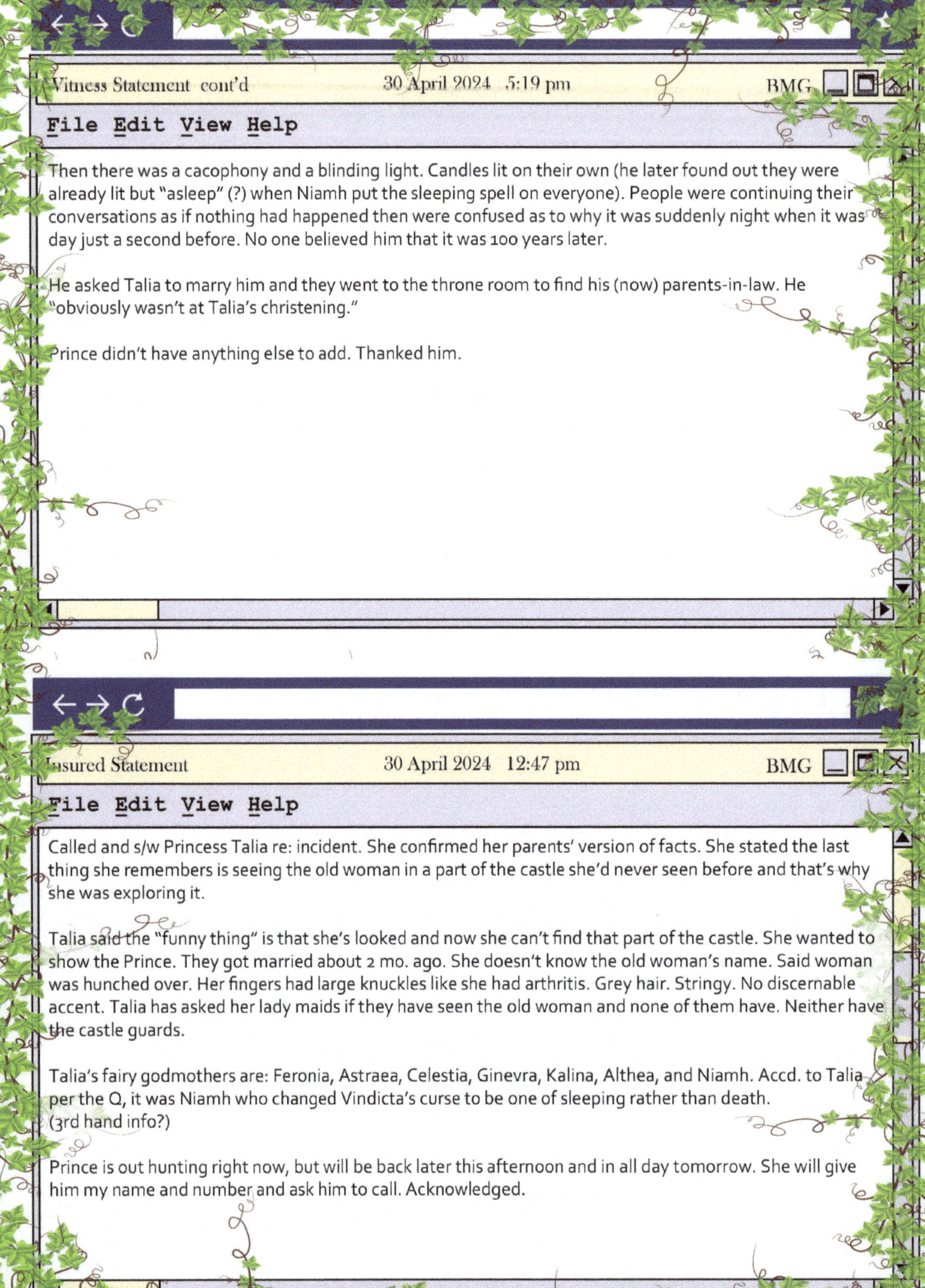

Witness Statement cont'd   30 April 2024   5:19 pm   BMG

File Edit View Help

Then there was a cacophony and a blinding light. Candles lit on their own (he later found out they were already lit but "asleep" (?) when Niamh put the sleeping spell on everyone). People were continuing their conversations as if nothing had happened then were confused as to why it was suddenly night when it was day just a second before. No one believed him that it was 100 years later.

He asked Talia to marry him and they went to the throne room to find his (now) parents-in-law. He "obviously wasn't at Talia's christening."

Prince didn't have anything else to add. Thanked him.

Insured Statement   30 April 2024   12:47 pm   BMG

File Edit View Help

Called and s/w Princess Talia re: incident. She confirmed her parents' version of facts. She stated the last thing she remembers is seeing the old woman in a part of the castle she'd never seen before and that's why she was exploring it.

Talia said the "funny thing" is that she's looked and now she can't find that part of the castle. She wanted to show the Prince. They got married about 2 mo. ago. She doesn't know the old woman's name. Said woman was hunched over. Her fingers had large knuckles like she had arthritis. Grey hair. Stringy. No discernable accent. Talia has asked her lady maids if they have seen the old woman and none of them have. Neither have the castle guards.

Talia's fairy godmothers are: Feronia, Astraea, Celestia, Ginevra, Kalina, Althea, and Niamh. Accd. to Talia per the Q, it was Niamh who changed Vindicta's curse to be one of sleeping rather than death. (3rd hand info?)

Prince is out hunting right now, but will be back later this afternoon and in all day tomorrow. She will give him my name and number and ask him to call. Acknowledged.

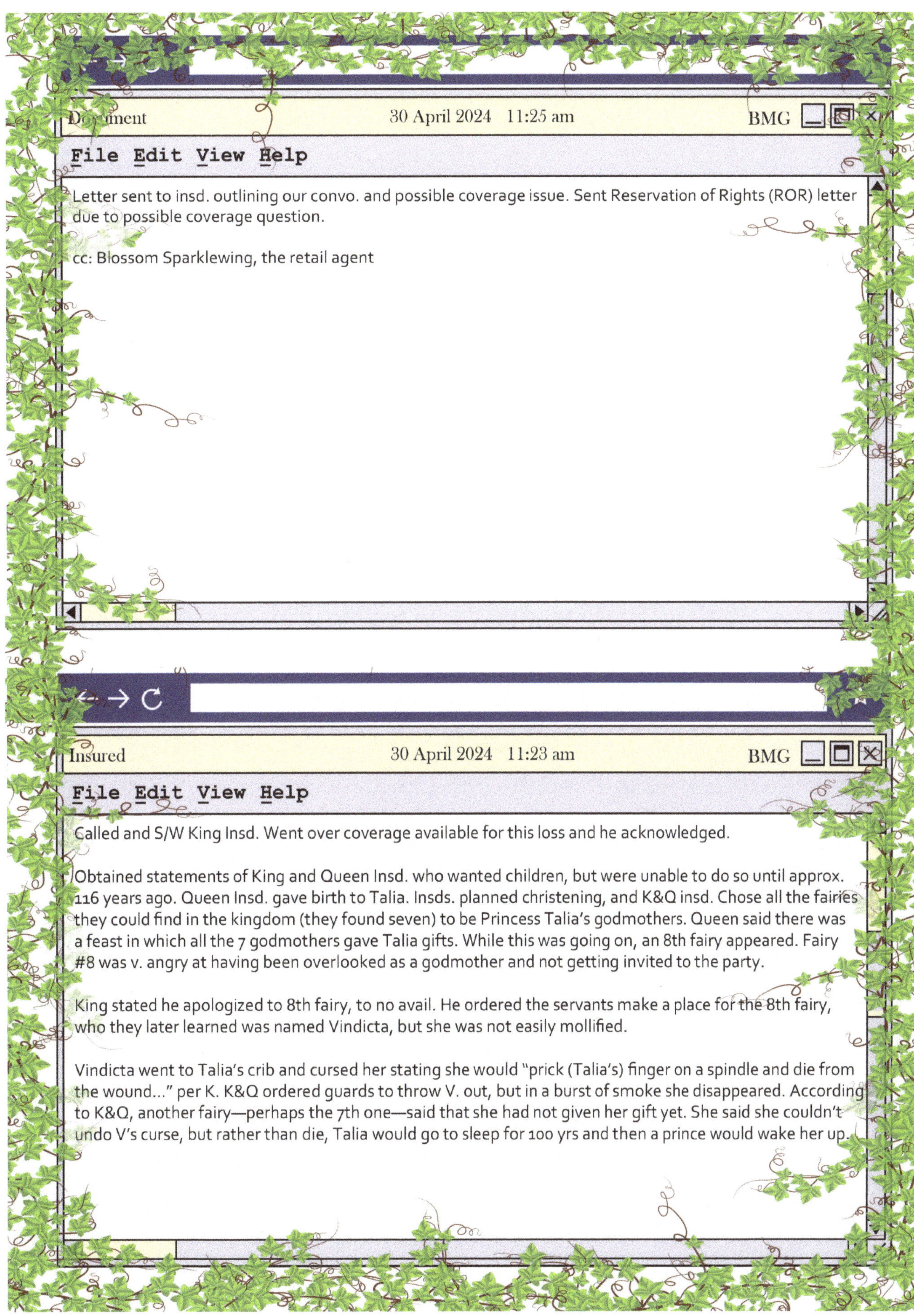

Letter sent to insd. outlining our convo. and possible coverage issue. Sent Reservation of Rights (ROR) letter due to possible coverage question.

cc: Blossom Sparklewing, the retail agent

Called and S/W King Insd. Went over coverage available for this loss and he acknowledged.

Obtained statements of King and Queen Insd. who wanted children, but were unable to do so until approx. 116 years ago. Queen Insd. gave birth to Talia. Insds. planned christening, and K&Q insd. Chose all the fairies they could find in the kingdom (they found seven) to be Princess Talia's godmothers. Queen said there was a feast in which all the 7 godmothers gave Talia gifts. While this was going on, an 8th fairy appeared. Fairy #8 was v. angry at having been overlooked as a godmother and not getting invited to the party.

King stated he apologized to 8th fairy, to no avail. He ordered the servants make a place for the 8th fairy, who they later learned was named Vindicta, but she was not easily mollified.

Vindicta went to Talia's crib and cursed her stating she would "prick (Talia's) finger on a spindle and die from the wound…" per K. K&Q ordered guards to throw V. out, but in a burst of smoke she disappeared. According to K&Q, another fairy—perhaps the 7th one—said that she had not given her gift yet. She said she couldn't undo V's curse, but rather than die, Talia would go to sleep for 100 yrs and then a prince would wake her up.

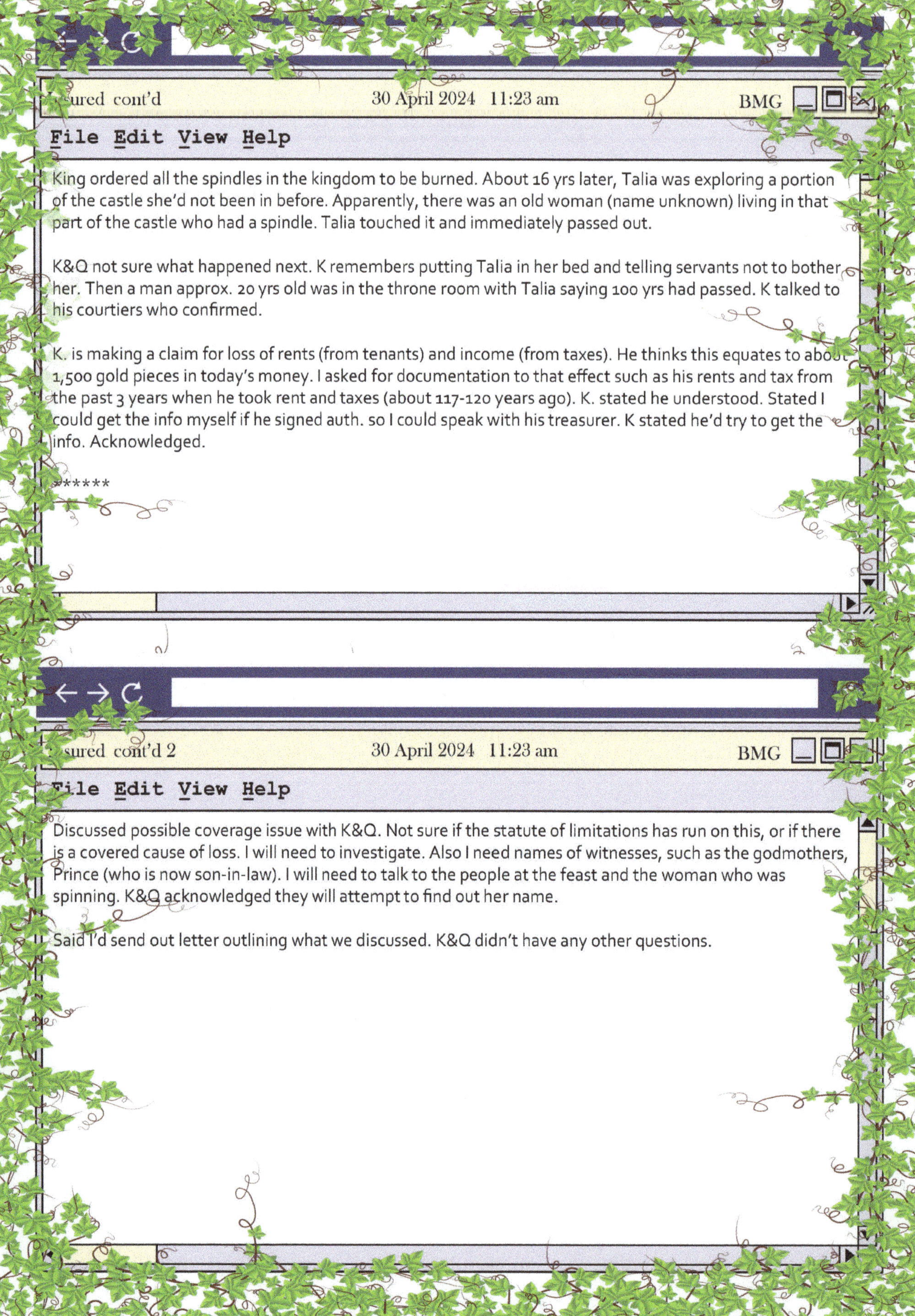

ured cont'd 30 April 2024 11:23 am BMG

File Edit View Help

King ordered all the spindles in the kingdom to be burned. About 16 yrs later, Talia was exploring a portion of the castle she'd not been in before. Apparently, there was an old woman (name unknown) living in that part of the castle who had a spindle. Talia touched it and immediately passed out.

K&Q not sure what happened next. K remembers putting Talia in her bed and telling servants not to bother her. Then a man approx. 20 yrs old was in the throne room with Talia saying 100 yrs had passed. K talked to his courtiers who confirmed.

K. is making a claim for loss of rents (from tenants) and income (from taxes). He thinks this equates to about 1,500 gold pieces in today's money. I asked for documentation to that effect such as his rents and tax from the past 3 years when he took rent and taxes (about 117-120 years ago). K. stated he understood. Stated I could get the info myself if he signed auth. so I could speak with his treasurer. K stated he'd try to get the info. Acknowledged.

******

sured cont'd 2 30 April 2024 11:23 am BMG

File Edit View Help

Discussed possible coverage issue with K&Q. Not sure if the statute of limitations has run on this, or if there is a covered cause of loss. I will need to investigate. Also I need names of witnesses, such as the godmothers, Prince (who is now son-in-law). I will need to talk to the people at the feast and the woman who was spinning. K&Q acknowledged they will attempt to find out her name.

Said I'd send out letter outlining what we discussed. K&Q didn't have any other questions.

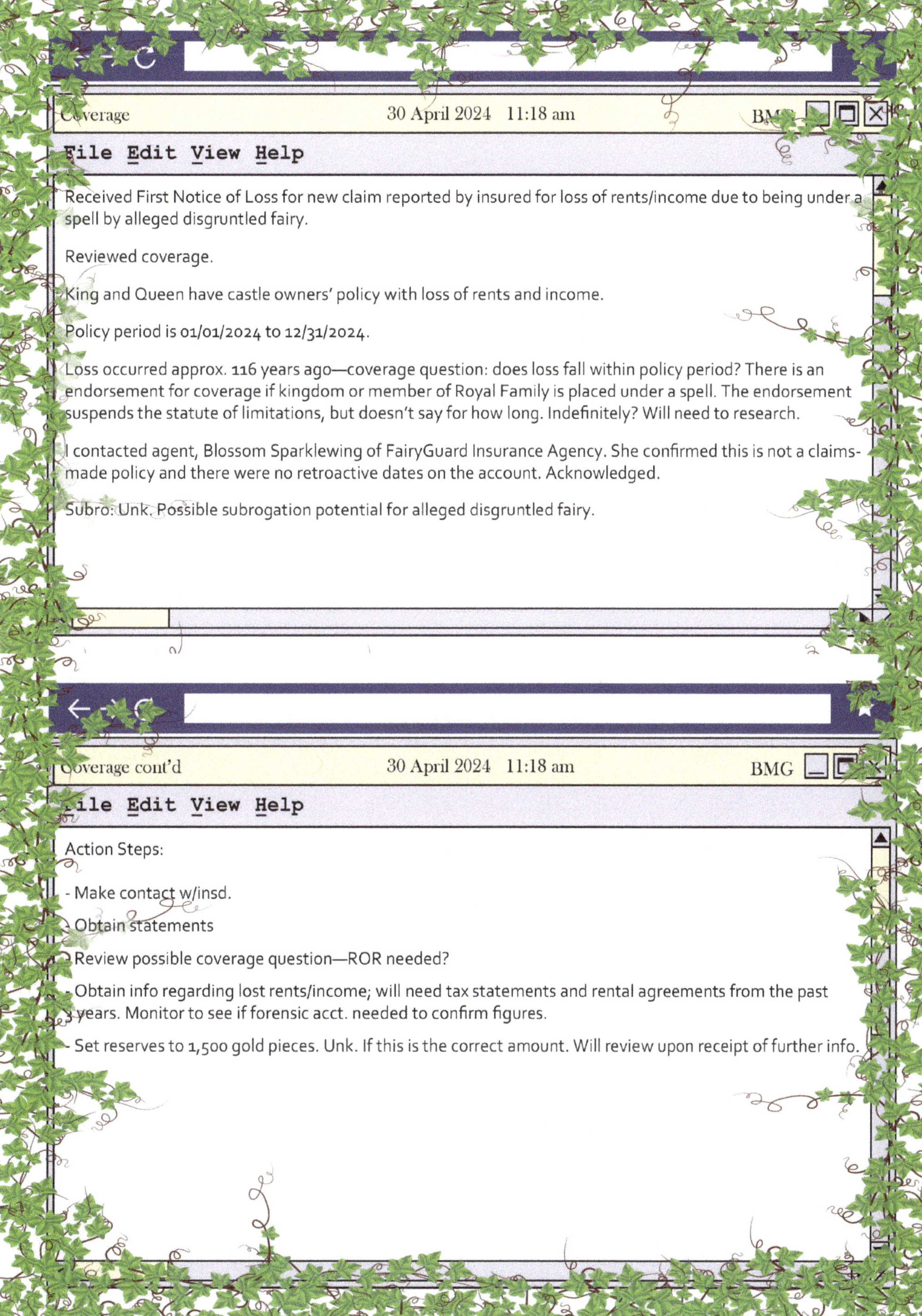

Coverage 30 April 2024 11:18 am BMG

File Edit View Help

Received First Notice of Loss for new claim reported by insured for loss of rents/income due to being under a spell by alleged disgruntled fairy.

Reviewed coverage.

King and Queen have castle owners' policy with loss of rents and income.

Policy period is 01/01/2024 to 12/31/2024.

Loss occurred approx. 116 years ago—coverage question: does loss fall within policy period? There is an endorsement for coverage if kingdom or member of Royal Family is placed under a spell. The endorsement suspends the statute of limitations, but doesn't say for how long. Indefinitely? Will need to research.

I contacted agent, Blossom Sparklewing of FairyGuard Insurance Agency. She confirmed this is not a claims-made policy and there were no retroactive dates on the account. Acknowledged.

Subro: Unk. Possible subrogation potential for alleged disgruntled fairy.

Coverage cont'd 30 April 2024 11:18 am BMG

File Edit View Help

Action Steps:

- Make contact w/insd.

- Obtain statements

- Review possible coverage question—ROR needed?

- Obtain info regarding lost rents/income; will need tax statements and rental agreements from the past 3 years. Monitor to see if forensic acct. needed to confirm figures.

- Set reserves to 1,500 gold pieces. Unk. If this is the correct amount. Will review upon receipt of further info.

At the beginning of time, animals were just starting to work for humans. Though there were already several species of animals, this story involves a dog, a horse, an ox, and a camel.

The first three lived with humans because humans took care of them, and in return, they worked for the humans, providing protection, transportation, and labor. However, the camel lived in Howling Desert because he did not want to work; he did not like company; and whenever someone spoke to him, he said, "Humph!"

Just "Humph!" and nothing more.

The camel ate grass, grains, tamarisks, milkweed, and oats. He was excruciatingly indolent and rude, and when the other animals spoke to him, he said, "Humph!"

Just "Humph!" and nothing more.

Monday morning shone bright. The sky was clear and the birds sang when Horse went to Howling Desert to look for Camel. By and by, Horse found Camel and said, "Camel! Come out and carry the humans and pull their carts with the rest of us. It is ever so much fun!"

"Humph!" said the Camel. Horse went away and told the others.

Tuesday morning burst forth to the rooster's crow. The sky was clear and the birds sang when Dog went to Howling Desert to look for Camel. By and by, Dog found Camel and said, "Camel! Come and protect the humans with the rest of us. You like to howl and spit. You will like this game, too!"

"Humph!" said the Camel. Dog went away and told the others.

Wednesday morning erupted into the world. The sky was clear and the birds sang when Ox went to Howling Desert to look for Camel. By and by, Ox found Camel and said, "Camel! Come and plow with us. You have a sturdy back. You will find it easy!"

"Humph!" said the Camel. Ox went away and told the others.

Thursday morning dawned peacefully, with a soft glow and a gentle breeze. The humans had seen Dog, Horse, and Ox speaking and asked what troubled them.

"We are very sorry for you. It is regrettable that Camel will not share in the work which must be done—as there is so much work since the world is new and all," commiserated the humans. "We will go out and speak with Camel and persuade him to help, since the more of us who work, the faster the work will be done."

The sky was clear and the birds sang when the humans went to Howling Desert to look for Camel. By and by, the humans found Camel and said, "Camel! You have been asked nicely by your fellow animals. You must now come to the farms and cities and cooperate with us. We expect you on Friday morning!"

"Humph!" said the Camel. The humans went away and told the others.

Friday morning arrived with vibrant energy of a new day. The sky was clear and the birds sang when the humans left their homes to begin their activities. They went to their barns and their pastures; Dog followed them as they hitched Ox to the plow and Horse to the cart. But there was no sign of Camel.

"We are very sorry for you. It is regrettable that Camel will not share in the work which must be done—as there is so much work since the world is new and all," commiserated the humans.

"Camel, if he wanted to cooperate, would have been here by now, so we are going to leave him alone. But you three must work double to make up for his absence."

Well, that made Dog, Horse, and Ox very angry, indeed, for there was much work to be done, with the world so new and all. They called an ***indaba*** on the edge of Howling Desert to discuss what they should do about Camel. While they were discussing amongst each other, Camel approached, chewing on milkweed. He was most excruciatingly indolent and laughed at them.

Then he said, "Humph!"

Just "Humph!" and nothing more.

Presently, the ***djinn*** in charge of all deserts came rolling in on a cloud of dust, and he attended the indaba with the three animals.

"Djinn of All Deserts," said the Horse, "Is it right for anyone to be idle, with the world so new and all?"

"It is not," opined the djinn.

"Well," said the Horse, "Camel, who lives in your desert, hasn't carried any humans or led any carts since Monday morning."

"Hmmmm," hummed the djinn, stroking his braided beard, for that is what djinns do when they are trying to buy some time. "Yes, that's my Camel, all right. Have you tried to talk with him?"

"He says, 'Humph!' and nothing more," whined Dog. "He won't even protect the humans. I asked him on Tuesday morning."

"Hmmmm," hummed the djinn, stroking his braided beard, "Yes, that's my Camel, all right. Have you tried discussing this with him?"

"He says, 'Humph!' and nothing more," grumbled Ox. "He won't even plow for the humans. I asked him on Wednesday morning."

"Hmmmm," hummed the djinn, stroking his braided beard, "Yes, that's my Camel, all right. Have you tried speaking to him?"

"The humans have," all three replied, "He says, 'Humph!' and nothing more."

"Hmmmm," hummed the djinn, stroking his braided beard, "Yes, that's my Camel, all right. I shall humph him. Please, kindly wait here for me."

Saturday morning rose with a warm and welcoming glow. The sky was clear and the birds sang when the djinn went to Howling Desert to look for Camel. By and by, the djinn found Camel and said, "Camel! You have been accused of doing no work since Monday by Horse, Dog, and Ox, who say the humans have also spoken to you about this. What say you?"

"Humph!" said the Camel.

"The humans have given Horse, Dog, and Ox extra work to make up for your lack of cooperation. What say you?"

"Humph!" said the Camel.

"I wouldn't say that again if I were you," counselled the Djinn, "You might say it once too often. Camel, I want you to work."

"Humph!" said the Camel. But no sooner had Camel spoke than he saw a great, big, gigantic, enormous hump on his back.

"Do you see that?" asked the Djinn. "That's your very own 'humph' that you've brought upon yourself by not working. Today is Saturday, and you've done no work since Monday, when the work began. Now, go to work."

"But how can I work with this hump on my back?" lamented Camel.

"Ah, that's the beauty of the hump," revealed the djinn. "Because you missed five days of work, you shall be able to go 5 days without eating or drinking. Your food and water are stored in your hump. Come out of the desert and cooperate with the others."

So Camel, hump and all, went and joined Horse, Dog, and Ox, but he has never caught up with them, which is why he still has a hump to this day.

Moral of the Story

Three Blind Mice pointed out that insurance policies are conditional contracts. The insured must perform an act, like paying the premium, for the policy to respond to a loss.

In this fairy tale, the camel does not believe he should perform any duties or do any work, so the djinn punishes the camel by giving him a capacity for working without stopping. Claimants must adhere to the conditions of the policy, one of which is the duty in the event of a loss. While this is mostly directed at policyholders with whom the insurer has a contract, for certain coverages, there are duties the third-party claimant must perform in order for the policy to respond. For the majority of policies, the duties are similar. Failure to follow the conditions of the policy may result in the claim being denied or additional work for the claimant.

In *Adjuster, Mend My Shoe*, the condition was that the insured must begin repairs of the damaged property, but it could also refer to the insured's duty to protect the property from further loss.

Jack and the Beanstalk, discussed later, is an excellent example of another duty in the event of a loss: the insured's duty to notify the police in the event of a crime such as vandalism, arson, or theft. The insured must notify the insurer of a loss "as soon as possible" or "promptly." These words are not defined in the policy, but it is wise to notify the carrier sooner rather than later so that an estimate of damage can be determined. It also stands to reason all information concerning the loss must be given to the carrier such as how, when, and where the loss occurred.

The policyholder must submit an inventory of the damaged and undamaged property to the insurer, as well as allowing the carrier (or representative) to inspect the property or records as often as necessary. This may sound like an insurmountable mountain. How is the average person to determine damaged and undamaged property or separate the two? Fortunately, adjusters are able to do this, notably because this is their job, and they will write estimates of the damaged property. If the adjuster needs records, for example receipts of spending or proof of ownership, they will request them. Some of these things are mentioned in other tales, such as *The Three Spinning Women* and *Suvannahamsa-Jataka*.

The carrier also lists that the insured's duty in an event of a loss is to submit to an examination under oath. An ***examination under oath (EUO)*** is a legal proceeding in which a person is asked to answer questions while under oath, typically as part of an insurance claim investigation. The EUO is conducted by an attorney or representative of the insurance company, and the person being questioned is typically the policyholder or someone making a claim under the policy.

During an EUO, the person being questioned is required to answer questions truthfully and fully, and failure to do so could result in the claim being denied or the policy being cancelled. The EUO is typically conducted in person, and the person being questioned may be required to provide documentation or other evidence to support their claim.

The purpose of an EUO is to gather information about the claim and to determine whether the claim is valid and covered by the policy. EUOs are often used in cases where there is suspicion of fraud or other wrongdoing, and the information gathered during the EUO may be used as evidence in a legal proceeding.

Another duty for the insured is to cooperate with the carrier in its investigation of the loss. For the most part, this would seem self-explanatory, especially when it is the insured's loss which is being investigated. Sometimes, however, insureds do not cooperate with the carrier in liability claims because they feel the claimant has put forth a fraudulent claim or is outright lying about the incident. Be that as it may, a claim is still alleged, and with the insured's cooperation, the adjuster can accurately and quickly determine liability, which is discussed more fully in *Humpty Dumpty*. The insured should remember their duty to report a claim "promptly." Again, some insureds do not want to report the claim for fear of an increase of premiums or because they do not believe the claimant has a valid claim. The best advice is to report the loss and discuss the suspicions with the adjuster.

The condition to submit a signed, sworn ***proof of loss*** is one of the insured's last common duties.

The proof of loss is frequently confused with a *release*. Both are legal documents. A release is used in a liability claim to indicate the file is completed. It is a document that is signed by the claimant (or their representatives) stating that in exchange for an item (usually money), the claimant will not pursue any future claims, additional damages, or sue the at-fault party (the insured) related to the same injury in the future.

A proof of loss, on the other hand, is a formal statement made by a policyholder to an insurance company, stating the amount of money being claimed as compensation for an insured loss covered by the policy. It serves as evidence of the loss incurred by the policyholder and includes a detailed description of the loss or damage, the date and cause of the loss, and the amount of the claim being made. It is rarely used by the more well-known carriers, although it is still a duty and a requirement if requested. Often, if required, the adjuster will complete the form, sending it to the insured for review; then, if accepted, to sign, notarize, and return it in exchange for the settlement check.

Regardless, since it is only a document, albeit a legal one, which formalizes the amount of loss (thus the name "proof of loss"), it is not a *release*, which releases all future responsibility of payment (thus the name "release of all claims"). By reviewing the fine print on a proof of loss document, the insured will note there is nothing which indicates a future claim cannot be submitted. A future claim in the case of a first-party loss is called a "supplement," which was discussed in *Adjuster, Mend My Shoe*.

As an aside, there is such a thing as a "***policyholder release***." It is even more infrequent than the proof of loss, since it acts in the same manner as a release for a third-party claimant indicating the insured may no longer seek additional payments for the loss in question. The author has only seen these used in suspicious claims where payment was being issued as a business decision.

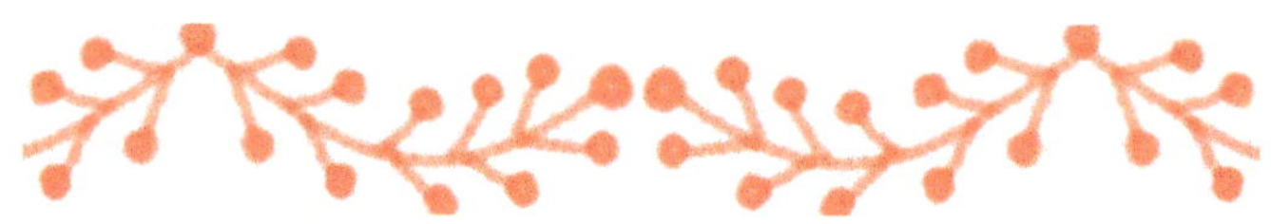

First-Party Property Claim Process

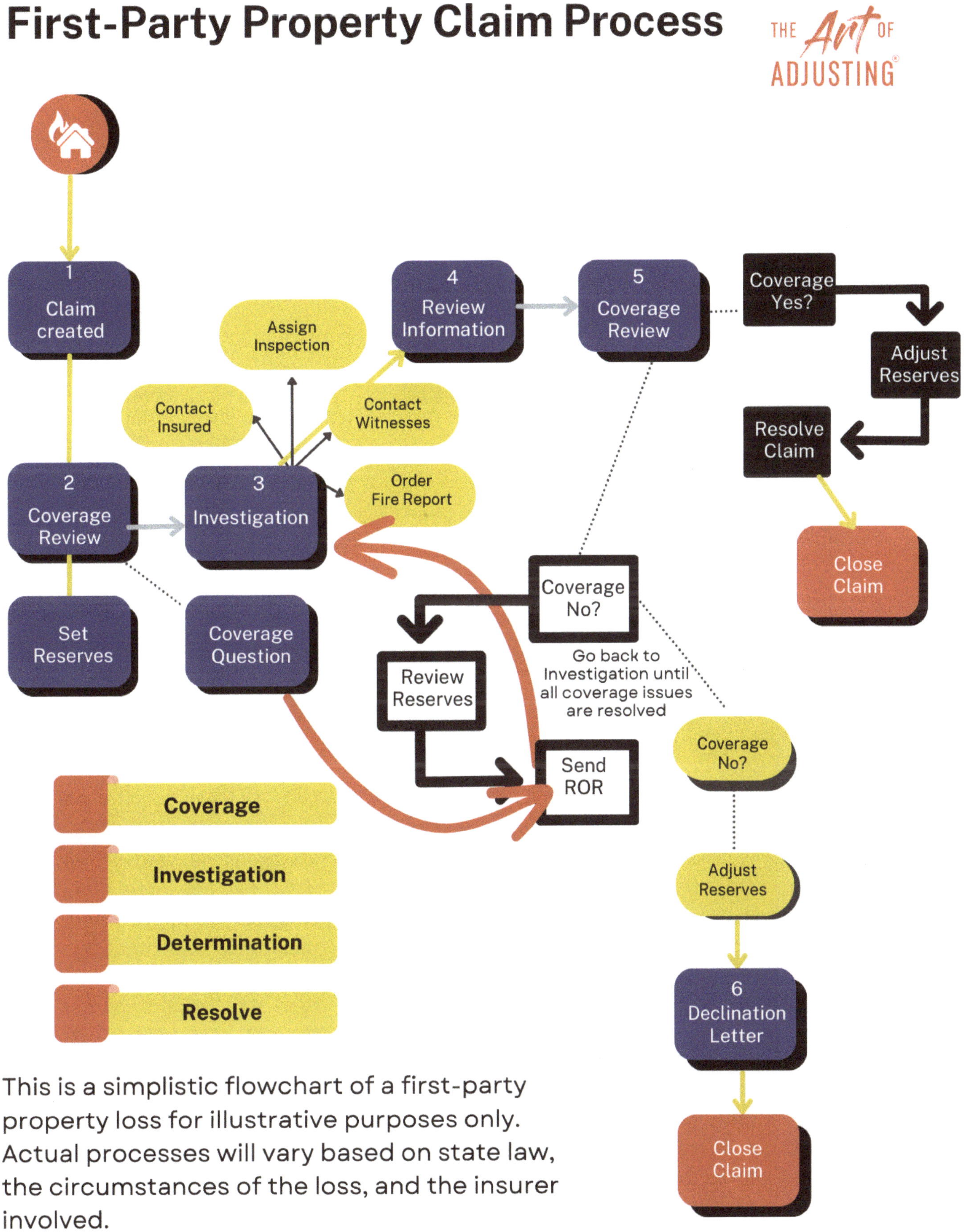

1 Claim created

2 Coverage Review

Set Reserves

3 Investigation

Contact Insured

Assign Inspection

Contact Witnesses

Order Fire Report

Coverage Question

4 Review Information

5 Coverage Review

Coverage Yes?

Adjust Reserves

Resolve Claim

Close Claim

Coverage No?

Review Reserves

Send ROR

Go back to Investigation until all coverage issues are resolved

Coverage No?

Adjust Reserves

6 Declination Letter

Close Claim

Coverage

Investigation

Determination

Resolve

This is a simplistic flowchart of a first-party property loss for illustrative purposes only. Actual processes will vary based on state law, the circumstances of the loss, and the insurer involved.

The Earthquake Fish

Long, long ago, the gods came down from heaven to conquer the earth and civilize the world. While the gods rested here, there were thousands of earthquakes, but the gods did nothing to stop them since the gods, themselves, were not affected by the continuous rocking of the earth. Yet people's houses and lives were never safe.

Now it came to pass that Kashima and Katori, the two gods tasked with subduing the northeastern part of the world, were particularly efficient. They had quickly and quietly restrained all enemies of the sun-goddess and decided to move on to the province of Hitachi. There, Kashima ran his sword into the earth, driving it down through the core until it emerged on the other side. Only the hilt was left above the ground.

Kashima left his sword in the ground when the gods returned to heaven, and over the course of the millennia, the sword turned to stone, and mankind took to calling it *Kanamé ishi*, or the rock of *Kanamé*.

As everyone knows, *Kanamé* is the rivet that holds all of a fan's ribs together; so the area where Kashima left his sword was called "Rivet Rock," since old men believed that the sword bound the earth together.

When ramming the sword through the core, Kashima speared a great catfish, known as *jishin-uwo*, or the earthquake-fish. *Jishin-uwo* is thousands of miles long and holds all the world on its back. Its tail is at Awomori in the north, and the base of its head is at Kyoto, the capital of Japan.

Being so speared caused *Jishin-uwo* great pain, making him restless and angry. Huge, looping feelers, which are as hideous as the moustaches the hairy-faced *Gai-Jin* wear on their lips, are attached to *Jishin-uwo*'s mouth. Movement of these feelers is a sign the monster is in wrath. When he gets angry and flaps his tail or bumps his head, there is an earthquake. When he flounders about or rolls over, there is terrible destruction of life and property on the surface of the earth above.

It was known to the ancient ones that the Rivet Rock could lull the fish back to sleep, but no one could ever lift this rock, except Kashima the mighty one who first set it into the earth. Thus, mankind called to the gods for help, who bade Kashima to watch *Jishin-uwo* since it was his sword which pierced the catfish's flesh, causing pain in the first place.

Yet Today, Kashima never raises the sword rock, except to stop an earthquake of unusual violence. Then, to quiet the beast, Kashima jumps up and straddles him holding him by the gills. Kashima puts his foot on *Jishin-uwo*'s fin. Only then, and only when necessary, Kashima lifts up the great rock of *Kanamé* to hold *Jishin-uwo* down with its weight. *Jishin-uwo* becomes perfectly quiet, and the earthquake ceases.

Hence children sing this earthquake verse:

"No monster can move the *Kanamé* rock
Though he tugs at it ever so hard,
When buildings tumble, people are in shock,
The claims adjusters are on their guard."

Another verse they sing as follows:

"These are things
An earthquake brings;
At nine of the bells, policyholders foretell
Their policy is boloney,
At four insurance is an abhorrence,
At six and eight I want my money."

Moral of the Story

Standard policies cover losses such as hurricanes, tornadoes, windstorms, fires, hail, vandalism, etc. Floods, earthquakes, landslides, mudslide or mudflow, subsidence or sinkholes (basically, dirt) are not covered perils for homes or businesses. This moral will look specifically at the homeowner policy.

Encompassing earthquakes is earth movement, earth rising, earth sinking, or earth shifting. None of these are covered. If the insured has the unfortunate luck of living near a volcano, and regular sacrifices to the volcano gods are not forthcoming, the shock waves from the volcanic eruption also are not covered.

On the bright side, however, ensuing losses caused by fire, explosion, or theft are covered. For example, if an earthquake broke a gas line and then the volcano god dropped some hot lava into the house and it exploded, that would be covered under the standard homeowner policy.

In an earthquake or property policy, the ***occurrence*** of an earthquake includes the quake itself and subsequent aftershocks within 72 hours of the initial quake. This is important because of the deductible, which is a percentage of the policy limits stated on the Declarations Page. The deductible applies either to the house or its contents, whichever is greater. As with every policy, the higher the deductible, the lower the premiums. It is not uncommon to see deductibles of 10-20% in areas where there is a high occurrence of earthquakes. Therefore, policyholders should be aware of how much they need to have in savings should an earthquake strike.

For example, if a home has a policy limit of $500,000 for the house, and the earthquake deductible is 15%, the deductible is $75,000.

$500,000 x 15%= $75,000

Imagine, then, if the damage to the home caused by the earthquake was appraised to be $45,000. The carrier would not issue any payment since the damage would be less than the deductible. If the damage was discovered to be $100,000, the insured would receive a check for $25,000.00 (assuming the insured was compliant with coinsurance requirements).

Whole Loss and Damage	**$100,000**
Deductible	**$75,000**
Net Settlement to Insured	**$25,000**

It may be possible to obtain coverage through an endorsement or a separate policy. If the policyholder has a mortgage and lives in an earthquake zone, the lender might require the owner to obtain insurance. If the homeowner doesn't obtain the earthquake policy, the lender will obtain it and add the premium to the mortgage payment, usually at an increased cost.

Old Mother Hubbard

Old Mother Hubbard
Lived in a house.
Her dog was so hungry,
He barked and he groused.
She went to the cupboard
To give him a snack,
But the door was stuck,
So she gave it a whack.

She looked in the fridge;
There was nothing to eat.
She looked in the pantry;
There was no treat.
She went to the store and
Bought some food and snacks.
When she came back,
Her dog had the facts.

Old Mother Hubbard
Went to the cupboard.
She saw that the door
Had been broken and bent.
The dog was confused and
He gave her a stare.
Mother Hubbard knew
Someone had been there.

Call the adjuster,
And you must trust her.
Call the police now,
Report the crime, *meine frau.*
They inspected the crime
That "someone" had come.
Breaking the door from
Whacks, slaps, and their thumbs.

The adjuster talked
This loss did not shock.
Unriddling things,
Explaining everything,
She said the old door
Had seen way much more
Damage from slings and dings.

Mother Hubbard was agog.
She was not a fraud!
Hoist the adjuster,
She would, by her petard!
Hubbard was flustered.
Of her furniture
She took very good care.
NO way this was wear and tear!

"This is not mischief,
"Vandalism, or
"Malicious Intent.
"The door is quite old;
"There were days not bent
"On hinges which bore
"Abuse through segments."
The adjuster relayed.

Old Mother Hubbard
Called a contractor.
The door needs to be
Replaced, but there is no
Good benefactor.
No payment from the
Insurer. Forgo
Payment for the cupboard.

Moral of the Story

Most people are not very perceptive about their possessions. Cars and home appliances are routinely serviced; holes are filled in; gutters cleaned, rooms repainted, yards mowed, raked, mulched, etc. People believe they are taking good care of their material possessions, but they don't necessarily see the cabinets' chipped paint, for example, as the years go by. So, it is natural that if there has been a break-in, people look at their home through fresh eyes. The homeowner may see damage they believe must have occurred during the break-in, but in reality, may simply be worn out items.

Most policies will cover riot, civil commotion, vandalism, malicious mischief, and theft. But no policy will cover wear and tear, which makes sense. It is up to the property owner to take care of their property and to replace it when it is worn. Remember, this is an insurance policy, not a warranty.

Laypeople tend to use certain insurance terms interchangeably. Unfortunately, it's uncommon for most policies to define the terms which are the subject of this nursery rhyme. As discussed in *Three Blind Mice*, words which have special meanings will be bolded or in quotes. If they are not, the common, everyday meaning is applied to a word, but there are times when adjusters, attorneys, and the courts will use different sources to define these words.

For example, most people think riot and civil commotion are the same, but legally they are different.

> **RIOT:** Black's Law Dictionary (11th ed. 2019) defines this as a group of three or more persons illegally disturbing the peace with the intention to act in a violent manner by threatening or terrorizing the public.
>
> **CIVIL COMMOTION:** This picks up where the definition of riot stops. It is an uprising, or an insurrection, by a large group of people who act to cause damage or harm to people or property.
>
> People also think the next two words are the interchangeable, but again, they have different legal meanings.
>
> **MALICIOUS MISCHIEF:** This is the deliberate, planned, and premeditated destruction of property. It is usually the name of the crime in criminal statutes.
>
> **VANDALISM:** Vandalism is willfully, wantonly, and recklessly damaging property for the sole purpose of causing damage.

Put in these clear-cut definitions, it's easy to see how some damage would not be the result of vandals or malicious mischief, but the result of the normal wear and tear that all property eventually experiences. While not defined in the policy, *wear and tear* means the deterioration of an item by its ordinary and reasonable use.

Often, it is absent landlords who confuse vandalism with the hard living of their property. Adjusters frequently see claims in which a tenant has been evicted. Then, when the landlord regains control of their property, they see cabinet doors off hinges, debris and trash left behind, and general nastiness everywhere.

This, for the most part, is not vandalism because it has not occurred by someone "willfully, wantonly, and recklessly damaging property for the sole purpose of causing damage." (see above) It is the result of a messy person having lived at their property.

The key to recognizing the difference between wear and tear, hard-living, and vandalism is the intent of the person who is damaging the property. Proving intent is difficult. The adjuster may know that the tenant willfully left fish on the kitchen counter in the middle of summer and turned off the air conditioning, but proving that will be nigh impossible.

The author is not entirely sure but believes it to be illegal to hoist an adjuster by their petard. Readers should consult with their attorneys for legal advice.

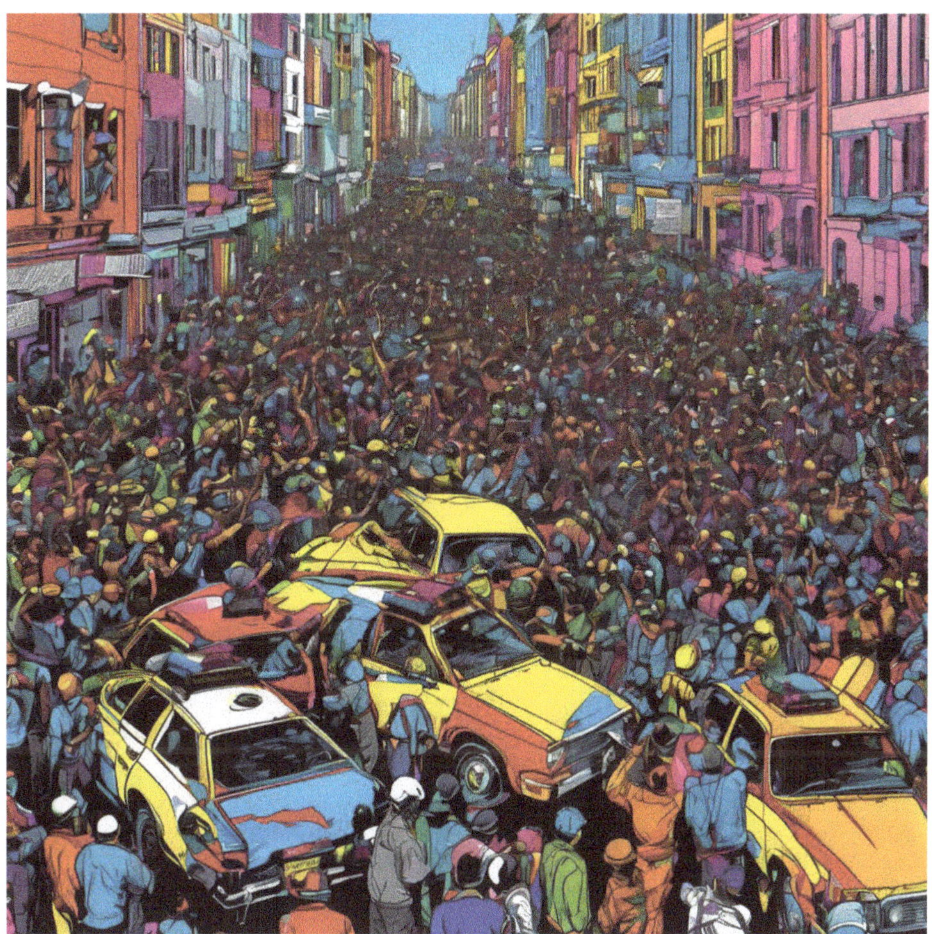

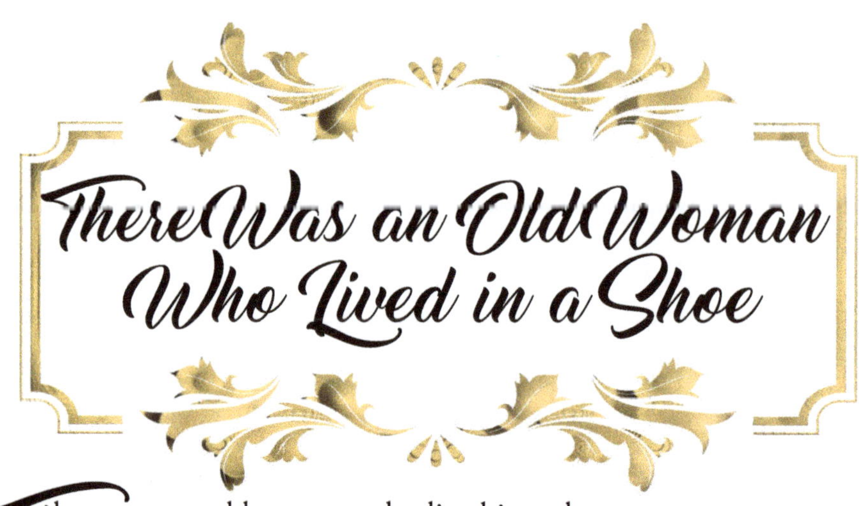

There was an old woman who lived in a shoe.
She had so much stuff she didn't know what to do.
A wind came from the south and blew and blew.
Taking her stuff to a place she had no clue.

She filed a claim for her books;
The pots and pans in which she cooks;
For all her gifts she looks and looks,
But she cannot find the family's photo book.

She had a claim and didn't know what to do.
She called her insurer who came to the rescue.
The adjuster investigated the old woman's issue
And found the shoe was undervalued.

This created a big ballyhoo,
Because the old woman previously eschewed
Raising her policy limits hitherto.

The agent attempted to help in this snafu,
But he could only offer to pursue
A redo on the old woman's miscue.
That it was his fault was simply her view.
The old woman was a co-insured, that is true.
She must pay a portion of the loss from her revenue.
But then came a terrific breakthrough!

Being underinsured had met its Waterloo.
And the next claim she had
Made her mighty glad
That her limits were no longer bad.

Moral of the Story

Coinsurance is rarely understood by insurance consumers. The simplest explanation is that the policyholder agrees to carry a specific percentage of insurance (policy limit) on the building; failure to do so means the insured will have to pay a pro-rata share of the loss.

If a loss occurs, then the original carrier will pay its portion of the loss, less the deductible, and the insured will pay their portion of the loss, plus the deductible. This condition in property policies encourages the policyholder to insure the property to the insurable value. The insurable value may be different (higher or lower) than the amount for which the insured purchased the property. This is because insurance excludes some things that a homeowner or building-owner purchases as part of the home/structure—namely land.

Because coinsurance is assessed *at the time of the loss*, inflation in the economy, alterations, renovations, and improvements to the building can result in the insured having to cover a significant portion of the loss if they haven't regularly reviewed their premiums and adjusted them accordingly. Inflation, home repairs since COVID, and labor and material shortages have all caused the cost of building materials to increase. Unfortunately, underinsurance has been a chronic problem in the insurance industry for decades. Some homeowners and businessowners are underinsured by as little as 25% to as much as 400% according to some sources.

Usually, the policyholder must have policy limits for the structure up to 80% of its value to receive 100% of the policy limit. The policy includes information about the way the insurable value of the structure will be determined in the case of a loss—usually it is replacement cost value (RCV) or actual cash value (ACV). Without going too far afield, the insurable value is what it will cost to rebuild the structure as it was at the time of the loss. Most structures are insured for replacement cost, so we will use that amount for our explanation here.

There are two main ways to value a claim: (1) Actual Cash Value (ACV) and (2) Replacement Cost Value (RCV).

There are three methods for determining and measuring actual cash value (ACV): (1) Market Value, (2) Broad Evidence, and (3) the mathematical formula of Replacement Cost less Depreciation.

As with everything in claims, where the policyholder lives (aka "jurisdictions") determines which method will be used.

When the policy or state law does not define ACV, most states use the broad evidence rule, which includes replacement less depreciation, purchase price, condition of the item, reproduction of the item, obsolescence of the item, and the item's fair market value.

Depreciation is the devaluation of an item due to wear, tear, and its condition. Many courts now use the definition of ACV to mean the broad evidence rule. The reason is that simply using the mathematic formula of RCV less depreciation can leave a policyholder with very little money to repair a shoe, where The Old Woman lives, based on its wear and tear.

For the most part, building supplies cost the same in a particular city, although they do fluctuate, and supplies will have a different value depending on where the insured lives in the country. As mentioned in *Adjuster, Mend My Shoe*, insurers use a computer program which can determine prices of building supplies down to the zip code.

The policy states how coinsurance is determined, but the shortcut adjusters use is:

$$\left(\frac{\boldsymbol{Did}}{\boldsymbol{Should}}\ \boldsymbol{x\ Loss}\right) - \boldsymbol{Deductible}$$

The adjuster will measure the old woman's home and input this information into the computer program. This amount is the "should." Then they will look at the current policy limits (*Did*) and divide that by what the valuation is (*Should*). That number should be 80% or greater. If that number is 79% or less, the old woman will become a co-insurer with her carrier.

EXAMPLES

Scenario #1:

A 3 bedroom, 3 bath, 2,600 sq ft house in Enchanted Hollow, Fairytale Land, is listed for \$570,275. The old woman's policy limit for her shoe home is \$570,000; the insurable value is \$650,000. The loss is \$25,000. The deductible is \$5,000.

First, Begonia Gemforest, the adjuster determines the "should" of the equation:

\$650,000 x .80=\$520,000

Begonia can see that the "should" is less than the "did" of \$570,000, and the insurer will pay 100% of the loss, less the deductible. In other words, the old woman will receive a check for \$20,000 (the amount of damages less the deductible).

Scenario #2:

Using the same information, but now increasing the insurance value to \$825,000. The old woman, then should have insured her shoe for \$660,000.

\$825,000 x .80=\$660,000

Begonia realizes the "should" is greater than the amount of insurance the old woman "did" have. Now Begonia needs to determine what portion of the loss Mother Goose Insurance Mutual will pay, which is 86% of the loss.

$$\left(\frac{\$570,000}{\$660,000}\right) = 86\%$$

In this example, the old woman will assume part of the responsibility of being an insurance company in addition to paying for her deductible. The carrier will issue a check in the amount of \$16,500 to the old woman. This was determined in the following manner:

$$\left(\frac{\$570,000}{\$660,000}\right) = (86\%\ x\ \$25,000) - \$5,000 = \$16,500.00$$

Whole Loss and Damage	**\$25,000**
Less Coinsurance Deduction	**\$21,500**
Less Deductible	**\$ 5,000**
Payment by Insurance Company	**\$16,500**

Then the old woman must pay $8,500 out of her pocket to repair the property—she is a co-insurer of the loss. This figure was determined in the following manner:

Whole Loss and Damage	**$25,000**
Less Payment by Insurance Company	**$16,500**
Amount Insured Owes	**$8,500**

The old woman will pay $3,500 for the damages ***plus*** the $5,000 deductible, or $8,500 as illustrated in the chart above.

There is a debate in insurance circles about the duty a carrier or producer owes someone like the old woman regarding compliance with the policy's coinsurance requirement. Most insurance professionals believe that it is the insured's responsibility to make sure they are insured to value on the structure.

After all, it's the old woman's property. She knows what she paid for it; she knows what improvements or repairs she has done. She should be aware of what happens if she is not properly covered.

If the ***insurance-to-value*** isn't the retail value of the house/building/structure, then how is it determined? We already discussed the national program that adjusters use, but this happens after the loss—it's too late at this point. There are two methods for structure valuations prior to the claim:

(1) Contractors can write an estimate for the rebuild cost;

(2) Agents may have access to a program similar to the one adjusters uses, post-loss.

For businessowners who have contents which may have a coinsurance requirement, an agreed value or a reporting form may be advantageous. An ***agreed value*** form lists the contents and their values. The carrier agrees to the values of the contents, and in the event of a loss, the insurance company will pay actual cash value in the case of a partial loss, or the value everyone agreed on in the case of a total loss. A ***reporting form*** is advantageous to businesses with seasonal fluctuations in their inventory. The policyholder will turn in a list of their contents at a prearranged time (e.g., monthly or quarterly). The insurer will adjust the policy limits for this fluctuation in contents so that the business is not underinsured in the event of a loss. The reporting form will create fluctuations in premiums as often as the reports are turned in, but it does offer some degree of comfort to know the insured is not underinsured.

Regardless, the old woman should routinely review her policy limits to make sure she will not become a co-insurer on a loss.

The Historic Fart

Kaukaban, a village of wondrous beauty, nestled amidst the rugged mountains of Yemen, is like a jewel, sparkling in the sun, with its whitewashed houses and ornate wooden doors, each one a unique work of art. The townspeople are as warm and hospitable as the Arabian sun, welcoming travelers with open arms and offering them a taste of their rich culture and way of life. And at night, Kaukaban is transformed into a magical realm, with the stars twinkling in the clear sky like diamonds and the distant mountains shrouded in mist. The air is filled with the sweet scent of jasmine and other exotic flowers, while the voices of storytellers echo through the streets.

One raconteur was a figure of great respect and admiration in the village of Kaukaban, where young and old, alike, eagerly waited to hear his stories. Hassan had a weathered face with deep-set wrinkles from too many years in the sun, and a long white beard that blended with his flowing white robe, making it impossible to tell where one began and the other ended. His hazel eyes were bright and twinkling, with a mischievous glint that hinted at the stories he had yet to tell. No one knew how old Hassan was. The children would ask, and his answers would always change. He would say, "My child, my age is a mystery only Allah and the Prophet, blessings be upon him, know. My years are as numerous as the grains of sand in the desert." Or he would smile and lean in, whispering, "Ah, my dear friend, age is but a number, a mere fleeting shadow that changes with the wind. For centuries, I have roamed the lands and seen empires rise and fall, but the fire in my heart burns as bright as ever. Perhaps I am older than the mountains and wiser than the sages, or perhaps I am but a sprightly youth with the soul of an old man. Who can say for sure? Some mysteries are best left unsolved, and the question of my age is one of them. Let us instead savor the tales I weave and the wonders they contain."

The night was calm and clear, and the moon shone bright and full, casting a silver light that bathed the village of Kaukaban in an otherworldly glow. Hassan had set up his storytelling spot in the village square, under the spreading branches of a majestic old fig tree. The tree was adorned with small oil lamps, their flickering flames casting a warm golden light on the faces of the eager listeners who had gathered around.

The air was alive with anticipation, as children and adults waited in hushed silence for Hassan to begin weaving his tales. In the distance, village dogs could be heard, and the call of a night bird lent an eerie yet enchanting quality to the scene.

"Does anyone have a story they want to hear?" Hassan's gentle voice drew in his audience and held their attention.

"I do." A man covered in ash declared. "My house burned to the ground. Ahmed, the carpenter, has given me an invoice of 5 gold coins to rebuild it. I went to Hakim, the wealthiest man in Kaukaban for aid and money. He gave me 2 gold coins, telling me my home was worth 2 gold coins at the time of the fire. This does not make sense. Explain that to me."

Hassan listened intently and nodded thoughtfully before he began to speak.

"My dear friend," he said, "your situation reminds me of a tale from long ago. It is the story of *The Historic Fart*."

As Hassan began his tale, his voice rose and fell like the waves of the sea, carrying his listeners on a magical journey through time and space. The night was alive with the magic of his words, and the stars seemed to dance in the sky in time with the rhythm of his tale.

"The elders tell a tale of Abu Hasan that happened right here in Kaukaban. Abu was from the Fadhli tribe which he had left to become a successful merchant here, amassing even greater wealth than Hakim. Abu was married to the love of his life who had, unfortunately, died during childbirth. Abu's friends were eager for him to remarry. When they would approach him about the subject, he would say, 'My friends, the elders' elders say, "Matrimony brings happiness for just one month and misery for a lifetime."'

"It is said that Abu, as he aged, grew weary of his loneliness, and ached for a son to carry on his legacy. Perhaps it was this longing that prompted him to entertain the proposal brought forth by the match-makers: the ***caliph*** sought his hand in marriage to his eldest daughter, said to be more beautiful than the moon over the sea. After much contemplation, Abu finally consented to the union, and all around him were filled with an immense sense of jubilation and elation.

"To celebrate his nuptials, a grand ceremony was arranged, the likes of which had not been seen for many moons. Tables were adorned with delicacies such as stuffed chickens with pistachios, roasted goats with fresh dates in their mouths, and pastries filled with cream and walnuts, rice in five different colors, sherbets and more. The finest musicians in the land played melodious tunes throughout the day, and as evening approached, Abu emerged onto the balcony and showered gold coins onto the outstretched hands of the poor. It was a night that would be remembered for generations to come, as a testament to how well loved Abu was in this very city.

"As the groom and his companions lazed on silk cushions, smoking pipes filled with the finest honey tobacco, the bride was brought forth. She was dressed in the first of seven dresses, each more stunning than the last. Adorned in a turquoise gown embellished with precious gems and silver, she shone as bright as the fullest moon. And as she removed each successive dress, her beauty grew, until she emerged in a simple white gown with a pearl necklace around her slender neck. Her lips were like the most precious coral, and the elders say that the angels in heaven were jealous of the bride's eyes which outshone the stars in the sky.

"The bride, blushing with anticipation, retired to her opulent chamber adorned with silken drapes and fragrant flowers, eagerly awaiting the arrival of her beloved husband. Meanwhile, the groom enjoyed the company of his esteemed guests, regaled them with his wit and wisdom, expounded on matters of faith and governance with equal aplomb, and won their admiration and respect.

"As the night wore on, Abu's desire grew stronger, and he rose to bid farewell to his guests and join his bride in the nuptial chamber. However, his overindulgence in the sumptuous wedding feast proved to be his undoing, for as he stood up, a mighty fart erupted from his bowels, resounding across the room and shattering the tranquil silence. All fell silent, shocked and bewildered by the sudden outburst, as Abu Hasan himself blushed with embarrassment, unable to hide his flatulence from the nose and ears of his guests.

"His friends, not wanting to offend, feigned ignorance of the affronting sound and resumed their merrymaking. Abu quietly exited toward the bedchamber, but as he neared his wife's room, he was overtaken by a sudden panic, and instead fled down a side corridor, mounted his trusty steed, and galloped with all haste toward the port. There, he boarded a ship bound for the East and sailed away that very night, casting a longing glance back at his beloved city, tears streaming down his face until the horizon consumed it from sight.

"Abu made landfall in Calicut on the Malabar coast in the southwest of India. With his gift for languages, fine manners, and impeccable character, he soon found himself in the service of a local ***rajah***. He was known for his pureness and moderation, never

partaking in vices such as smoking the ***hookah*** with other men, and he soon rose through the ranks to become responsible for the welfare and discipline of the rajah's personal guard.

"Despite being loved and respected by all in the court, Abu never so much as cracked a smile. At nightfall, he would often climb to the highest battlement and gaze toward the west, in the direction of his homeland, and sigh heavily. The servants knew better than to disturb him. His demeanor led many to believe he was a great man who carried a heavy burden.

"After ten long years of serving the rajah and tired of being homesick, Abu finally gathered his few possessions and set sail for his homeland. As the ship approached the coast, he paced the deck anxiously, wondering what fate awaited him upon his return. Abu rode toward the city and couldn't help but feel a sense of trepidation, unsure if he would be welcomed back with open arms or shunned for his long absence.

Eventually, he found himself wandering through the hills, for seven nights and seven days, until one night, he stumbled upon a humble shepherd's hovel and heard a mother singing her child to sleep. Curiosity getting the better of him, he pressed his ear to the side of the hut and listened as the child asked, 'Mummy, how old am I?'

"The mother spoke softly to her daughter, saying, 'My beloved, on the night that you were born, a great sound echoed through the halls of Kaukaban, a sound that shook the very foundations of the earth. That was the night that Abu Hasan farted.'

"As soon as Abu overheard these words, his heart sank within him. He realized that his reputation was forever tarnished by that one embarrassing moment, and he could not bear the thought of facing his fellow citizens. With a heavy heart, he fled from the hut, muttering to himself, 'My fart has become a date that will be remembered forevermore.' And with that, he disappeared into the night, never to be seen in Baghdad again."

"What's that got to do with the invoice amount and the money received?" The man and Ahmed demanded.

Hassan smiled and said, "The…

Moral of the Story

There Was an Old Woman Who Lived in a Shoe discussed actual cash value (ACV) and replacement cost value (RCV) in property losses. This story also deals with valuation in a claim.

Whether the insured likes it or not, the carrier wants to assure itself that the property insured (the home, for example) will be repaired or the damaged property replaced. This is why many insurers will pay ACV even if the insured has an RCV policy. Essentially, the carrier is presenting a carrot to the insured: repair this damage, and we will pay the entire loss, less the deductible.

When reviewing the estimate of damages, the insureds and their contractors may notice the carrier has depreciated intangible items such as general contractor overhead and profit, labor, and even sales tax. How, exactly, can the insurer depreciate something that does not exist in a physical form? After all, the labor to install the damaged item (in the case of our story, the burned structure) may still exist if part of the structure is still standing. Or seen another way, policyholder advocates argue the labor to install a shingle is still applicable even if the nail and the shingle are damaged as a result of wind damage.

An intangible item is something that cannot be touched. The labor from a person installing a shingle, for example, cannot be touched. Abu's fart cannot be touched, yet it is, arguably, a thing that has had an impact on other things (people, and perhaps a reputation).

When an insurance company calculates the value of a damaged property, they take into account the depreciation of the materials used in the construction process, which includes the cost of labor, the general contractor's overhead and profit, and the taxes/fees/permits. If the insureds have RCV, they will receive, ultimately, full reimbursement for their expenses when the work is done. Again, this is an incentive to the policyholder to repair the damaged property.

Everyone agrees a tangible item (something that can be touched) is subject to wear and tear and therefore depreciable.

Advocates for the insureds often state that repairs cannot be funded because contractors, while used to the idea of depreciation of materials and aware that insureds do not receive 100 percent payment for the loss (because of the deductible), cannot reduce their labor costs, overhead, and profit since that is what allows them to pay their workers, their utility bills, etc. In other words, the insureds will not have enough money to pay the contractors.

Think of it like this: after a meal in a restaurant, the diner is charged for the entire meal, even if they have eaten only half the food. The customer is not permitted to pay for half the meal, take the other half home, and then the next day, when the diner reheats the leftovers for lunch, pay the restaurant for the other half of the meal. A restaurant could not pay its servers or order food if it was consistently operating on half its budget, with only a "maybe" on collecting the rest of the payment. Yet, policyholder advocates argue, this is what the insurance industry is doing to contractors and insureds when carriers deduct wear and tear to intangible items like profit and labor.

Setting aside the fact that one does not (and should not) pay the contractor 100% up front for the proposed work, how does this difference in understanding about what could and could not be reduced occur?

As always, it stems from the definitions in the policy. "Actual cash value" is not defined in the property policy; so, some insurers began depreciating intangible items. Lawsuits ensued. Courts were split. The Illinois State Court of Appeals said in 2020 that labor cannot be depreciated when considering ACV of a loss; other states, California among them, have passed legislation stating carriers cannot depreciate labor; South Carolina's insurers, however, may deduct wear and tear from labor; yet, the Vermont Department of Insurance issued a bulletin in 2015 addressing the issue, in which they asserted that insurers are violating the unfair claim settlement practices if they depreciate labor. In Pennsylvania, insurers cannot depreciate labor unless the policy says they can.

A fart, as in Abu's case, can be a bad thing and a detriment to one's social life. On the other hand, passing gas indicates the sign of a good meal for the Inuit tribe of Canada. As always, it is of utmost importance that the insured read, and *understand*, the policy and be aware of what the state allows regarding depreciation of intangible items.

Jack and the Beanstalk

LOST PROPERTY REPORT

Completion of this report will document the loss of Personal Property **other than FIREARMS**. If the loss includes Firearms, **DO NOTCOMPLETE THIS FORM.** (To report the loss of a firearm, call the Fairy Godfather Task Force.)

Mail Completed Form to: Police Department Records Division
400 Goldfinch Street
Enchanted Hollow, FTL 00002

ATTN: Fairy Godmother Task Force

REPORT NUMBER: ______________________

Call the Fairy Godmother Task Force and ask for a "Lost Property" report number. If this number is not filled in, your report will not be recorded bythe Department.

NAME OF PERSON OWNING PROPERTY

NAME Kragsog Blunderboore

STREET 153172 Beanstalk Lane

SUITE/APT ______

CITY/ST/ZIP Enchanted Hollow, Fairytale Land 00002

TELEPHONE Stone # Bean-15

Address of Loss 153172 Beanstalk Ln **Zip** 00002

Type of Location of Loss Residence

Date Property Last Seen February 26, 2023 **Time** 10:30 ☒ **AM** or ☐ **PM**

Property Discovered Missing February 26, 2023 **Time** 10:30 ☒ **AM** or ☐ **PM**

REPORTING PERSON AND WITNESS INFORMATION
(This is NOT public information.)

PERSON MAKING REPORT (RP) (If Different from Owner) **Race** Giant **Sex** M **Birthday** 06/30

Name: Kragsog Blunderboore **Contact Phone #** **H** (Stone) Bean-1515 **Other** (Stone) Bean-26

Street 153172 Beanstalk Lane **City** Enchanted Hollow **ST** FTL **ZIP** 00002

PROPERTY

QTY	DESCRIPTION – (Serial Numbers if Available)	COST EACH $	TOTAL COST $
1	Sack of gold coins (Mother Goose on one side; beanstalk on the other)	1,000 gold pieces	1,000 gold pieces
1	Hen who lays golden eggs on command (red feathers; clucks a lot)	1 gold egg/day	Unknown
1	Golden, Magical Harp (Serial #: 18-MH-0482961; Model: Self-playing)	500 gold pieces	500 gold pieces
	Use Additional Sheets if Necessary **Total Loss**		Unk. See below

NARRATIVE : (Briefly describe what happened.)

I don't know when Jack Englishman stole the hen, but she lays a golden egg every day. The cost will be the number of days the Englishman has had my hen.

I came home one day and I smelled an Englishman. They stink, but my wife said there wasn't any boy in the house. I counted my money and fell asleep. The next day the same thing happened, but that was the last time I remember seeing my hen. But my wife said there was no boy in the house. The third day I took a nap, but my harp woke me up saying an Englishman was kidnapping her. He got away down the beanstalk before I could go after him. I wasn't going to go down there and fall and break my neck. I think you should talk to my wife, too, because she's obviously in on the theft. She was the one who kept saying "Oh, no, there's no boy here." When obviously there was a boy. But it was Jack Englishman who stole all my property. And my wife was in on it.

In an effort to assist citizens of Fairytale Land who have lost personal property while still allowing police officers to remain available for emergency situations, the Fairy Godmother Task Force has authorized citizens to complete their own Lost Property Reports. These reports are available to all citizens with the following stipulations:

- Lost firearms cannot be reported when using this form. In the event of a lost firearm, call the Fairy Godfather Task Force to make the report.
- As this is an official document, any falsifications on the form may result in criminal charges for "Filing a False Police Report."
- Lost Property is not a criminal action and therefore will not generate any police follow-up. If lost property is the result of a crime being committed, you will need to call the Fairy Godmother Task Force to make your report.
- Property listed on this form WILL NOT be entered into any crime databases.
- Property lost outside Enchanted Hollow City Limits or last seen outside Enchanted Hollow City Limits may not be reported to the Enchanted Hollow City Police Department. It must be reported tothe agency with jurisdiction for that location.

To file your report:

1. Complete the ***Lost Property Form***, leaving the Report Number blank. Be as thorough as possible, including a description of the lost item and a brief explanationof where and how the property was lost.

2. Call the Fairy Godmother Task Force to obtain your Report Number. Inform the operator that you need a Report Number for a Lost Property Form.

3. Write the Service Report Number in the appropriate box (located near the top ofthe form on the left-hand side).

PLEASE NOTE: A FORM WITHOUT A REPORT NUMBER IS NOT AN OFFICIAL DOCUMENT AND WILL NOT BE RECORDED BY THE POLICE DEPARTMENT.

4. Make a copy of the completed form – this will be your official police report.

5. Mail the completed form to the following address:

Police Department
Records Division
400 Goldfinch Street
Enchanted Hollow, FTL 00002
ATTN: Fairy Godmother Task Force

02/24/21-fgtf

Moral of the Story

Just like *Old Mother Hubbard*, Mr. Blunderboore's homeowner policy states he must file a police report in the event of a theft. He has done so.

Most policies, and specifically the homeowner policy, have special limits the carrier will pay on certain types of contents. This is called a "***sublimit***." The reason for these sublimits is that most property can be easily stolen, and the insurer wants to limit its responsibility; further, determining a value of these items, if they had not already been appraised, would be difficult after the fact. Some of the sublimits involved in this tale are:

Type of Property	Amount
Money, bank notes, bullion, gold, silver, platinum, coins, medals, stored value cards, and smart cards	**$200**
Jewelry, watches, furs, and precious and semiprecious stones	**$1,500**
Firearms and related equipment	**$2,500**
Silverware, goldware, platinumware, and pewterware	**$2,500**

Domesticated animals, such as the hen that lays the golden eggs, are excluded in the unendorsed homeowner policy. Of course, her product—the golden egg—would only be covered for $200, since it's gold.

If this loss were to be adjusted, the most Mr. Blunderboore would receive is $200 because of the sublimit for gold. If he had wanted to fully protect his property, he should have talked to his agent about an endorsement, rider, floater, or schedule. All of these words can mean the same thing—in essence, Mr. Blunderboore would obtain a mini-policy to attach to his main homeowner policy to specifically cover those items for a higher policy limit. This would result in an additional premium.

There also is an interesting coverage issue related to the golden harp. On the one hand, she's not really in the same category as gold, coins, and money. On the other hand, she is gold—perhaps she's goldware? So, would the harp be affected by the sublimit?

Moreover, the harp seems to be a sentient being, since she could yell for help while being abducted. Therefore, would she fall under the definition of "insured" in the policy, as discussed in *Three Blind Mice*? And if she should fall under the definition of "insured," would Mr. Blunderboore list her in a police report for theft and submit her on his inventory sheet? Or would her taking be reported as a kidnapping?

The Three Spinning Women

There was a girl who was lazy and would not spin flax. No matter what her mother said, the girl would not do any work. Finally anger and impatience got the better of the woman, and she beat her daughter, who began to cry loudly.

Her royal majesty was riding in a carriage when she heard the girl's crying. The queen ordered her carriage to stop, went into the house, and asked the mother why she was beating her daughter so that her cries could be heard out on the road.

The woman was ashamed of her daughter's laziness and lied, "I cannot make her stop spinning. She wants to spin on and on. She never stops! I am poor and do not have the money to get more flax."

The queen smiled, "There is nothing that I like more than to hear spinning. I am never happier than when the wheels are humming. Let your daughter come with me to the palace. I have flax enough. Your daughter can spin to her heart's content."

The woman was pleased with her scheme, and the girl left with the queen. Arriving at the palace, they went upstairs where three rooms were filled top to bottom with the finest flax.

"Now you must spin this flax," the queen commanded, "and when you are finished, you shall have my oldest son for a husband. You will be better suited for my son because you are not soft like that Princess who complained about a lump under her mattress. Your poverty matters not. Your work ethic will do for a dowry."

The girl was locked inside, and she was frightened since she would not be able to spin the flax. Not even if she had lived until she was three hundred years old, sitting at it every day from morning until evening could she have spun as much flax as the queen had in those rooms. When she was alone, she began to cry. For three days the girl sat without moving a hand. The queen was surprised when she entered the room on the third day and saw that not one length of flax had been spun.

"Why, child, have you not spun anything? Do you not wish to marry my son and become Queen when I die?" she inquired.

The girl excused herself saying, "Oh, that is my most ardent wish, but I am so sad because I miss my mother. I cannot yet begin."

This satisfied her majesty, but as she left, she looked the girl directly in the eye, and coldly said, "Tomorrow you must begin my work."

When the girl was alone again, she was overwhelmed by the chore. She did not know what to do or where to turn for help. So, rather than work, she went to the window to see what kinds of animals she could see in the clouds. Outside, she saw three old women coming up the path toward the castle. The first one had a wide flat foot, the second one had such a large lower lip that hung over her chin, and the third one had a thick thumb.

They stopped outside the window, looked up, and asked the girl why she was crying. The girl was lazy, but she was also clever like her mother. She said that she and the prince had fallen in love, but the queen was evil and locked her in the tower commanding her to spin flax.

And so it came to pass that thc threc old women offered her their help, saying, "If you will invite us to your wedding unashamed of how we look, call us your aunts, and let us be seated at your table, we will spin all the flax for you, and in a very short time, too."

"Yes! Of course," replied the girl. "Come right in and begin at once."

Then the lazy, clever girl let the three strangers in. The woman with the wide foot pulled the thread and peddled the wheel; the woman with the large overhanging lip moistened the thread; the last woman twisted it, then struck the table with her thick thumb. Each time she struck the table, a skein of the most finely spun thread fell to the floor.

The girl kept the three spinners hidden from her royal majesty, but whenever she came, the girl presented the great quantity and quality of thread that had been spun. The queen was so very pleased, murmuring to herself that sleeping on flax sheets was so nice.

When the first room was empty, the women went to work on the second room, and then onto the third one, which was quickly finished. The three women waved good-bye and said to the girl, "Do not forget what you have promised us. It will bring you good luck."

When the girl showed the queen the empty rooms and the large pile of thread, the monarch made preparations for the wedding. The bridegroom was happy that he was getting such a wise, industrious, and most of all, humble wife. He had thought the Princess who slept on all the mattresses and then had the audacity to complain that they were lumpy was rude and ungrateful.

"I have three aunts," the girl said in a low voice because she was ashamed at how the women looked. "They have been very kind to me; I want them to celebrate with me in my good fortune. I would like to invite them to the wedding and allow them be seated next to us at the table."

The queen and the bridegroom were shocked that the girl would think they would object to this and said, "Why would we not allow that? Of course, you may invite your aunts. We will even send our carriage to fetch them!"

The young couple was perplexed because the three women did not appear in the cathedral for the royal wedding, but after the feast began, they appeared dressed in strange clothing.

The bride said, "Welcome, dear aunts. I was worried you would not come."

"Oh," said the bridegroom, "what brought you to look this hideously?"

The women replied in unison, "We were in a carriage accident, your Grace, but we told the driver to hurry on so we would not miss our dear niece's wedding."

Then the Prince went to the woman with the broad, flat foot, and asked, "Where did you get such a broad foot?"

"From peddling, sir," she answered.

Then the bridegroom went to the second one, and said, "Did you get this fat lip from the accident?"

"No, it is from licking and moistening the flax."

Then he asked the third sister, "Where did you get this broad thumb?"

"From twisting thread," came her response.

These physical conditions alarmed the prince, and he decreed, "My beautiful bride shall never again touch a spinning wheel."

And so, it was with that she was freed from flax spinning and work in general since she was now a princess.

Moral of the Story

Readers may take the moral of the story to be that sometimes laziness can pay off; or, lying to someone can land one a cushy gig. The author would encourage her readers to review *Snow White and the Huntsman* and *Pinocchio*, concerning insurance fraud.

This story is close to *Adjuster, Mend My Shoe*, in that the insured or the claimant must buckle down and get the job done, even if the carrier has paid actual cash value (ACV) and additional funds are needed to complete the project. The difference between *Adjuster, Mend My Shoe* and this story is that the girl must first perform the work before she can receive the benefits of the deal (i.e., marriage to the prince). In insurance parlance this is called "incurred costs."

As discussed in *Three Blind Mice*, if a term is not defined in a policy, then its normal, everyday meaning is taken, unless there are special meanings used by the courts, as illustrated in *Old Mother Hubbard*. "Incurred" is often debated because it is not defined in the policy. It is an important term because it is a trigger for claim payment—meaning that when this particular event happens, the claim must be paid. Naturally, the insureds would rather be paid sooner than later, while the carriers have a different interpretation of the word.

Insurance carriers interpret "incurred" to mean an act has been "*performed* and *paid*." Policyholders and their representatives interpret "incurred" to mean a loss has been "*suffered*." In other words, it is the difference between interpreting something that ***has been*** paid versus something that is expected ***to be paid***.

In this example, the carrier's position would be that the girl has not "incurred" the expense of her time and energy until she "performed or completed" the task of spinning all three rooms of flax (i.e., actually did the work by expending time/energy). The insured's position would be that the girl "incurred" the ability to marry the prince as soon as she was locked in a room (in other words, it's a foregone conclusion that the girl must spin the flax to get married; so, the wedding can go through right now before the girl even does the work).

The issues with "incurred" costs are usually seen with additional coverages, such as debris removal, additional living expenses, increased construction costs, and permits/fees. Various states' departments of insurance have weighed in on this topic to give guidance to insurers. Because this is a hotly debated subject, lawsuits are often filed over this issue. Courts in New York opine that "incurred" means "to become responsible for" while "suffered" means "paid."

Using the New York interpretation, if an insured had a property damage estimate for their house with a $2,500 fee for debris removal, the carrier should pay that because the insured had "incurred" that loss, even if they have not yet suffered the fee—the policyholder would be *responsible for paying* the fee even if they *had not paid* the invoice yet.

As with all things, there is a dissenting view. Wisconsin courts, for example, opined that the policyholder had not incurred the cost of removing the debris because they had not yet paid the invoice; therefore, the carrier would not yet owe the payment to the insured.

This is a very fine line which essentially comes down to the question of when the insured will be paid. Make no mistake that, in the examples used, the policyholder is owed money. It is a matter of determining when the insured will be paid: before they pay for the repairs (pre-payment by the carrier) or after the insured pays for the repairs (reimbursement by the carrier).

Carriers are now beginning to specifically state that "incurred" means the policyholder must pay for the item or the repair. In this and in all instances with a claim, the insured should keep all receipts and forward them to the adjuster for consideration. It cannot be stressed strongly enough that, although the insured may have undertaken to pay for the repair or replacement of an item, this does not mean the carrier will pay the entire invoice. The insurer will pay what is reasonable and what is covered.

To learn more about the princess with a lumpy mattress, please see *The Princess and The Pea*. For more information about what happened to the three women in the carriage accident, read *The Shahzadi in the Suit of Leather*.

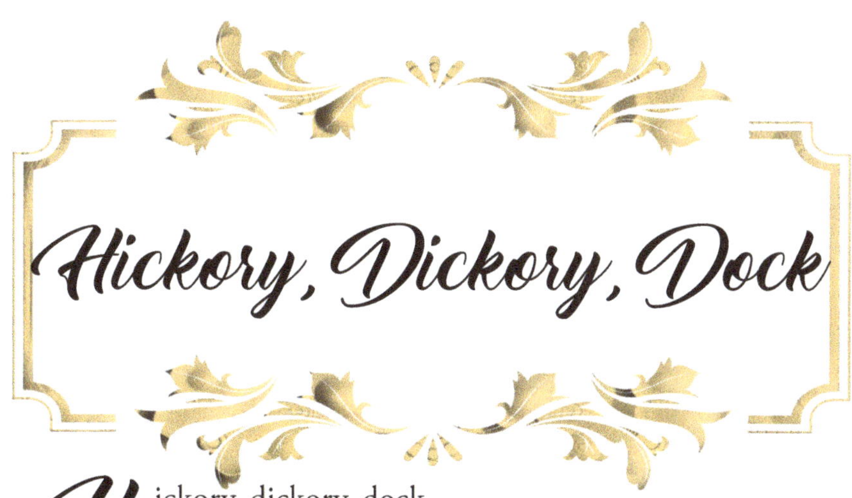

Hickory, Dickory, Dock

Hickory, dickory, dock,
The mouse ran up the clock;
The clock struck one,
But the damage was done.
There's an exclusion for rodents;
And the denial was sent with a condolence.

Little Miss Muffet

Little Miss Muffet
Sat on a tuffet,
The morn of a Tuesday.
Along came a spider,
Who sat down beside her,
And frightened Miss Muffet away.

She threw a bowl which
Made the spider flinch.
The bowl was in pieces;
The tuffet was broken;
Furniture bespoken,
Coverages denied and ceases.

Moral of the Stories

As mentioned previously, policies have exclusions. Damage caused by birds, rodents, insects, and animals owned by or kept by the insured is not covered. If the insured owns a pet rat and that rat damages the house, that damage is not covered; the same is true of the insured's dog—if that dog damages the insured's home, that damage is not covered.

But if the neighbor's dog causes damage at the insured's home, that damage would be covered.

Vermin used to be listed in the exclusion, and some policies still have that wording. Be sure to read the policy to know what is and is not covered.

Spiders, squirrels, and rodents are considered vermin. Racoons, on the other hand, are neither rodents nor vermin. Nesting, infestation, discharge, or release of waste products or secretions by animals is not covered.

Suvannahamsa-Jataka

A rich man who lived in Sāvatthi, the glittering capital of the ancient Indian kingdom of Kosala, near the Rapti river, sent for his bailiff and gave orders that he would offer the local Buddhist monastery of nuns a supply of garlic. If the sisters came, the bailiff was to give each two handfuls of the pungent vegetable. The nuns were grateful for the man's generosity and made a practice of coming to his house or field for their garlic.

It came to pass that on one holiday, the supply of garlic in the house ran out. When Sister Fat Nandā approached the house with three of her fellow nuns, the bailiff ran out to meet them on the road and lamented their poor luck. However, he stated his master had invited the nuns to go into the field and dig for it themselves. So away to the field Sister Fat Nandā went. She succeeded in finding garlic, but she carried off an excessive number of heads! The bailiff grew angry and remarked what a greedy lot these nuns were! This piqued the more moderate nuns; the monks, too, were indignant at the taunt that was repeated to them. The monastery approached the Blessed One and told Him their woes.

Rebuking the greed of Sister Fat Nandā, the Master said, "Brethren, a greedy person is harsh and unkind even to the mother who bore him; a greedy person cannot convert the unconverted, or make the converted grow in grace, or cause alms to come in, or save them when they come in; whereas the moderate person can do all these things."

In such a wise manner did the Master point the moral, ending by saying, "Brethren, as Sister Fat Nandā is greedy now, so she was greedy in times gone by." And thereupon He told the following story of the past:

Once upon a time when King Brahmadatta reigned in Varanasi, which was once spelled Baranasi, which was once spelled Banaras, a Bodhisattva, or an Enlightened One, was once a man born into the priestly caste we know as Brahmin. The man resolved to become enlightened. And he did. When he died, he was born again into the world as a golden mallard endowed with the consciousness of its former existences. He decided to check on his family, who had survived him.

In his human life, the man had married a bride of his own caste, who bore him three daughters, named Nandā, Nanda-vatī, and Sundari-nandā. Now, the Bodhisattva viewed his magnificent size and golden plumage but was saddened to see that after his death, his wife and daughters had been taken in by neighbors and friends and were living on the charity of others. The mallard thought of his plumage like hammered and beaten gold, and how by giving them one golden feather at a time, he could enable his wife and daughters to live in comfort. So away he flew to where they dwelt and alighted on the top of the central beam of the roof.

Seeing the golden bird, the wife and girls asked where he had come from. The Bodhisattva told them he was their father who had died, that he'd been reborn a golden mallard who desired to put an end to their misery and reliance on others.

"You shall have my feathers," said he, "one by one, and they will sell for enough to keep you all in ease and comfort."

So, he gave them one of his feathers and departed. And from time to time, he returned to give them another feather, and with the proceeds of their sale these brahmin-women grew prosperous and quite well-to-do.

But one day the mother said to her daughters, "There's no trusting animals, my children. Who's to say your father might not go away one of these days and never come back again? Let us use our time and pluck him clean next time he comes, so as to make sure we have all of his feathers."

The daughters refused thinking this would cause their father pain. Their mother took no heed and greedily called the golden mallard to her. When he appeared, she took him with both hands and plucked him clean. Now the Bodhisattva's feathers had this property that, if they were plucked out against his wish, they ceased to be golden and became like a crane's feathers. The poor bird, though he stretched his wings, could not fly. The woman flung him into a barrel and gave him food there.

As time went on his feathers grew again (though they were plain white now), and he flew away and never came back again.

At the end of this story the Buddha said, "Thus you see, Brethren, how Fat Nandā was as greedy in times past as she is now. Her past greed caused her to lose the gold in the same way her current greed will cause her to lose the garlic. Observe, moreover, how her greed has deprived the entire Monastery of its supply of garlic, and learn to be moderate in your desires and to be content with what is given you, however small that may be."

In saying this, he uttered this stanza:

Contented be, nor itch for further store.
They seized the swan—but had its gold no more.

The Master soundly rebuked Sister Fat Nandā and laid down the precept that any sister who should eat garlic would have to do penance. Then, making the final connection for his followers, he said, "Fat Nandā was the brahmin's wife of the story, her three sisters were the brahmin's three daughters, and I myself the golden mallard."

Moral of the Story

Dearest readers, before discussing the Moral of the Story, the author would like to clear up any confusion there may be, since Brahmins are Hindus and Bodhisattvas are Buddhists. The Jataka tales are stories of the Buddha's past lives; in some of the tales, he is human and in some he's an animal.

This story can easily fit into several parts of an insurance lesson: fraud, assault, theft, but it is intended for additional living expense. Additional Living Expense (aka Loss of Use) is a homeowner coverage benefit available to insureds if their home is unlivable. Business owners may also have similar coverage if they bought coverage that covered a cause of loss preventing them from working in their office. This coverage is called business interruption (aka business income loss). For the sake of ease, this moral will relate to homeowner insurance, but the concept is similar for business interruption with a few key differences. See *Snow White and the Seven Dwarfs* for more information.

Additional Living Expense (ALE) pays for the ***additional*** expenses of living because the insured cannot live in their home. In other words, the expenses in excess of what the insured normally would experience.

What does this have to do with stripping a golden duck of his feathers and taking more than garlic than Sister Fat Nandā needed?

All too often, insureds believe ALE coverage will pay for everything, including an upgrade in their living conditions. If Sister Fat Nandā had an ALE claim, the policy would not pay for the excessive amount of garlic she took; it would not pay for the two-to three-handfuls she normally received. It would pay for a fourth handful of garlic she received because it was in addition to her normal amount of garlic.

In a modern context, the policy would pay to put the insured in a hotel, apartment, or rent a similar sized home. The insured would still be responsible for their original mortgage, utility invoices, and normal grocery bills. If repairs to the home will take several weeks, the insured may find the carrier has rented an extended stay with a small kitchenette. It is expected that the insured will cook some (if not all) their meals, just as they would if a loss had never occurred.

The point is that this coverage is not meant to be a vacation or an upgrade in the policyholders' living condition. It is meant to keep the insured in a close-as-possible-to-pre-accident condition.

There are times when the carrier can find a hotel or home which may cause the insured to spend additional time on the road driving to and from work, dropping the children off at school, or to their array of after-school activities. Increase in the mileage and fuel to accommodate those added expenses might also be covered in this policy benefit.

It is the policyholder's duty to provide documentation, which the author has mentioned several times. The adjuster will ask for proof (documentation) that the insured has had an increase in expenses. To be blunt, the adjuster will need several months of bank statements, bills, and receipts to determine the insureds' baseline expenses and see that there has been an increase in expenses.

There are many examples and ***permutations*** which can be used and created about ALE. As in so many cases with insurance, claims will differ. The policyholder should speak with the adjuster to obtain a clear view of what is and is not covered—and preferably speak to the agent so that they understand this prior to any loss occurring.

Row, Row, Row Your Boat

Row, row, row, your boat,
Gently down the stream
Merrily, merrily, merrily
Life is but a dream

Row, row, row, your boat,
Gently down the stream
Watch the water rising warily
You will want to scream.

Row, row, row, your boat,
Gently down the stream
Covering dry land temp'rarily
That is flood's main theme.

Row, row, row, your boat,
Gently down the stream
Get coverage now voluntarily.
Claims will be a dream.

Rain, Rain, Go Away

Rain, rain, go away
Come again some other day
We want to go outside and play
Come again some other day

Rain, rain, go away
Flooding is not OK
Too much water causes delay
Come again some other day

Rain, rain, go away
My homeowners doesn't pay
For excess water today
Come again some other day

Rain, rain, go away
The NFIP may pay
If I bought it the other day
Come again some other day

Rain, rain, go away
But I was not wise—no, nay!
And now the house is filled with clay
Come again some other day

Moral of the Stories

Policyholders believe their policies cover everything. Unfortunately, they do not. Flood happens to be one of those risks (or perils or causes of loss) which is not covered. Flood damage is covered by the government insurance program which is necessary because these types of perils are difficult to insure privately. Not to mention that private carriers could not offer affordable premiums.

Flood can be defined as:

> *A general and short-term state where at least two acres of typically dry land or two properties (in which one is owned by the policyholder) are partially or fully submerged due to the overflow of inland or tidal waters, sudden accumulation or surface runoff of water from any origin, or mudflow.*

Adjusters will use this or a similar definition to determine whether the policyholder's property flooded or if there was a back-up or overflow of water.

The government's flood insurance policy is called the National Flood Insurance Program (NFIP). The Federal Emergency Management Agency (FEMA) administers the NFIP.

The government has maps of flood plains showing the likelihood of an area to flood. The bar for be-

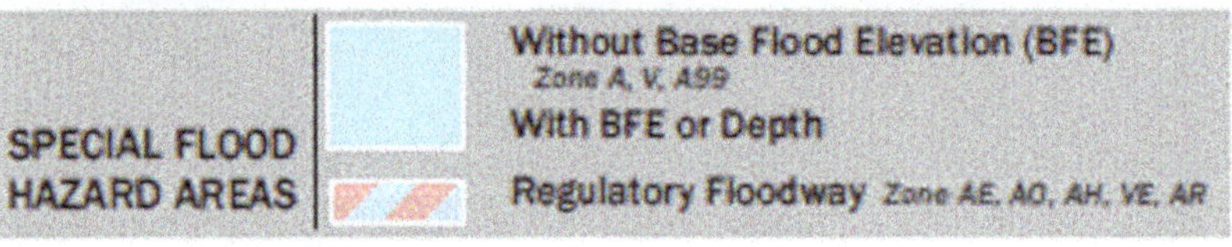

ing in a flood zone is extremely low: any location with a 1% chance of experiencing a flood each year is considered a high risk according to FEMA. Homeowners are more likely to have a flood event than they are a fire, yet so many people go without flood coverage.

Homeowners can go online to the FEMA Flood Map Service Center to enter an address and see the likelihood that location will flood and if a flood policy is needed. (**http://bit.ly/3OEVFjF**)

It was mentioned earlier that private insurers do not write flood insurance, but that is only partially true. More than 50 private insurers sell federal flood policies under their names, collect the premiums, and receive payments from the government for the policies they write and the claims they pay. However, the government is the actual insurer and is responsible for all payments. Insureds can obtain policies from agents or directly from the NFIP.

The NFIP covers both the building and contents, but limits are generally low. For example, building coverage is limited to $250,000 on the dwelling (house) and $100,000 on personal property (contents). Considering that even an inch of flood damage can cause an average of $25,000 (based on experience, flood waters are usually measured in feet, not inches), it is obvious how this policy is necessary if the standard homeowner policy does not cover flood. And $25,000 is a lot of money to be out of pocket.

As with standard homeowner policies, the insured must have policy limits equal to at least 80% of the replacement cost of the building ***at the time of loss.*** Or, the insured must have the maximum limit available at the ***inception of the policy***. If this condition is not met, then the insured will pay a pro-rata portion of the loss, as explained in *The Old Woman Who Lived in a Shoe*. Reimbursement for the dwelling

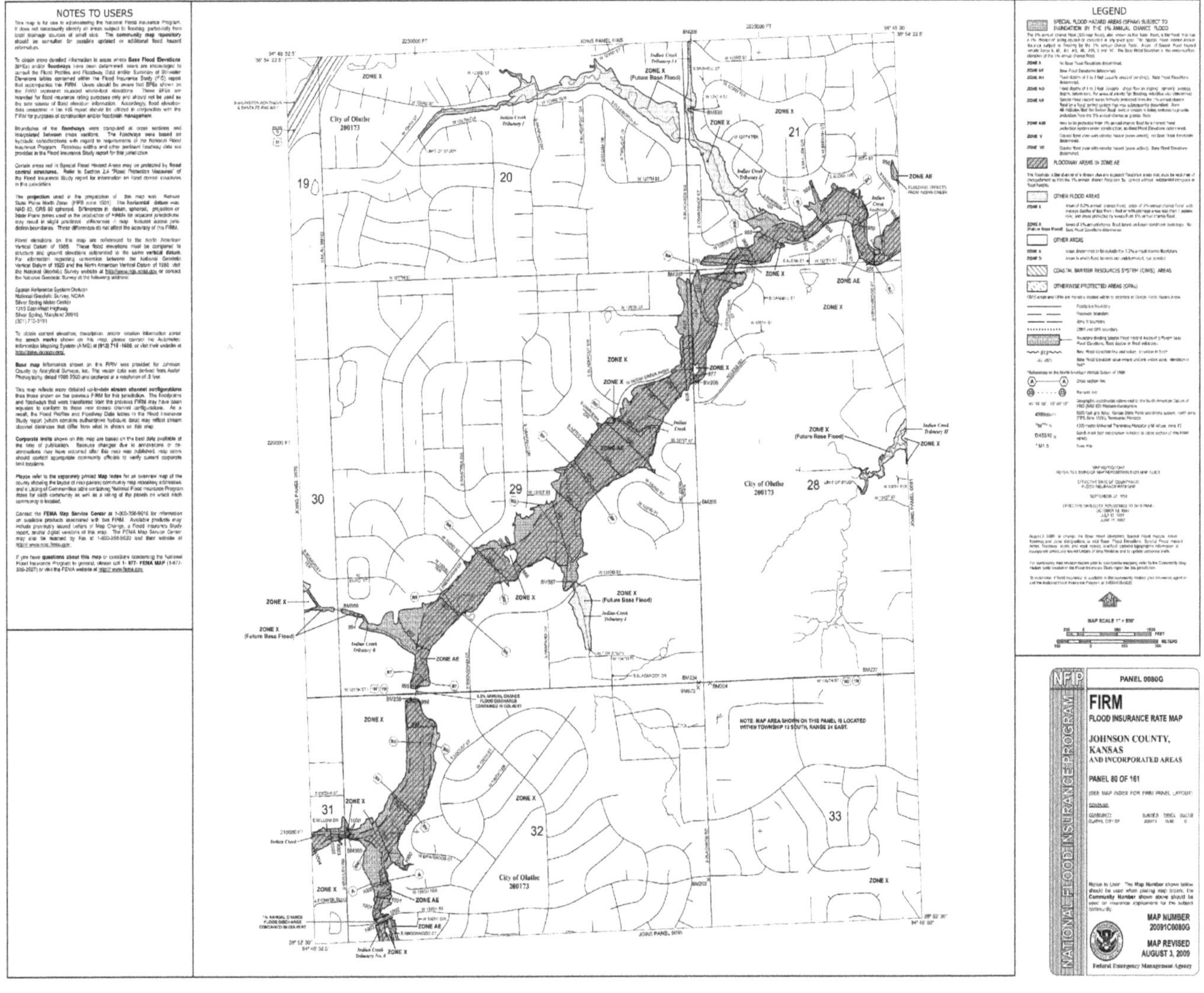

is settled on a replacement cost and contents are settled on actual cash value. See T*he Old Woman Who Lived in a Shoe* and *Old Mother Hubbard.*

In the case of a hurricane, a policyholder can have the unfortunate circumstance of having not only a windstorm claim but also a flood claim, which is often caused by storm surge. The flood policy does not cover the wind damage to the home, and the standard HO 03 homeowner policy does not cover the flood damage. Because of these limitations, in both cases, the homeowner will likely receive a reservation of rights letter for potential uncovered claims, which is further discussed in *Snow White and the Seven Dwarfs.*

Adjuster Begonia Gemforest

A homeowner will need to have both flood and homeowner policies to be covered in the event of a similar loss. However, claims involving this kind of loss require a delicate coordination of several people at the time of a catastrophe when manpower, patience, and time are in short supply. Begonia Gemforest must coordinate with the flood adjuster (*or vice versa*) for inspection of the home.

Unfortunately, the author finds this cooperation and joint inspection an uncommon occurrence, but it can be helped when the insurers share information with one another. To accomplish this, the homeowner may need to do a bit of matchmaking, for lack of a better term, to get the two adjusters together.

Adjuster Gemforest should arrange her damage inspection with the flood adjuster, Lotta Wadda, and the totals of their two damage estimates (property and flood) should match closely enough that they cover the vast majority of the homeowner's loss.

Even though there are computer programs which help write these kinds of estimates, determining the amount of damage is not an exact science. By coordinating inspections—or even using the same field adjuster to write both estimates—the two insurers can ensure their mutual insured is not left with a large gap or uncovered claim.

For the example below, Gemforest and Wadda's estimates will pay for 100 percent of the damage to the home. (It is beyond the scope of this book to discuss potential uncovered losses which neither the homeowner policy nor the flood policy cover.) The two insurers will each pay their pro-rata portion of the loss, less their policy's applicable deductible.

For example, the two adjusters may decide to split the damage for the following claims in this manner:

Damage	Flood Policy	Property Policy
No flood damage to the home	0% of damages	100% of damages
No wind damage to the home	100% of damages	0% of damages
Majority of damage caused by wind; minor flood damage	25% of damages	75% of damages
Majority of damage caused by flood; minor wind damage	85% of damages	15% of damages

It is not the goal of insurance to pay as little as possible. The policy's goal is to put the insureds back to where they were prior to the loss. There is, literally, no way to tell what damage is caused by which peril in most hurricane losses. Therefore, Gumdrop and Wadda are going to adjust their estimates to match the damages and fully indemnify the insured.

It could confuse some that Wadda is paying 25% of the damages, or that Gumdrop may pay a minority share of the damages. Why wouldn't the policy with the majority of the damage pay the entire loss? Simply put, the policy does not pay for what is not covered. This may sound self-evident, but this fact often surprises policyholders. Therefore, giving the insured every benefit of the doubt, the property insurer should pay for a portion of the damage, and the flood policy should pay the other portion in order to avoid a gap in coverage.

As a final note on this damage, the neatly split percentages between the two carriers described above are entirely fictional. In reality, the two adjusters would discuss the damages and come to an agreement regarding how much would be paid from each carrier so that the insured was fully paid for the damage.

Little Dutch Boy

All the way to the east of Fairytale Land, there was a little kingdom named Kleinlandje, which sat lower than sea level. The people there, though, were industrious and clever. They built a wall as tall as it was thick in order to keep out the sea. The wall was so wide that merchants could drive carts led by teams of eight side-by-side oxen and never touch. It was so tall that the king's subjects never saw the sunrise unless they were standing on the wall.

It had to be so tall and wide to protect the kingdom, for if it was not, the Sea King would come in with his tide and cover all the crops and houses and shops and stables. When they were very small and went to school, all the residents of the kingdom learned that an accident to the wall would be a calamity. So it came to pass that the entire kingdom relied on the sturdiness and stability of the wall which had been built so long ago that no one alive even knew anyone who helped build the original wall.

This did not stop the Sea King from daily crashing against the wall in his attempts to weaken it and bring it down. Every so often, the Sea King would convince his brother Wind to howl at the wall and endeavor to blow down the wall, yet the wall still stood after all those years.

The wall did not surround all the eastern kingdom, because the land gradually rose to be higher than the sea. Where the wall fell away because the land was high, there lived a family who had two sons: Hans, who was the elder, and Jan, who was the younger. Hans and Jan were on their way to Kleinlandje because their father asked them to take some important documents to his office there.

Despite the long journey and the difficult terrain, the boys had set out early in the morning, determined to complete the task their father had entrusted to them.

The sun had not yet risen to the midday point when Jan complained of being tired of walking. He said, "Look at the fields where the lambs jump and play. Look at the flowers and the colors!"

For, indeed, there were ever so many flowers and green fields to admire and smell. Hans admitted he, too, was a bit tired of walking, so he climbed up onto the wall, which had since become a road, and sat down. Jan continued playing in the field with the lambs.

Hans began to feel sleepy, lulled by the Sea King's waves, when he heard Jan call out, "Oh, what a clever thing the farmer built to water the lambs, flowers, and fields. It's a little hole that bubbles with water!"

Alarmed, Hans sat up.

"Hole? Where?"

"Here in the wall," said the little brother. "But it does not taste good. The water is salty."

"What!" exclaimed Hans, and he slid down as fast as he could to where Jan was playing.

Although all school children in Kleinlandje knew about the wall and the need to keep it safe, Jan was only four and had not yet attended school. There, in the wall, was a teeny-tiny, little hole—no bigger than Hans' pinky finger—where a drop of sea water trickled through and ran down to the ground.

"O jee!" cried Hans, who was terrified because the Sea King had managed to make a hole in the wall. "What shall we do?" He fretted as he looked all round; not a person or a house was in sight, for the brothers were still a mile from town.

He looked at the little drops which oozed steadily through the wall. Mr. Van de Meer, the terse, tedious, and tiring schoolmaster, who was always looking at the sea, had taught Hans' class that the sea would make a big break in the wall if given half a chance. Hans and his classmates laughed and laughed at Mr. Van de Meer, but now Hans remembered that "van de meer" means "of the sea." Could his schoolmaster be a loyal vassal of the Sea King?

"What shall we do?" Hans cried again.

Hans could instruct Jan to put his finger in the hole while he ran the mile to town. But Jan was young and easily distracted. If told to keep his finger in the hole to plug it, Jan might see a butterfly and go chasing it, along with a lamb.

Hans stared at the hole in amazement—it was growing larger and more water was now trickling through! Hans yelled for help, but there was no one near enough to hear. The town was so far away—if they both ran for help it would be too late; what should he do?

Hans had to send Jan to town while he plugged the hole with his forefinger, because now the hole was even larger and the water came out in a tiny stream.

With his finger tightly in the hole, Hans instructed his little brother, "Run, Jan! Go to the town and tell Papa and the men that there's a hole in the wall. Tell them I will stop it until they get here. But be careful not to tell Mr. Van de Meer. I think he must have planned this."

Jan knew by Hans' face that something very serious was the matter, even though he had not been to school. He ran along the base of the wall toward Kleinlandje, as fast as his little, chubby legs could carry him. Hans watched Jan run and become smaller and smaller until he was only a speck of dust.

Hans knelt at the base of the wall; he was afraid because he was alone. Yet his finger still plugged the hole, and no water seeped through. By-and-by, his finger began to feel numb. Hans saw that the sun had slipped past the midpoint of the sky toward the tops of the trees, when Mother would usually send Jan to bed for a nap.

Slap, crash, slap, crash. Hans heard the Sea King's army on the other side of the wall, and although the wall was as thick as it was tall, the army of waves seemed very nearby.

Gurgle, rumble, gurgle, rumble. Hans heard the Sea King's generals telling the soldiers to look for other weaknesses in the wall to exploit. He tried to flex his hand, but he could not move his fingers without unintentionally enlarging the hole. So, his hand became very cold, and it no longer felt numb.

The sun now touched the horizon where princesses went to university and pigs had straw and brick homes. Yet there was no one on the road. Had he made a mistake sending Jan? It had been more than six hours—his Papa and the townsmen should be here before now.

Slowly but surely, the chill crept up his arm, starting at his wrist before spreading to his elbow and then up to his shoulder, as Hans realized just how cold he had become. As the sun disappeared below the horizon, the last sliver of its light and heat vanished with it.

The wall, having faced the sun for more than half the day, was still warm, and Hans sat near it, attempting to get most of his body pressed to the wall to keep it warm. His legs began to ache from standing. His finger, long having been numb, began to have shooting pains, as if something was biting it. He was dizzy as he was thirsty and hungry—having had nothing to eat since breakfast that morning.

His head listed to the side, and he heard the Sea King sing,

"I am the mighty Sea King,
Ruling over land and wave.
I'll tear down any obstacle
That stands in my way, brave.

"No one can stop my power,
Not even a little child.
I'll flood your streets and homes
Until you're broken and beguiled.

"You may think you can hold me back,
But I am wild and free.
I'll find another path to take,
And you'll bow down to me."

Hans was frightened. He felt a shiver begin at the back of his neck and go all the way down his spine. It was hours since Jan had gone to town. He felt very lonely, and the hurt in his arm grew and grew. It was now dark with only the stars to light the fields. Hans could not see the men if they came, but it mattered not, because the only sound was the crickets and the army of the Sea King.

Hans began to think Jan must have gotten lost. He was frightened as the moon peaked over the wall. Hans knew something was not right. The sea went on beating at the wall.

"I am the terror from the deep,
Rising up with every leap.
My waters churn with rage and might,
Beware my wrath, you have been warned tonight.

"I'll burst through pipes and back up your streets,
My power overwhelming, none can compete.
I'll claim your homes, your shops, your halls,
You'll beg for mercy, but my wrath never stalls.

"Run, run, while you still can,
Before my wrath descends like a great wave,
a tsunami plan.
No wall can keep me from my goal,
My power unstoppable, I shall take it all."

Hans was in such pain that tears welled in his eyes. He began to pull out his finger when a tear fell on his quivering lip. Hans remembered what Jan had said—the water was salty—and knew that minute how much everyone in Kleinlandje was relying on him even if they did not yet know it. Taking out his finger from the hole would only make things worse. The water would rush in, and eventually break down the dike, leading to the sea flooding in and destroying all the houses and land. With gritted teeth and a determined spirit, Hans held onto the hole tightly, refusing to give up, and continued to plug it with his finger, fighting to save his town from the inevitable disaster.

"Sea King, I will not run or hide,
Nor will I let this city be destroyed by
your tide.

I will keep my finger in this hole,
And protect my home, with all my soul.

"Though your power is great and your wrath is strong,
I will stand firm, and I will not be gone.
So come with all your fury, come with all your might,
I'll face you with courage, and I'll win this fight."

Hans had no sooner declared his willingness to fight than he heard and felt rumbling through the ground.

"Oh, no!" he thought. "The Sea King has burrowed underneath the wall!"

Far in the distance he saw fireflies bobbing up and down. Confused, he blinked his eyes. No, not fireflies. Lanterns. On horseback. The ground carried the pounding of the horses' hooves as Papa and the townsmen raced toward Hans. They carried hoes, pickaxes, and shovels.

The townswomen came running after the men with cakes, ***stroopwafels***, and tea, for they knew Hans had been there since morning and had had nothing to eat.

Hans' father jumped from his horse and said, "Take heart, son. We're here!"

When the townspeople saw Hans, with his finger still in the wall, they gave a great cheer. The men toiled the rest of the night repairing the wall, while the women stuffed Hans with food and gave him so much tea he thought he might float away.

By the time the sun came up in the east—which the townspeople couldn't see because of the wall—the hole had been plugged and the wall reinforced. Everyone in Kleinlandje lifted Hans up, carried him into town, and told him that he was a real hero. They said that he had saved the town.

But Hans frowned, "Papa, where is Jan?"

Papa laughed and said, "I wondered what was taking you boys so long to deliver the papers. I went to look for you. I found Jan still asleep under a tree from his nap. He was so sleepy it took several minutes to figure out what had happened. We thought he was joking."

"Then Jan told us what Mr. Van de Meer had taught you about the sea and the wall," said the king of Kleinlandje, "and I don't mind telling you that I fired him right on the spot. The last we saw of him was jumping into the sea where his feet became a fish tail!"

"So," Papa said, "I gathered up some men, took Jan home to your mother, and we came here!"

And to this day the people of Kleinlandje tell the story of how a little boy saved the wall.

Moral of the Story

The story of the little Dutch boy and the dike (wall) is often told to children as an example of how quick thinking and self-sacrifice can avert disasters, even with limited strength and resources. By using his fingers to plug the hole in the dike, the little boy demonstrated how one individual could make a difference and save the whole town from the devastating effects of the sea. This parable encourages children to be brave and resourceful in the face of adversity, and to understand that even small actions can have a big impact.

This fairy tale could easily be about flooding, but it is more about avoiding water damage from backups or overflows of drains, sump pumps, etc. Water damage is not a well understood peril by most home- or businessowners. In general, water damage is covered if it is caused by something that is not excluded. This is a very confusing way to say, "Water damage is covered if it is caused by a covered cause of loss."

This may seem self-evident, since the only time a policy responds is when there is a covered cause of loss. Insurance policies are contracts; contracts are written by attorneys; attorneys like to make things complicated. In the general property exclusions of a standard homeowner policy, there is a section which is known in the insurance sphere as "***anti-concurrent causation doctrine***" language. This is a difficult concept for adjusters to understand, let alone consumers.

The anti-concurrent causation doctrine means that a loss is not covered when it is the result of two or more risks/perils/causes of loss, and one of those risks/perils/causes of loss is excluded in the policy.

Imagine that the Sea King's brother, Wind, created a storm, picked up enough water to force it over the dike and into Kleinlandje, where homes flooded due to the water. Wind damage is a covered cause of loss, but flooding is not. Absent the anti-concurrent causation language in the policy, Mother Goose Insurance Mutual would pay for the entire loss even if flooding was specifically excluded.

With the anti-concurrent causation language, the carrier would not pay for anything—including any wind damage to the structure.

Just like multiplying any number by a negative number will always result in a negative number, if any cause of loss is excluded (by the anti-concurrent causation doctrine), then the entire loss will be excluded, regardless of any other unexcluded causes of loss.

The third exclusion in the homeowner policy concerns water, which has a specific meaning that would be relevant to a specific policy. Water which overflows or backs up from a drain, sewer, sump pump, dike, dam, levee, or something similar is not covered. However, there is coverage for water overflowing or backing up if the reason for the water overflowing or backing up is caused by fire or explosion or any other ***exception to the exclusion***. An exception to the exclusion limits the exclusion of coverage in specific circumstances.

In other words, if Mr. Van de Meer had placed explosives at the base of the wall (rather than trying to subvert young children's minds) causing the wall to collapse and flooding all of Kleinlandje, then *that* loss would be covered because that kind of loss is the specific circumstance where there would be coverage.

Understanding the anti-concurrent causation language is important for both insurers and policyholders in insurance claims. It helps to determine whether a loss is covered or excluded under an insurance policy. If any cause of loss is excluded under the provision, then the entire loss will be excluded, regardless of whether another cause of loss is covered.

The Magpie's Nest

Back when Earth was young, even before the animals began working for humans, the magpie was a master builder of nests. All the birds wanted to emulate her work, and so it came to pass that she decided to host a seminar on nest-building.

One bird from every species gathered around on the appointed day.

First the magpie took mud and fashioned a domed structure. The thrush thought, "Well, that's how it is done. Now I am very busy and must be off!" This is why the thrush makes her nest this way.

The magpie then took twigs and arranged them around the mud, to which the blackbird thought, "I now know all about it. I best leave to get the best mud and twigs before the other birds try to take them." He flew off; now all his children and grandchildren make their nests this way.

The instructor added a second layer of mud which satisfied the owl, who claimed he was the wisest of all animals and did not need any further instruction. The magpie continued her seminar as she lined the nest with a second layer

of twigs. The sparrow, who was somewhat of a lazy fellow, thought, "Geez! This is too much work!" And so he left and his offspring are known today to have rather messily constructed nests.

Lastly, the magpie lined the inside of the nest with feathers to make it comfortable for her children. The starling, who came late to the seminar and was sitting in the back, saw this and thought it was a wonderful idea. This is the reason starlings have such comfy and cozy nests.

Having completed her nest, the magpie looked up from her work and saw that all the birds had left, save one: the turtle-dove, who asked the magpie to make a double nest.

"A single nest is enough," the magpie said. But the turtle-dove, who lives with her spouse, insisted a double be made. The magpie and turtle-dove went round and round, for you see, the turtle-dove is always with her mate.

Finally, the magpie got angry and said, "One is enough, I tell you!" She flew away and refused to help any other birds or host another seminar on nest-building again. This is why all birds' nests have different forms of construction.

Moral of the Story

The magpie's building technique is a good starting point to discuss condominiums, or condos for short, because the nest has multiple layers: initial mud, initial twigs, second mud, second twigs, and feathers. Further explanation of homeowner policies is in order.

There are several types of homeowner policies, some of which were discussed in *Three Blind Mice*. The standardized forms are as follows:

Form	**Coverage**
HO 00 01 (edition date)	**Homeowner Basic Covered Perils**
HO 00 02 (edition date)	**Homeowner Broad Covered Perils**
HO 00 03 (edition date)	**Homeowner Open Perils**
HO 00 04 (edition date)	**Renter coverage**
HO 00 05 (edition date)	**Homeowner Comprehensive (provides replacement cost on the building and contents)**
HO 00 06 (edition date)	**Condo Owner form**
HO 00 07 (edition date)	**Mobile Homeowner form**
HO 00 08 (edition date)	**Modified Homeowner form (covers older and unique homes)**

The homeowner policy, HO 03, encompasses the entire wall from the outside material to the inside paint/wallpaper (we will use paint for simplicity). The HO 04, called the renter's policy, covers the policyholder's contents—not the building where the insured resides.[1] The HO 06 is the condo policy, which melds the HO 03 and HO 04 policies. This will be explained further below.

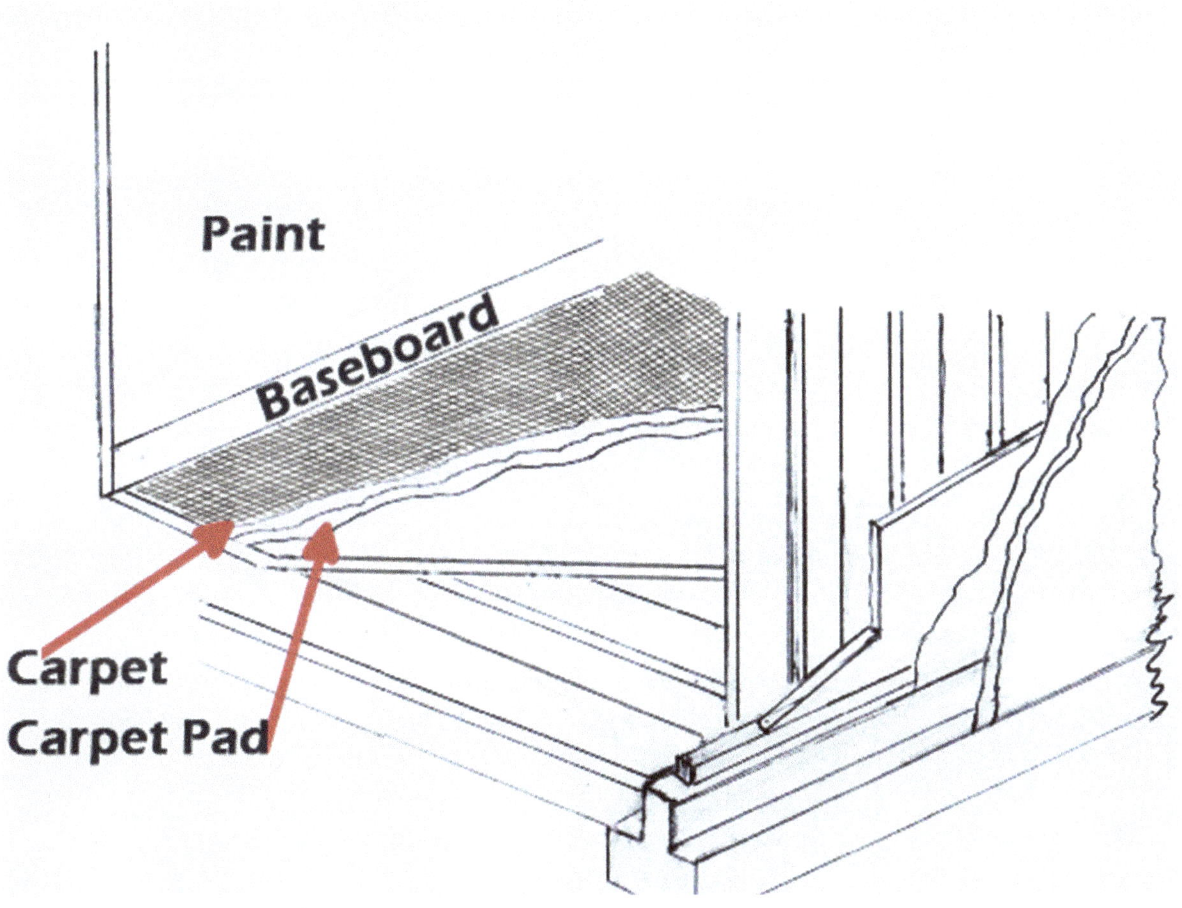

Returning to the magpie's nest, the mud and twig layers will be, for the sake of illustration, the composition of a wall; the feathers will be the condo owner's belongings (contents). Buildings are erected much like the magpie's nest. There is the frame (initial mud layer), the outside of the building (initial twigs), drywall (2nd layer of mud), and then paint (2nd layer of twigs).

Condos have associations: the group of individual owners, and the individual owners themselves. Therefore, two policies cover a condominium building: (1) the condo association, aka the master policy, and (2) the policy belonging to owner of the individual condo unit.

Apart from other homeowner policies, condo association bylaws play an important role in the adjustment of the condo claim. The bylaws will state what is owned by whom, and whether a loss assessment is needed. Therefore, when there is a claim with a condo, the adjuster will ask for a copy of the bylaws.

The individual condo owner's policy will cover contents, the property ***fixtures*** the owner added to the condo, and what insurance adjusters like to refer to "paint in" or "walls in." The phrase "paint in" is the

1 Homeowner policies also have ***liability*** coverage. This coverage is not discussed here, since this section focuses on property damage. Liability covers not only damages such as bodily injury but also property damage. A familiar example is a car accident. The claimant's bodily injury is covered under the insured's liability section of the auto policy, as is the damage to the claimant's car.

highly unscientific adjuster jargon to say that the condo policy covers the "box of air" the policyholder owns (the condo itself) and the layer of paint on the wall. This is important to understand because the condo owner does not, like the homeowner, own the drywall or the wall cavity.

Here is an example of condo bylaws stating what the *association* will insure:

> **1.18. Cost Center**
> Cost Center shall mean one or more Improvements or maintenance areas on a portion or portions of the Common Area or Association Maintenance Areas, the expenses of the operation, maintenance and repair of which are to be borne solely by the Association. The (i) exterior surfaces and roofing (excluding glass areas) of the Dwelling Building (including detached Dwelling Buildings) in the Dwelling Area, (ii) landscaping and other Improvements in the front yards of the Dwelling Building(s) in the Dwelling Area (including the unit in the Dwelling Area which contain detached Dwelling Buildings), (iii) the structural portions and fixtures and floor coverings originally installed by the Association in accordance with the original plans and specifications therefore, and (iv) all insurable Improvements and fixtures originally installed by the Association in the Common Area or remaining portions of the Association Maintenance Areas shall constitute a Cost Center with the operation, maintenance and repair of such items to be borne by the Association.

In plain English, this means that the condo association will provide insurance coverage for the exterior of roofs, landscaping, outside walls, wall cavities' fixtures (such as pipes and wires), and for property and liability in the common areas.

The condo association master policy will include the drywall, ceiling, and floors of the unit, but not anything attached to them. For example, if the condo owner adds travertine tile to the condo unit, that tile is owned by—and needs to be insured by—the condo owner.

Here is an example of what the association's bylaws require for the condo *owner*:

> **12.2 Insurance Obligations of Owners**
> Subject to the provisions of Section 12.1 concerning the Association's insurance of the Dwelling Units in the building, each Owner shall insure the Improvements on their unit, including their entire Dwelling Unit, against loss or damage by fire or by any other ***hazard*** or risk, under the standard form of extended endorsement now in use in Fairytale Land under such other insurance as may be required by the Beneficiary of the first Mortgage on their unit.

It is the responsibility of each Owner to provide insurance on their personal property and upon all other property and improvements within their Dwelling Unit for which the Association has not purchased insurance in accordance with Section 12.1 hereof. It shall also be the responsibility of each Owner to carry general liability insurance in the amount such Owner deems desirable to cover their individual liability for damage to person or property occurring inside their Dwelling Unit or elsewhere upon or within their unit.

Again, in plain English, the condo owner will insure the changes or "improvements" they have made to the condo unit. A sharp reader will realize there is nothing in the bylaw examples which specifically say "walls-in" or "drywall-out" and wonder where the adjuster got such jargon.

The phrase is a visual aid to explain to new adjusters and insureds what the condo owner's policy covers. Unlike the HO 03 policy, which covers the dwelling or residences, the HO 06 covers fixtures and improvements found at the condo location that is owned by the policyholder. Since the condo owner does not own the drywall, wall cavity, roof, pipes, and wires, the condo owner isn't responsible for insuring it.

In the event of a claim in which drywall and paint are both damaged, the condo master policy adjuster and the condo owner policy adjuster work together, much like the flood and property damage adjusters, to agree to the damages and split them between the two policies so there is no gap.

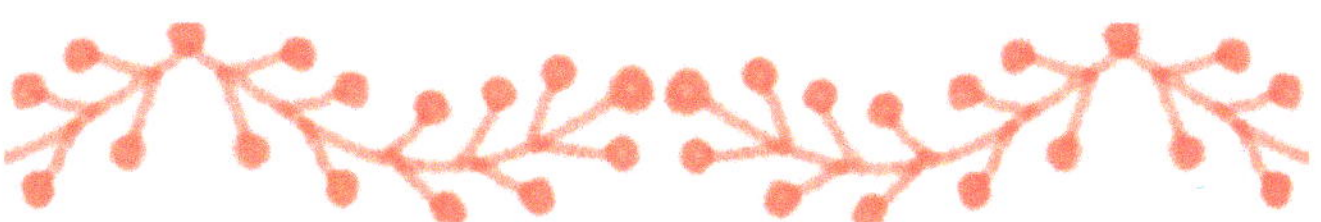

Third-Party Claim Process

1 Claim created

2 Coverage Review

Set Reserves

3 Investigation

Contact Insured

Contact Claimant

Contact Witnesses

Recorded Statement(s)

Coverage Question

Coverage No?

Review Reserves

Send ROR

Go back to Investigation until all coverage issues are resolved

Coverage No?

Adjust Reserves

6 Coverage Declination Letter

6 Letter to Claimant re: Coverage

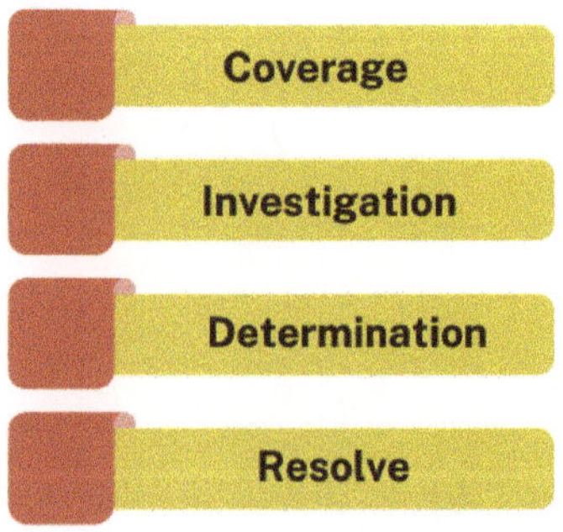

4 Review Information

Review and adjust reserves

5 Coverage Review

Coverage Yes?

Liability Yes?

Obtain Records

Liability No?

6 Declination Letter

Close Claim

6 Check MSP Eligibility

7 Send Release

8 Receive Release

9 Send Check

Close Claim

Coverage

Investigation

Determination

Resolve

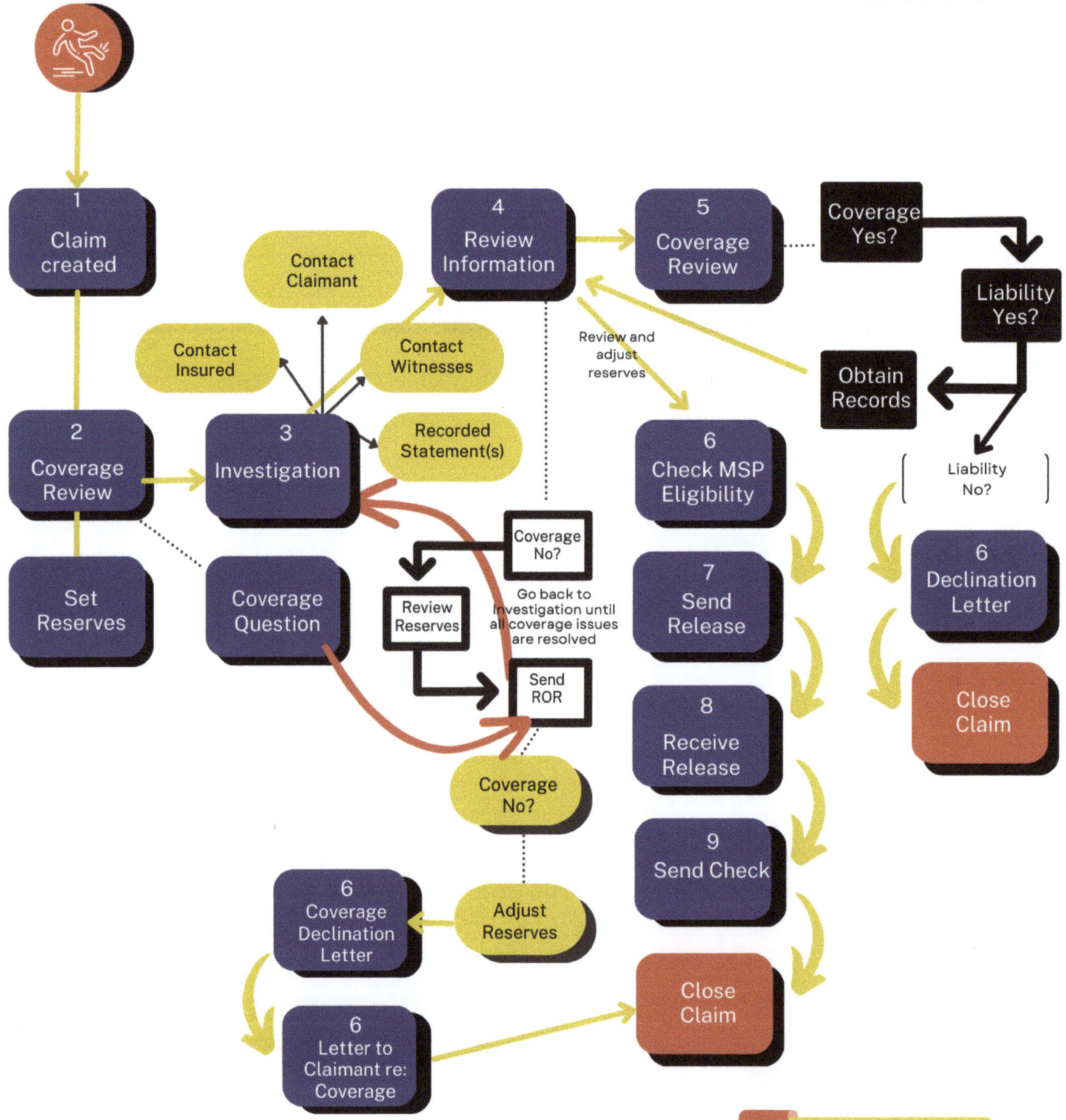

This is a simplistic flowchart of a third-party liability loss for illustrative purposes only. Actual processes will vary based on state law, the circumstances of the loss, and the insurer involved.

Humpty Dumpty

Humpty Dumpty sat on a wall,
Where he placed a personal call;
Humpty Dumpty began to wobble,
Which was quite frightful;
When his friend made him giggle,
The motion made him wiggle;
Humpty Dumpty fell with a plop,
Due to the drop!
So now we eat our eggs scrambled,
All because his friend caused him to chuckle.

Jack and Jill

Jack and Jill went up the hill
For a pail of water to fetch;
He tripped over a rock
Which caused Jill to retch.

Up Jack got, and began to rot,
Because he was a zombie.
He ate Jill's brain, as she ran in the rain
But soon she felt less achy.

Moral of the Stories

Fault is known by several words in the insurance world, namely as "***liability***" or "***negligence***." Fault, liability, and negligence all mean similar things, but they are slightly different and beyond the scope of this book. However, it is important to understand one's As, Bs, Cs, and Ds in order to determine who is at fault in a loss.

A Duty Owed—discussed in *Rapunzel* and *Goldilocks and the Three Bears*. The owner of the premise has a duty to the people on the property.

Breach of Duty—if the duty (to provide a safe environment, for example) is breached, then the owner may be responsible for the other person's injuries.

Caused by the breach—the breach of the duty must proximately cause the loss. There are no intervening events between the breach and the loss.

Damage—if the other person suffered injury or damage as a result of the breach, the responsible person will owe monetary compensation (like paying medical bills, or repairing the vehicle).

Rapunzel and *Goldilocks and the Three Bears* discuss how, based on the status of the guests (the prince and Goldilocks), the duties of the property owners change. One could argue the friend who caused Humpty Dumpty to laugh and fall off the wall is responsible for his death, but one could also argue that the fall is Mr. Dumpty's fault—he should not have been sitting there in the first place. Likewise, no one is at fault for Jack tripping over a rock. So, if Jill had survived the Zombie Apocalypse, she could not have filed a claim for Jack's death, because (1) he wasn't really dead—he was a zombie; and (2) he caused his own non-death by not watching where he was going.

This brings up a good point that is often forgotten in today's Everyone's-Responsible-But-Me society. Aside from a safe environment, not laying a trap for someone, etc., no one owes anyone anything. As a visitor on another person's premises, an equal responsibility lies in being attentive to one's surroundings, just as the property owner is accountable for maintaining a dry floor or providing a cautionary notice if it is wet.

This logic is why Mr. Dumpty's friend is not responsible for his death. Humpty should have been sitting closer to the ground. His friend didn't make him sit on the wall. Mrs. Dumpty will just need to admit she was married to an eggshell claimant. (That's a joke only insurance professionals and attorneys reading this will get.)

Rumpelstiltskin

"All rise. The Court is now in session. The Right Honorable Yarrow Willowwitch of Fairytale Land Superior Court presiding."

The bailiff's voice was a gunshot, a sharp crack reverberating through the room. He barked commands. His words carried a weight that left Puss quaking in his boots. He had no doubt as to his role in the legal system.

He was a tree—tall and sturdy, with broad shoulders and a stern expression. He wore a well-tailored uniform that hugged his frame, emphasizing his muscles and the power he wielded in the courtroom—and in the bedroom. He had strong legs which made women's knees weak.

The life lines etched on his face could cut diamonds. His eyes were the same steely color of the jail walls in the bowels of the courthouse. With a single eyebrow, he could silence even the rowdiest of spectators, restoring order with a solitary gesture.

He carried himself with the confidence of a man who knew his place in the world and was not afraid to enforce the law with an iron fist. He was a man of few words, but when he spoke, people listened. His reputation preceded him, and even the most hardened criminals like Big Bad Wolf, Schattenhexe, the witch who captured Hansel and Gretel, and Queen Morganna, Snow's Evil Stepmother, knew better than to cross him. In a world of gray areas and shifting loyalties, the bailiff was a beacon of unwavering justice, a force to be reckoned with in the dark and dangerous world of Fairytale Land.

"Has the jury reached a verdict?" Judge Willowwitch inquired.

"We have, Your Honor."

My eyes followed the bailiff's hands that held my future in black letters. Willowwitch unfurled the scroll and looked at me. She was a sight for sore eyes—if you like your sights to be nightmares. Her face was a map of wrinkles and creases, like an old leather wallet that had been left out in the sun too long. Her eyes were beady and small, like a rat's, and her nose was crooked and bulbous. Her hair was thin and stringy, like a nest of tangled wires, and her skin had a sickly, jaundiced hue. I wondered if she was related to Schattenhexe. She was the kind of woman who could make a scarecrow look like a supermodel. Even her voice was grating and harsh, like nails on a chalkboard. It was hard to look at her, let alone talk to her, without feeling a shiver run down your spine.

It was a spinning wheel that got me here. That, some straw, and a dame. A real looker, with legs that went on for a country mile and curves that dipped in all the right places. But it wasn't her beauty that made me uneasy. It was the way she moved, like a snake in the grass, all slithery and smooth. And her eyes—they were like daggers, cutting through your soul with a single glance. She had a way of sizing you up that made you feel like a piece of meat on a butcher's block. She was trouble, all right—the kind that gave the Beast thoughts about throwing Belle over.

"I was desperate. My father, the miller, had told the king that I could spin straw into gold. It was a lie. Of course, it was. But the king believed him and locked me in a room with a spinning wheel and a heap of straw. I knew that if I couldn't turn the straw into gold by morning, I'd be done for. That's when he appeared..."

Sure, I knew him. Her old man. He was a shadowy figure with a reputation to match. I'd heard the rumors about him. A predatory figure, lurking on the outskirts of Enchanted Hollow like a vulture waiting for its prey. When he heard someone talking about gold, he'd lick his lips like he was eating a T-bone steak that cost more than his monthly rent. I used to wonder if he had any tastebuds left.

We went way back. Used to work together. Pulling off small-time scams and cons to make some quick coin. We were a tight duo. Me using my cleverness and wits to come up with the schemes, and him using his charm and silver tongue to sell them to unsuspecting marks.

One day, the miller came to me with an opportunity, something we'd never attempted before. A big job. One that would allow the miller to retire.

"So, what are you gonna do after this job? Retire on a beach somewhere?"

He drew on his cigarette, "Nah, nothing like that. I'm gonna go straight. Get married, settle down, have a son."

"A son, huh? What if it's a girl?"

"It won't be."

"But what if it is?"

"It won't be, I tell ya! I'm going to have a son. If it's not, there are always ways of getting rid of girls."

"All right, keep your britches on. What's so special about having a son?"

"Well, I always wanted one," he got a dreamy look in his eye, like he was looking far into the future. "You know, to carry on the family name and all that. Plus, I never had a pa myself, and I don't want my son to grow up like I did. So, I'm going to take real good care of him."

"I see. And what's your special lady like? She pretty?"

The miller's face lit up like a Christmas tree at the mention of his lady. He began to describe her in great detail, her beauty, her grace, her intelligence, and her charm. He spoke of her as if she were the rarest gem in the world, and he was the luckiest man alive to have won her heart. I couldn't help but feel a pang of envy at his description.

"Yeah, she's a real looker. Smart, too. She's got a good head on her shoulders. I think we're a good match. And she don't know about you or our funny business so let's leave it that way."

I nodded along, pretending to be interested, but all the while I was thinking about the job. The miller had said something about spinning straw into gold, and that was all I needed to hear. My mind began to race with possibilities, schemes and cons that could make us rich beyond our wildest dreams.

We talked for a while longer, hammering out the details of the job, and before long we had a plan. It was risky, but we were confident we could pull it off.

"Sounds like you got it all figured out. But let's focus on the job for now, all right?"

The night of the heist arrived, and everything seemed to be going smoothly. But then the miller got greedy. He wanted to take more than we'd planned, and in the chaos, we were caught.

It was the kind of pinch that would've put the

miller away for a long stretch since he was the front man. But he made a deal with Madam District Attorney Mirage. He turned on me, a little man with a sharp wit and a talent for spinning gold out of straw and lies out of thin air. The miller walked away with a slap on the wrist, and I went up the river. Spent a few years behind bars. I emerged a bitter and jaded man while the miller went straight. But I could still see the ghosts of his past in the way he carried himself—the way he looked over his shoulder, the way he talked to people like he was sizing them up, looking for angles. He knew the game and he knew the stakes. But he was out now and he wasn't going back in. Not for nobody.

Except there was one last con he couldn't resist, and I knew it.

The miller thought putting me in the slammer was the end of our partnership, but he was wrong. When the miller's daughter was born, I saw the opportunity to get revenge. Sure, the miller was as greedy and desperate as ever, so I hatched a plan to use his daughter as a pawn in a new con game. One I'd win this time.

"Well, well, well. What's a beautiful woman like you doing crying over some spent straw?"

She slowly raised her face. Her tears were like drops of acid, burning through the facade of the world. Her sobs were a practiced performance, each one expertly crafted to manipulate the emotions of those around her. But to the trained eye, her cries were as phony as a three-dollar bill, as artificial as the cheap makeup that caked her face. There was no real sadness in her heart.

I got into her cell thanks to a corrupt guard and a sly courtier. I knew them from another little scheme that hadn't panned out, only that time I'd saved them and they knew it. I had them by their necks, and they'd do anything to keep my mouth shut.

The guard stationed outside the daughter's room was a burly man with a face that looked like it had been chiseled out of granite. He had a thick neck and shoulders like a bull, and his unyielding gaze could intimidate even the bravest of souls. But he's the type of person who's always looking for a way to make a quick buck, even if it means betraying his country or his fellow guards. He's not above taking bribes or turning a blind eye to criminal activities happening within the castle walls, as long as he gets his share of the profits. He manages to keep his job by being cunning and manipulative, always knowing how to play the right cards and make the right connections, like me and the courtier.

The courtier was a slick, slimy man, always dressed to impress with a neatly trimmed mustache and that $500 custom-made suit. It would have been a significant investment for most people, but for a wealthy and powerful courtier, having a suit from Master Bespoke, hand-sewn with fairy thread, well, that was a necessity if he wanted to maintain his image before the king. He had a way with words, charming and manipulating those around him to get what he wanted. But beneath his polished exterior lay a heart as black as coal, willing to do whatever it took to advance his own interests, including selling out his own country. He moved like a snake, slithering through the shadows, always watching, always waiting for the right opportunity to strike. His eyes were dark and calculating, always searching for his next victim.

The treasonous plot was as dirty as they come, a scheme that could overthrow the kingdom and place the two crooks on the throne. The guard and the courtier had been planning it for months, exchanging hushed whispers in shadowy corners and plotting their next move like chess masters. Their pawns were the unsuspecting knights, bishops, and rooks that dotted the court, all played with a cunning hand that was as cold as ice.

The plan was simple yet effective: they would frame the king's closest allies for a heinous crime, one so terrible that it would leave the kingdom in a state of chaos. With the king and his loyal followers out of the way, the guard and the courtier would swoop in and claim the throne for themselves.

Unfortunately for them, I had sniffed out the plot like a bloodhound after an escaped con. I had all the evidence of their scheme and confronted the guard and the courtier, forcing them to see that they were playing with fire. And I was fuel for the flame. Now they owed me their necks, and I owned them like a pair of dogs on a leash.

"You need some help with that, honey?" I jutted my chin out toward the bundle of straw in the corner.

"What's it to you, Mister?"

"Hey, I'm just here to help, baby. I heard you crying and thought you might need a shoulder."

"Name is Lana. And unless you can spin gold outta straw, I don't need yours or anyone else's shoulder. My neck won't be on my own shoulders tomorrow unless I get some gold."

"It's a mighty pretty neck, I'd hate for anything to happen to it. How much gold do you need?"

"How would I know? I don't know the ratio of straw to gold. Oh, if I get my hands on my fath-…"

"Sweet cheeks, get me a whisky and make it a double. Neat. I hate to see a pretty dame like you cry."

She got up from the spinning wheel and went over to the liquor cabinet to pour my drink. Without looking at her, I said, "What'll you give me if I spin this straw into gold?"

The sound of the pouring whiskey stopped.

"Whaddayawant?" There was an edge to her voice. She was wary. Yeah, she was her father's daughter, all right. Right down to the cold calculations that drove her every move.

"Not much. I'll take that pretty li'l trinket around your neck."

"That was my mother's."

"I could take something else."

"I could scream."

"You think the guard who let me in would save you?"

"All right. Here." She threw the gold chain and locket at my feet.

I picked it up and threaded the first piece of straw around it. By the time the sun rose, all the straw was gone and in its place was a pyramid of gold coins. I was gone, and Lana was asleep looking like the angel she portrayed herself to be.

The door to the chamber opened violently. The king's presence filled the room, his tall frame looming over everyone else in the chamber. He wore a long black overcoat that hugged his broad shoulders and tapered down to his polished boots. His piercing blue eyes were icy daggers, scanning the room with a fierce intensity. A perfectly groomed beard framed his strong jawline, adding to the intimidating aura he projected. After he entered the room, his entourage followed like little ducklings, the air grew colder, and the sound of his heavy footsteps ominously stopped in the middle of the room.

He saw the gold, and his eyes became bluer. He grabbed Lana by the shoulders, lifting her up until she was on her tippy toes, "How did you do it?"

His voice was more terrifying because it was a soft whisper.

Lana looked at the king coolly, "Your Grace, I have a gift."

The king's eyes took in the woman's face. "Is this true?"

She nodded; her eyes downcast. The king let Lana go and stroked his beard thoughtfully, then turned to her, "I have a proposal for you."

I was drinking two-bit whiskey at The Fallen Sparrow Tavern. It was dimly lit, with flickering candles casting eerie shadows on the grimy walls, walls you didn't want to touch with your bare hands, and floors your boots always slightly stuck to. The air was thick with smoke, mixed with the pungent scent of rotgut and piss. The bar itself was made of weathered wood, scarred and stained from countless spills and brawls. The bartenders were a pair of gruff, burly men, their arms thick with muscle from years of hauling kegs and breaking up fights – or noses, if the king's guards got too curious. It was a lawless area. Used to be a neighborhood of upward-moving people, but now is a place for folks brought down by circumstances of their own making. The patrons were a rough and rowdy crowd, their faces lined with years of hard living and shady dealings. The room was so loud with drunken revelry that I barely heard the message boy tell me over the din that Part 2 of my plan was in motion.

The king had moved Lana to the stables. I smiled to myself. So the king was human after all. He saw the glint of gold and he got greedy, just like the rest of us.

"Be careful in there. She's hot under the collar."

"You scared of a broad, Frank?" The guard slid the key into the lock as I slipped him a small purseful of coins. If looks could kill, Frank and the courtier woulda done me in several times over the past decade. This time was no different.

I walked into the room, and Frank closed the door, then locked it. I wondered, not for the first time, if he'd open it again when I asked him to.

Lana was waiting for me right inside the door.

"Where have you been?" she hissed.

"Whoa there, sweet cheeks. Don't get your garter in a twist. You know the score. More straw, more gold. And don't forget who's doing you the favor here."

"Yeah, I remember, all right. But the king thinks I did that job last night, and now he wants me to spin this straw into gold."

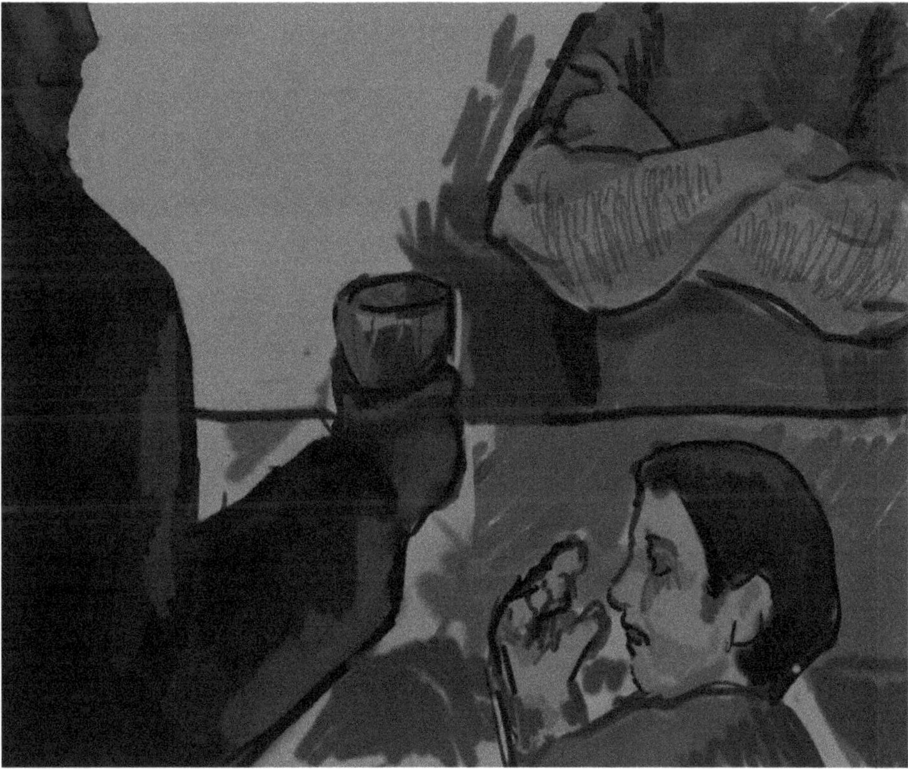

"Life ain't fair, doll. And if you think this is tough, wait till you see what Enchanted Hollow's got in store for you. But you got a good thing going here. A roof over your head, meals on the table, and a sweet deal with the king."

"Oh, it's a sweet deal. For him. He gets the gold. I get hitched. To him. Maybe that's not what I want."

Lana's eyes smoldered with a fierce intensity, her fiery gaze an attempt to ensnare me with her feminine wiles. But her flame was ice-cold, the chill of desperation seeping from her every pore. I saw right through her feeble attempt like a pane of glass, unfazed by her cheap seduction.

"You don't want me, baby. I'm no good."

"You gotta help me. He'll kill me if he finds out I didn't turn that straw into gold!"

"I don't gotta do nothing, sweet cheeks. Not without a little *quid pro quo*."

She looked at me and pouted. "What do you want?"

"You're going to be queen as soon as I finish this. So, cut the crybaby act and give me that gold ring."

"And on the charge of breach of contract, how does the jury find the defendant?"

The courtroom was tense with anticipation as the judge's voice cut through the silence like a sharpened knife. The air was thick with the stench of sweat and fear, the rustling of clothes sounded like the fluttering of frightened birds.

"We the jury find the defendant, Queen Lana, guilty," the jury foreman announced. The words hung in the air like a heavy fog, engulfing everyone in the room.

The Queen's face went ashen as she swayed on her feet. The verdict was a lightning bolt striking the courtroom, igniting a frenzy of reactions. Some gasped for air like fish out of water, while others simply sat, mouths agape, staring blankly into space. The echoes of Willow-witch's gavel reverberated through every heart in the room, as if signaling the end of something much larger than just this trial. Some saw justice being served, while others smelled the stench of a corrupt system. It was a moment frozen in time, like a snapshot of a collective conscience, split in half by the weight of the verdict. Suddenly, the

Queen's eyes rolled back, and she slumped over, fainting from the shock. Her attendants rushed to her side, fanning her with a perfumed handkerchief as they tried to revive her.

Willowwitch's voice boomed over the chaos, but no one was listening. The Bailiff tried to do his job, but it was too little, too late. I looked over at the prince, who was sitting quietly in his seat, watching the spectacle with a bemused expression. Nothing would stand in my way now. I had been waiting for this moment for too long.

As the chaos continued to rage around me, I couldn't help but smile to myself. I had played my cards perfectly, and now I had the ultimate prize: the miller's grandson.

The prince would be mine, and there was nothing anyone could do about it.

Moral of the Story

Although "breach of contract" is mentioned, this story highlights the importance of *"**reasonableness**"* in an insurance claim. It is not at all reasonable to spin gold out of straw, and if it is, expect it to be done in one night, and even if one can do that, play a ridiculously long game to get back at one's Partner-in-Crime by duping his daughter and stealing his grandson.

The concept of reasonableness in insurance claims is an important one. Insurance companies have a duty to act in good faith when handling claims, which includes adjusting claims and determining the value of the loss in a reasonable manner. This means the insurance company must act in a manner that a reasonable person would expect, considering all the circumstances.

A reasonable person is a hypothetical individual who exercises average care, skill, and judgment in conduct and behavior. The concept of a reasonable person is used in various legal contexts to determine whether someone has acted with reasonable care or negligence in a particular situation. A reasonable person is expected to act in a manner that an ordinary or average person with the same background and under the same circumstances would behave. Companies—such as insurers—must also pass the "reasonable person" test.

For example, if a person makes an insurance claim for damage to their car, the insurer must determine the damage in a reasonable manner. This may include investigating the cause of the loss, obtaining estimates for repairs, and reviewing the policy terms and conditions. If the insurance company unreasonably denies the claim or delays in processing it, they may be acting in bad faith and could be subject to legal action.

Similarly, claimants also have a duty to act in a reasonable manner when making an insurance claim. This may include providing accurate information, cooperating with the insurer's investigation, and mitigating damages where possible. If a claimant acts unreasonably, such as by making false statements or exaggerating the extent of their damages, their claim may be denied or reduced.

Overall, the concept of "reasonableness" is an important one in the insurance industry, as it helps to ensure that claims are assessed and handled fairly and in good faith.

The Ugly Duckling

One bright spring morning, Mama Duck—a distant relative to Mother Goose—sat on her nest, squirming with anticipation. As the sun approached lunchtime, Mama's six eggs began to crack.

One, two, three, four, five little ducklings appeared and began looking about. They shook their little yellow wings, and all began quacking at once.

"Look at all my pretty ducklings!" cooed Mama Duck. "You are the most beautiful ducklings ever there were! No other duck has had such handsome ducklings! Except, of course, your Grandma Duck—my mother —because I am an exceptionally pretty duck!" Mama Duck exclaimed.

"I will teach you your first lesson. Line up and we will go to the pond.

"One, two, three, four, five, si… Where's the sixth duckling?"

Mama Duck turned and looked at her nest. There in the middle was an egg that was larger than the rest. Mama Duck sighed.

"Come here, my pretty ducklings. We must wait for your nest-mate."

When the sun began to set, Mama Duck felt a poking in her belly. She got up to see the big egg was cracking open. It took all night for the occupant to come out, but as the sun came up the next day, a dark gray…*animal*…was in the nest next to his brothers and sisters.

No one knew what to make of him. He was taller than the rest of the ducklings; he was not fuzzy yellow; he honked rather than quacked; and he walked all wobbly.

"Now," said Mama Duck, "let's get on with our first lesson. Line up and we will go to the pond.

"One, two, three, four, five, six. Here we go!" And with that, Mama Duck took her ducklings to the pond and jumped in. Five of the ducklings followed suit, but the sixth one lagged behind because he walked funny.

Finally, Number Six made it to the pond's edge where his brothers and sisters said, "We've never seen such an ugly duckling! You cannot be a duck. You're too ugly!"

"Shut your beaks!" Mama Duck commanded. "He was born in the same nest as you, and you will love your brother, no matter what."

But the ugly duckling hung his head as he waded into the pond.

"At least he can swim," thought Mama Duck, because she, too, thought her son was quite ugly.

When Mama Duck was around, all the farm animals were nice to the ugly duckling, but she was not always around, as she liked to visit and gossip with the other mothers on the farm. All the other ducklings, piglets, kittens, calves, and puppies would say to Number Six, "We don't want to play with you. You can't run because your legs are weird. You should just leave."

That night, as Mama Duck was asleep, the ugly duckling flew over the pond.

The temperatures gradually got warmer, and the ugly duckling had many adventures meeting a chicken, encountering a mean tomcat, and weathering many a storm.

But everywhere he went, the animals told him he was ugly and they didn't want him around.

One evening, as the nights got colder, the days began to get crisp, and the trees started to change color, the ugly duckling heard a host of trumpets in the sky. He looked up and saw the most beautiful flock of white, long-necked birds flying overhead.

"Oh," he breathed to himself, "They are so beautiful! I wish I were beautiful."

Soon, the ground was as white as those beautiful birds, but the water in the ugly duckling's new pond had become very, very cold. He was hungry and needed to fish; so, he got into the cold, cold water. Every day, the ice in the water became a bit thicker and more difficult to move. Until one day, he became trapped and knew he was going to die on the pond. He began to cry, a sad and plaintive honking.

Before he knew what had happened, he was lifted from his watery grave and ensconced in a warm wool jacket. A kind, old man who had a farm in the dell, had picked him up and said, "You poor thing. You're frozen half solid. You'll come home with me, and I'll keep you warm this winter."

As he placed the ugly duckling in front of the roaring fireplace, the man explained, "We had a windstorm a few months back, and RePete Pig's old house was blown down. He left, so I took his wood home to use as fire logs for the winter. I don't mind saying it saved an ol' man like me a lot of hard work."

All through the winter, the old man cared for the ugly duckling and told him stories about when he had a pumpkin farm and a claim with a Fairy Godmother, or how he knew about a guy who'd gotten hurt stealing from a giant, or about the local Little People who had a business income loss claim because of a princess.

Then one day, the ugly duckling saw the old farmer hastily wiping away tears. "I'm not crying," the farmer denied. "I was cutting onions earlier, but it's time that you go and be with your own kind."

The farmer picked up the ugly duckling and took him back to the pond where he'd found the stricken bird in the early winter. Now the trees were budding, and flowers were popping up out of the ground as the sun got warmer.

The farmer placed the ugly duckling into the water and felt him push away, very strong, indeed. The duckling craned his neck just in time to see the farmer wave goodbye. As he watched the farmer turn to leave, he heard some splashing.

The ugly duckling looked into the water to see a reflection of one of the beautiful white birds he'd seen in the fall. When he moved his head to the right, so did the reflection. He moved his head to the left, and the reflection followed him. It was very confusing.

"Hello," said an old swan, "Where did you come from?"

"It's OK. I'll leave."

"No, don't. I was at a farm once. I didn't like it there. Everyone was preening and mean if you weren't pretty. I had an egg, and I knew my cygnet would be teased mercilessly when he hatched. Unfortunately, when I was ready to leave the farm, I couldn't find my egg. I bet that old biddy, Mama Duck, hid it from me.

"Anyway, my son would be about your age."

The ugly duckling could not believe his luck. This beautiful bird was describing the farm from whence he came! And as the beautiful bird's reflection continued to follow him around on the water, it began to dawn on him. The no-longer-ugly-duckling told the woman, whom he soon determined was his mother, his short, sad story about life at the farm and his happy winter with the old farmer.

While the pen was happy to have found her cygnet, she was furious at the farm animals. She immediately filed a liability claim against the farm for bullying.

Moral of the Story

Bullying is conduct where one or more persons harass another over time. It is characterized by methodical, hurtful, inappropriate, and threatening behaviors and can be either physical or psychological such as:

- Repeatedly sending offensive, rude, and insulting messages
- Posting or sending offensive photos (taken with or without consent) of the person being bullied, with the intention to humiliate and embarrass the victim
- Hacking into an email, social networking, or any electronic account and using the victim's virtual identity to send, upload, or distribute embarrassing materials to or about others
- Distributing personal or embarrassing information, or tricking the victim into revealing personal or embarrassing information and sharing it with others
- Repeatedly sending messages that include threats of harm or engaging in online activities that cause the victim to fear for his or her safety

In this example, the bullying of the ugly duckling was psychological. Thirty states have passed anti-bullying legislation because bullying has become so common now in schools and in workplaces.

Children and teenagers have been particularly aggressive in the use of cyber bullying through social media. Many others have become their victims. Parents of the bullied children are holding the bully's parents liable—or responsible—for their child's actions, based on the theory of "negligence" in claims and lawsuits. Specifically, if the bully's parents do not stop the bullying, they will be held responsible for failing to take any action to protect the child who is being bullied. In other words, the law makes it clear that adults should protect the child whom their child is bullying. (Please consult with an attorney for any legal advice on this topic.)

Homeowner policies and business policies (if the bullying occurs at work) will not cover an insured parent of a bully, because they deem the acts of a bully as "intentional." Therefore, the people filing a claim on behalf of a bully will receive no settlement from the insurance company. Their claim will be denied, and the at-fault person (or their parents) will be forced to pay out of pocket.

In the event of mass shootings, insurers consider this to be a criminal act, which also is not covered. Again, there is no insurance coverage for these acts. See *Humpty Dumpty* and *Jack and Jill* for a discussion of liability.

Many bullies claim, "I was just teasing. So-and-So just can't take a joke!" This is gaslighting, where the bully attempts to negate the other's perception of reality. It's also a form of bullying through manipulation. The courts take a dim (no pun intended) view of this so-called "defense."

So, the moral of the story is to shut the bullying down before it begins, because there is no coverage in the event of a lawsuit. Alternatively, because there is no coverage, even in the event that the insured was responsible/liable/at-fault for the bullying, the policy will not respond and no payment will be issued from the carrier.

London Bridge Is Falling Down

London Bridge is falling down,
Falling down, all around,
London Bridge is falling down,
My fair Lady.

Build it up with bricks and clay
Bricks and clay, don't delay,
Build it up with bricks and clay,
My good Fellow.

Bricks and clay will fall away,
Fall away, and decay,
Bricks and clay will fall away,
My fair Lady.

Build it up with iron bars,
Iron bars and crossbars,
Build it up with iron bars
My good Fellow.

Iron bars will bend and break,
Bend and break, rust and flake,
Iron bars will bend and break,
My fair Lady.

Set a man to watch all night,
Watch all night, not daylight,
Set a man to watch all night,
My good Fellow.

Suppose the bridge has bad design,
Bad design, I underline,
Suppose the bridge has bad design,
My fair Lady.

I cannot solve everything,
Everything, it's baffling,
I cannot solve everything,
My good Fellow.

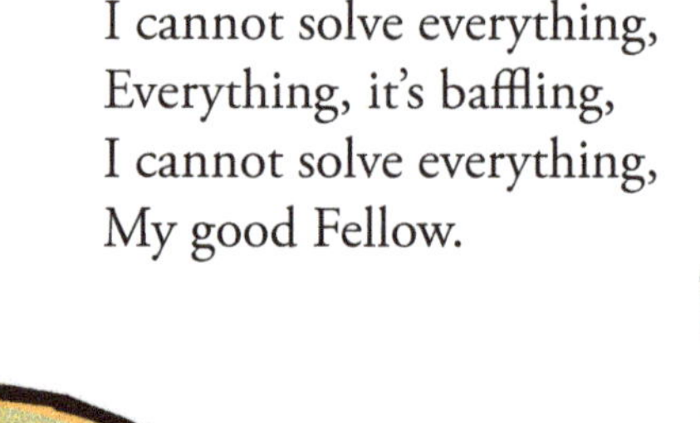

Moral of the Story

Collapse is covered due to the weight of rain which collects on the roof, rodents and vermin whose presence are unknown to the insured, and hidden decay (again, unless the insured knew of the decay). However, collapse is not covered due to a faulty design.

There was once a woman who had, for a very long time, wanted a child of her own.

Outside the woman's house could be seen a beautiful garden, full of the most gorgeous flowers and herbs. It belonged, unfortunately, to a powerful and frightening enchantress. One day, the woman was standing by her window, looking down into the garden, when she saw a bed of rampion, and suddenly a powerful hunger overtook her.

The woman told her husband, "I shall have no peace until I have some of that rampion."

The husband gathered his nerve and knocked on the enchantress' door to ask for some ***rampion***, for it was too late in the season to plant it. Alas, no one answered his call, so he took some of the rampion.

The woman ate it with relish, and the next day she desired even more. The man again went to the garden and took the rampion, thinking that what the enchantress didn't know wouldn't hurt him or his wife. Unhappily, when the man stood up with the rampion in his hands, he turned around to see the enchantress, who was very angry.

"How dare you, peasant," she spat, "come into my garden and steal my rampion like a crook's daughter recently raised to royalty? I will make you suffer!"

"Oh, powerful enchantress," the man stammered, "please be merciful. As I'm sure you know, 'a happy wife is a happy life,' and I only took it out of necessity. My wife saw your rampion from the window, and she was overcome with such a longing for it that she would have not left me in peace if she had not got some to eat."

The enchantress allowed her anger to be placated, and said to the man, "If that is the case, I will allow you to take as much rampion as your wife needs, on one condition: she must give me the child she will bring into the world; it will be well treated, and I will care for it like a mother."

The man, who also understood that 'a happy enchantress means no curses,' agreed to the trade without first consulting his wife. The man also understood it was easier to ask forgiveness than permission.

Soon after, the woman went into labor, and the enchantress appeared to whisk away the girl-child, whom she named Rapunzel.

Rapunzel grew into the most beautiful girl anyone had ever seen. When she was twelve years old, the enchantress shut her into a secluded forest tower, which had neither stairs nor door. At the top of the turret were windows to allow the sun and air. Around the base of the tower she planted Devil's Walking Sticks and rose bushes.

Rapunzel had magnificent, glossy, black hair, soft as the spring breeze. It contrasted with her *café-au-lait* skin. When the enchantress visited, she would yell, "Rapunzel, Rapunzel, let down your hair." Upon hearing the enchantress' voice, the girl would unfasten her layered and looped tresses, which she kept braided, and throw them over the window, where they fell down, nearly touching the ground below. The enchantress would climb up to visit Rapunzel, who was not afraid of the enchantress since she was the only mother the girl knew.

And so, it came to pass that a prince rode through the forest and noticed the tower. He heard a song, which was so sweet that he listened, dumbstruck. This, of course, was Rapunzel, who in her loneliness, passed her time singing. The prince desired to meet her and looked for the door of the tower, but none was to be found. He rode home, defeated, but the singing had so deeply moved him that daily he went into the forest and listened to Rapunzel. Once, as dusk crept across the sky and the prince was standing behind a tree listening, he saw the enchantress come and cry, "Rapunzel, Rapunzel, let down your hair."

Rapunzel let down her braids, and the enchantress climbed into her room.

"I would never have guessed that is the ladder by which one enters the tower," thought the prince to himself. "Happily, I will try my fortune tomorrow morning." And the next day, when dawn broke, he went to the tower and exclaimed, "Rapunzel, Rapunzel, let down your hair!"

Rapunzel was shocked and frightened when a man appeared at her window, rather than the enchantress. But the prince told her that his heart had been struck dumb by her singing, and he had to see her. The prince, with his royal manners, began to court Rapunzel, who soon lost her fear. The prince asked for Rapunzel's hand in marriage. She thought he was young and handsome, and she said to herself, "He will love me more than my old mother does," so she said yes, and laid her hand in his.

She swore, "I will leave this tower, but I do not know how to get down. Bring a coil of silk every day, and I will weave a ladder with it. When that is ready, I will descend, and we will ride on your horse to your castle."

They agreed that until that time, he should come to her every morning, for the enchantress came by evening.

Sadly, Rapunzel, having been sheltered from the evil ways of the world, did not understand how to dissemble well. One evening, as she and the enchantress supped, she asked, "Tell me, mother, how are you so much heavier for me to draw up than the young prince who comes during the day?"

"Naughty child!" cried the enchantress. "First, you shame my weight! I thought I had separated you from all the ugliness of the world, but I was wrong. Second, you have deceived me."

In her anger, the enchantress clutched Rapunzel's beautiful black braids, wrapped them twice 'round her left hand, and with a pair of scissors in her right, snip, snip, she cut the braids were off, and they lay on the floor, now useless.

The enchantress was so unforgiving that she dragged Rapunzel to the Howling Desert, where she was forced to live in great grief and misery. The enchantress then flew back to the tower, climbing the exterior walls like a cat, to the very top, where she laid in wait for the prince, who soon appeared like the morning dew.

"Rapunzel, Rapunzel, let down your hair!" the enchantress heard the prince's manly voice shout. And so the enchantress let down Rapunzel's discarded braids, and it came to pass that the prince climbed up the tower as he had every morning, but to his shock, he saw the enchantress in place of his fair maid.

This startled him so much that he lost his grip on the braids and fell backward onto the Devil's Walking Sticks and rose bushes. The thorns pricked his eyes, making him blind. Lamentably, the prince never saw his beloved Rapunzel again.

Goldilocks and the Three Bears

Now in the very same woods where the enchantress had kept Rapunzel, there lived three bears: a papa bear, a mama bear, and a baby bear.

Each had a bowl for their porridge: a little bowl for the baby bear, a mid-sized bowl for the mama bear, and a great big bowl for the papa bear. And they each had a chair to sit in: a little chair for the baby bear, a mid-sized chair for the mama bear, and a great big chair for the papa bear. And they had each a bed to sleep in: a little bed for the baby bear, a mid-sized bed for the mama bear, and a great big bed for the papa bear.

And so, it passed that one fall morning, before the three bears lay down for their winter nap, Papa Bear poured porridge in their bowls. The Bear family then walked out into the forest while the porridge was cooling, because they did not want to burn their mouths by eating too soon, for they were ever-so-polite, well-mannered bears.

Near the Howling Desert, where the enchantress had deposited Rapunzel, lived a woman with her daughter who was called Goldilocks because her hair was like golden strands of silk. Also this fine fall morning, Goldilocks was en route to meet her mother at Little Red Riding Hood's Grandma's Bistro for brunch.

Goldilocks skipped by the Bears' house and looked in the window because she was a nosey little girl. Then she peeped through the keyhole, because, unlike the Bears, she was not well-mannered. Seeing nobody home, she lifted the latch. The Bears never locked their door because they were bears who would roar and stand on their hind legs if necessary, so they never suspected

anybody would harm them or break into their house.

Goldilocks opened the door and went in. Upon entering the Bears' cottage, the smell of porridge filled the girl's nose, and her stomach grumbled its dissatisfaction. Since she was a rude little girl, she walked over to the table to help herself to some breakfast.

First, she climbed into the great big chair and tasted Papa Bear's porridge.

"Mgh! Da's too haught!" she exclaimed with her mouth full, attempting to cool her tongue from the scalding porridge. "And this chair is too hard."

Next, she slid into the medium-size chair and tasted Mama Bear's porridge.

"Ech," she said, repulsed, "this is too cold." Mama Bear's chair was too soft, and when Goldilocks sat in it, the bottom of the chair fell out, so down she plopped upon the ground which made her very cantankerous. Already nosey and hungry, she was now a grumpy little girl.

Next, she hopped down and sat in the little chair and tasted the porridge Baby Bear's porridge, which was neither too hot nor too cold.

"Ah!" she sighed in contentment, "this is just right." Goldilocks ate all of Baby Bear's porridge without a "by your leave." Then she sat in Baby Bear's chair, because it was neither too hard nor too soft.

Goldilocks began to doze off, since she'd eaten all those carbohydrates which had made her tired. She trudged upstairs, where she definitely knew she should not go, and went into the Bears' bedroom.

First, she lay down upon Papa Bear's bed, but it was too high and too hard for her so she could not get comfortable.

Next, she lay down upon Mama Bear's bed, but that was too low and too soft for her. She nearly suffocated because the mattress folded in on her.

Then she lay down upon the Baby Bear's bed, which was neither too hard nor too soft and exactly her size. So she tucked herself in and fell fast asleep.

By the time Goldilocks was in Dreamland, the Bears came home from their morning constitutional. Sadly, Goldilocks was not used to doing chores since she was a spoiled girl and her mother picked up after her, so she'd left the spoon in Papa Bear's great big bowl.

"SOMEBODY HAS BEEN EATING MY PORRIDGE!" Papa Bear's gruff voice harrumphed.

Mama Bear looked at her mid-sized porridge bowl, and noticed the spoon left in her bowl, too. *"Somebody's been eating my porridge!"* whispered soft-spoken Mama Bear in her mid-sized voice.

Then Baby Bear looked at his just-right bowl. He saw the spoon there, but the porridge was all gone! "Somebody's eaten all my porridge!" he said in his just-right voice.

Mama Bear wanted to call the Fairy Godmother Task Force to report a break-in, but Papa Bear began to look around for other signs of an intruder.

Goldilocks never cleaned her room, so the hard cushion on his chair was askew.

"SOMEBODY HAS BEEN SITTING IN MY CHAIR!" Papa Bear's gruff voice harrumphed.

Mama Bear looked at her mid-sized chair with her cloud-soft, fluffy cushion and saw that the bottom of her chair had come out. *"Somebody's been sitting in my chair!"* whispered soft-spoken Mama Bear in her mid-sized voice.

Then Baby Bear looked at his just-right, oh-so-comfortable chair. He saw his comfortable cushions were all akimbo. "Somebody's been sitting in my chair!" he said in his just-right voice.

Seeing that their chairs had been sat in, Papa Bear decided he should go upstairs to the bedroom to see if anything else was disturbed. After Goldilocks found Papa Bear's bed too hard, she hadn't bothered to remake the bed.

"SOMEBODY HAS BEEN SLEEPING IN MY BED!" Papa Bear's gruff voice harrumphed.

Mama bear looked at her mid-sized bed with her cloud-soft, fluffy mattress and saw that it had nearly folded in on itself. *"Somebody's been sleeping in my bed!"* whispered soft-spoken Mama Bear in her mid-sized voice.

Then Baby Bear looked at his just-right, comfortable bed to see a lump under his covers and golden hair on his pillow! "Somebody is still sleeping in my bed!" he said in his just-right voice.

Upon hearing Baby Bear's voice, Goldilocks woke up and saw all three bears staring at her. She was so frightened, she leapt out of the just-right bed and hurled herself toward the open bedroom window where she plummeted to her death.

Moral of the Stories

An owner of a property has three types of visitors:

Invitee

People who are invited onto the property of the owner are owed the highest duty of care from the owner. This person has a contractual relationship with the owner. An invitee might be a guest in someone's home or person who uses a convenience store restroom while they are pumping gas.

Licensee

These people have no contractual relation with the property owner but are still allowed to be on the property. The owner owes a duty to the licensee to make sure the premises are safe. A licensee is a person who uses a convenience store restroom without purchasing gas or snacks.

Trespasser

A trespasser is someone who enters the property without permission and remains there without consent. Most people do not know, though, that the premises owner still has a duty to trespassers. A premises owner cannot set traps for a trespasser; they must mark dangerous land as such. A trespasser is a person who breaks into a convenience store to take a Diet Coke. The owner cannot rig the coolers to shock the burglar when touched, as that would be a trap, but the owner could warn of the dangerous situation. In other words, the owner owes the duty to announce the coolers may cause an electrical shock when touched, but he is not allowed to place live wires on the coolers to allow them to give shocks when touched.

If the danger is "open and obvious," as was the case with the enchantress' Devil's Walking Sticks and rose bushes, not only would the enchantress not be liable for the prince's injuries, but she also would not owe a duty to warn an adult (like the prince) of their existence. Further, because the prince had visited the tower many times, he definitely knew about the thorny situation (see what the author did there?).

The duty to children is usually the same as that to an invitee. The premises owner must take great care to protect children from harm on the property.

There is the concept of "***attractive nuisance***" for children, which means something that might be of particular interest to a child—a swimming pool, or a bowl of porridge, perhaps.

The Bears would need to take steps to keep an ill-mannered child safe by locking their doors so the child doesn't get in while they are away; or closing a window so the child didn't jump out of the second-floor window and literally break her neck.

In some instances, a premises owner can be held "***strictly liable***" for children's injuries, even though the children were trespassers. This means the landowner is responsible for the injury (or death), even if that person did nothing wrong.

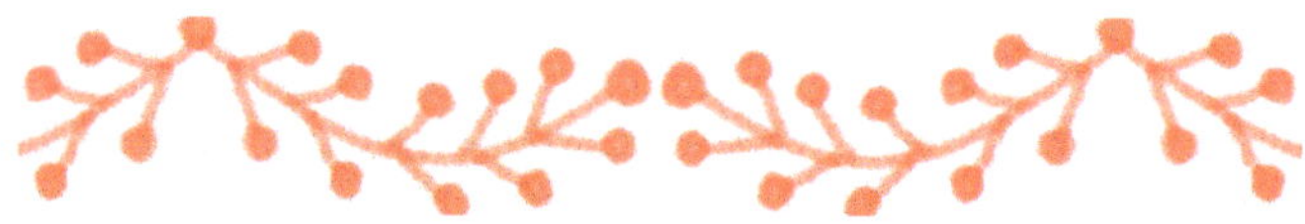

It's Raining, It's Pouring

It's raining, it's pouring,
But my worries aren't soaring.
My policy's got me covered
From downpour to puddles discovered.

An umbrella policy's the key
To keep you dry and worry-free.
When coverage isn't enough
It gives protection that's tough.

Liability claims can pour
But your umbrella will soar,
Above your home and car
To shield you from financial scar.

It's raining, it's pouring
My peace of mind's not storming.
Umbrella is the policy
I'm covered, safe, and worry-free.

Moral of the Story

Laypeople, and even insurance professionals, tend to use the terms "***umbrella***" and "***excess***" interchangeably, but these two policies are different. Their differences will impact how the claim is handled.

Both policies are types of liability insurance that provide an additional layer of protection beyond what standard insurance policies (sometimes called the "underlying policy") cover. They interact with the underlying policy in a way that provides additional coverage for liability claims that exceed the limits of the underlying policy. These policies are a wonderful source of protection, because if the insureds are found liable/negligent/at-fault for causing an accident or injury and the underlying insurance policy doesn't provide enough coverage (money) to pay for the damages, an umbrella or excess policy can help protect the insured from personal financial ruin by covering the additional costs.

The excess policy is a separate policy which is activated when the limit of the underlying policy has been pierced. In other words, the underlying policy, homeowner, auto, etc. must first pay out its full limit before the excess policy starts to provide coverage, in most instances. There are two types of excess policies which impact the way claims are handled. First there is the "***following-form***," and second there is the "stand-alone" policy.

As the names imply, if the insured has a "following-form" excess policy, that excess policy follows the terms and conditions of the underlying policy. To oversimplify things, the only difference between an underlying policy and a following-form excess policy are the limits of coverage.

The "***stand-alone***" excess policy has its own policy provisions and conditions, which could lead to gaps in coverage. Insureds should review these policies closely and discuss them with their agent to ensure complete coverage.

Either way, if a claim is not covered in the underlying policy, it is not covered by the excess policy.

The umbrella policy's ***trigger*** is similar. It generally covers the same types of liability claims as the underlying policy, such as bodily injury or property damage claims. However, it can also provide coverage for certain types of claims that are excluded from the underlying policy, such as libel or slander claims. This is called "***drop-down***" coverage and is a particularly good aspect of having umbrella coverage.

Overall, an umbrella policy is designed to provide additional liability coverage that can help protect assets in the event of a major claim or lawsuit or drop-down and cover a claim which is not covered by the underlying policy.

Both policies provide an extra layer of protection and peace of mind. If the insured's excess/umbrella coverage is not with the same insurer, the umbrella/excess adjuster will need to contact the underlying policy's adjuster to coordinate claims handling. The insured has the duty to report the claim and to cooperate with both insurers as a condition of coverage.

March 5, 2024

Messrs Grimm
Brothers Grimm News
2507 Fable Ln
Enchanted Hollow, FT 00002

Editors of *Brothers Grimm News*:

Please allow this letter to serve as notice that this firm represents Jin-Li, the mother of Jun-Li, widow of the recently departed Wu Li, and stepmother of Ye Xian. This firm also represents Miss Jun through her mother, as she is currently a minor.

It has come to our attention that the editors of the *Brothers Grimm News* have characterized Mrs. Li and her daughter, Jun, as "unattractive," "lazy," and "unloving and cruel" in no less than five (5) separate articles on five (5) separate days.

History:
Wu Li's First Wife, Miss Ye Xian's mother, unfortunately died, and shortly thereafter Mr. Li also passed away. Miss Jun is the daughter of Wudong's chief's Second Wife (Mrs. Li) and is an eligible maiden. She is fit to become a chief's First Wife.

Once a year, young maidens such as Miss Jun celebrate the New Year Festival in attempt to meet potential husbands. Miss Jun had a great many suitors prior to this year's Festival. Because Mr. Li left no sons, Mrs. Li must depend on her daughter to care for her in her sunset years, yet without Miss Jun's potential to marry a rich man, both Mrs. Li and Miss Jun face a life of extreme poverty and servitude amongst the savages of Wudong.

(Stone) Legal-1

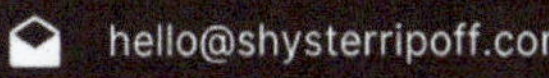
410 Goldfinch St.,
Enchanted Hollow,
Fairytale Land 00002

hello@shysterripoff.com

Damages:

You have libeled and defamed the good characters of Mrs. Li and Miss Jun. While truth is an absolute defense to libel claims, you cannot, in good conscience, assert your published statements were "opinions," as they were not printed in the Op-Ed section of your paper. Neither were these assertions quotes from alleged sources.

Even if these incendiary statements were the opinion of the articles' authors, those "journalists" are employees of *Brothers Grimm News*; therefore, as their employer, you are responsible for their actions under vicarious liability pursuant to the doctrine of *respondeat superior*.

Mrs. Li and Miss Jun will testify that the number of beaux for Miss Jun has significantly declined since the printing of your articles.

Because of your irresponsible "journalism," Mrs. Li's step-daughter, Ye Xian, now believes Mrs. Li and Miss Jun created a "burdensome life filled with chores, housework, and ceaseless abuse," when nothing could be further from the truth.

Mrs. Li loves Miss Ye Xian, but she wished to spare her the public humiliation if Miss Ye Xian's mental state was revealed. For example, Miss Ye Xian believed a 10-foot fish in the local lake to be her long-deceased mother's spirit, and if she kept the fish's bones under her mattress, this "spirit" would grant Miss Ye Xian wishes.

As you know, Miss Ye Xian claims the fish gave her a gown of sea-foam green silk, a cloak of feathers from a kingfisher, and golden slippers. However, Miss Ye Xian was discovered by the king attempting to steal said slipper from "an unknown lady of the court" according to Mrs. Li. While His Most August Majesty may believe Miss Ye Xian's far-fetched tale, Mrs. Li's heart truly breaks, because it is clearly obvious that her step-daughter has lost touch with reality and blames Mrs. Li and Miss Jun for her trials and tribulations. Therefore, Mrs. Li and Miss Jun cannot rely on their newly appointed royal relative to aid them in their time of need, since she is still suffering so many delusions.

Demand:

Mrs. Li strenuously objects to such language in reference to her daughter and herself by the *Brothers Grimm News* and immediately demands:

1. A retraction be issued for 7 consecutive days on the front page in no less than 8-inch font;
2. An accompanying apology to Mrs. Li and Jun for the same duration in the same font, size, and space;
3. Mrs. Li and Miss Jun's statement regarding the *actual* facts of the incident be printed on the front page of next Sunday's newspaper;
4. $50,000 in gold pieces to my client Mrs. Li to help alleviate her suffering from poverty;
5. $75,000 in gold pieces to Miss Jun, immediately, plus $2,500 per annum payment due to *Brothers Grim News*' irresponsible publication of gossip without verification of the facts; and
6. All reasonable attorney's fees, which to date amount to $3,284.72 in gold pieces.

You may send the money to our attention.

All of Mrs. Li and Miss Jun's demands must be met and carried out without alteration within fifteen (15) days of receipt of this letter. Failure to do so will result the filing of a lawsuit.

We look forward to your next week's publications.

Best regards,

Peter G. Shyster

Peter G. Syster Esq.
Managing Partner
PGShyster@shysterripoff.com

Enclosures: Mrs. Li written statement
Miss Jun written statement
Wire Transfer instructions
Attorney invoice to date

Moral of the Story

The person who is publishing an account about another—be it verbal or written, in a newspaper, on social media, or on television or radio—must know that the statement is true or must obtain the other person's permission to publicize a false statement about that person.

Libel is printed or written publication of false and defamatory statements about a person. These reports can, as Mrs. Li suggests, lower a community's opinion of the defamed person. In this instance, because Miss Jun is now seen as "lazy" and "unattractive," a rich man would not want her for a wife.

Of course, there's more to it than just that.

A. The untrue (read: false) report must be reported as fact.

B. The false fact must be communicated to a third person.

C. The person who published/said the false statement must be negligent (See *Humpty Dumpty* and *Jack and Jill* for a discussion on negligence and liability).

D. The statement must have caused provable harm to the person.

Needless to say, opinions are not facts. Unfortunately for the modern era, everyone has forgotten what a "fact" is. Harken back to high school English classes, where a paper had to have at least three reliable, independent sources. That is a fact. Facts can be proven with evidence, such as humans need oxygen to survive.

Opinions can be ***based*** on facts, but they can't be proven by multiple, reliable, and independent sources. For example, one might say water is the most important thing for a human to survive, while the author might strenuously argue that Diet Coke is the thing most important to human survival. Neither can be proven, although cable news stations might line up a number of pundits to support one belief or the other.

Written statements, whether delivered via blog, Facebook, LinkedIn, Threads, Carrier Pigeon, etc., cannot hide behind the phrase, "Well, this is my opinion." Neither can the spoken word in reels, TikTok, Instagram, Telegram, or whatever "kids these days" have migrated to in effort to keep one step ahead of the previous generation.

Slander is false and defamatory statements which are spoken. The memory aid to distinguish between slander and libel is: Slander is Spoken.

Most liability policies (like homeowner and business) have a section called Personal and Advertising Injury Liability coverage, and it covers a wide range of concepts, such as false arrest and libel/slander. Personal injury and advertising injury claims are seen in the commercial insurance space.

The term "Personal Injury" does not solely encompass bodily injury, despite its name. Such claims can also pertain to cases of libel or slander, as discussed earlier, as well as wrongful eviction (which became more prevalent due to the pandemic and housing shortages), and false arrests (such as when a store security guard detains someone mistakenly suspected of shoplifting).

The scope of "Advertising Injury" extends beyond just advertisements. It can also encompass cases of copyright infringement and theft of intellectual property. A homeowner who runs a business out of their home and doesn't have a businessowners policy could purchase this type of coverage. Advertising itself can be a means of attracting supporters, but it can also take the form of a child on social media making inappropriate remarks. While the latter example may be more a case of libel or slander, it illustrates how social media can quickly become a liability. To learn more, see *The Ugly Duckling*.

Businessowners, beware that there is an endorsement which the carrier can add to the policy which reduces coverage. The CG 24 13 endorsement to the commercial general liability policy removes coverage for any written or verbal release of information that violates someone else's right to privacy. In other words, if this endorsement is on the businessowners' policy, there is no coverage for libel, slander, advertising injury, etc.

Finally, umbrella policies are a terrific policy to have since they can drop down to extend coverage in the instance that a policy does not cover the loss.

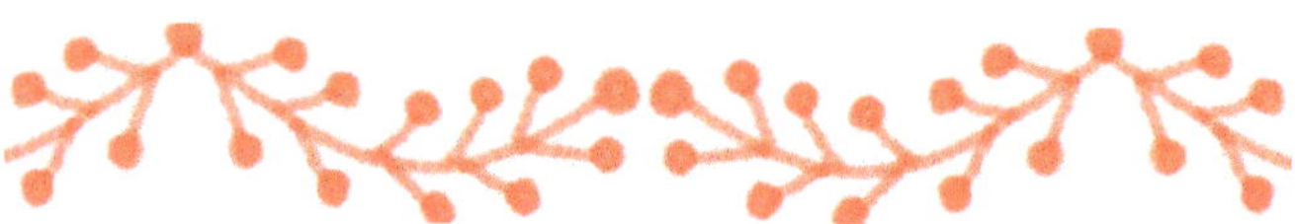

Rock A-bye, Baby

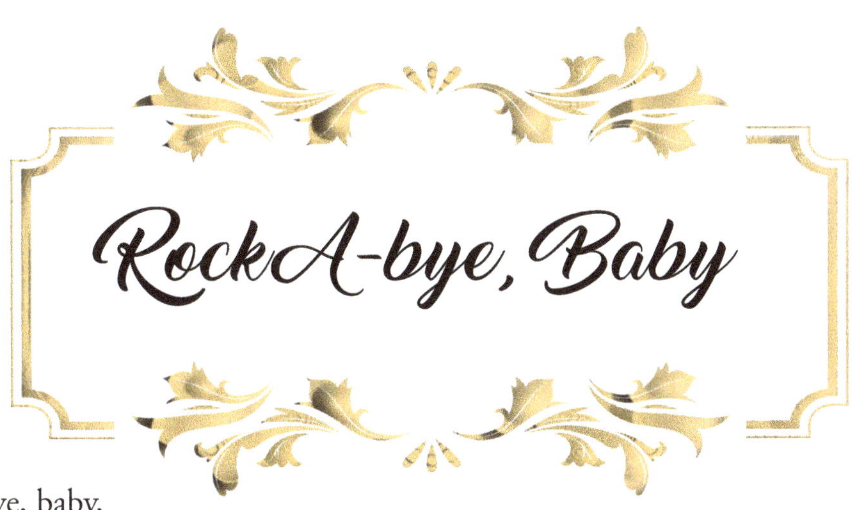

Rock a-bye, baby,
On the treetop.
When the wind blows,
The cradle will rock.
When the rope breaks,
The cradle will fall.
And down will come baby,
Cradle and all.

The policy covers,
For negligence,
Caused by the rope,
That's made so poorly.
The rope's fibers used
Were old and were spent.
So down came the baby,
Cradle and all.

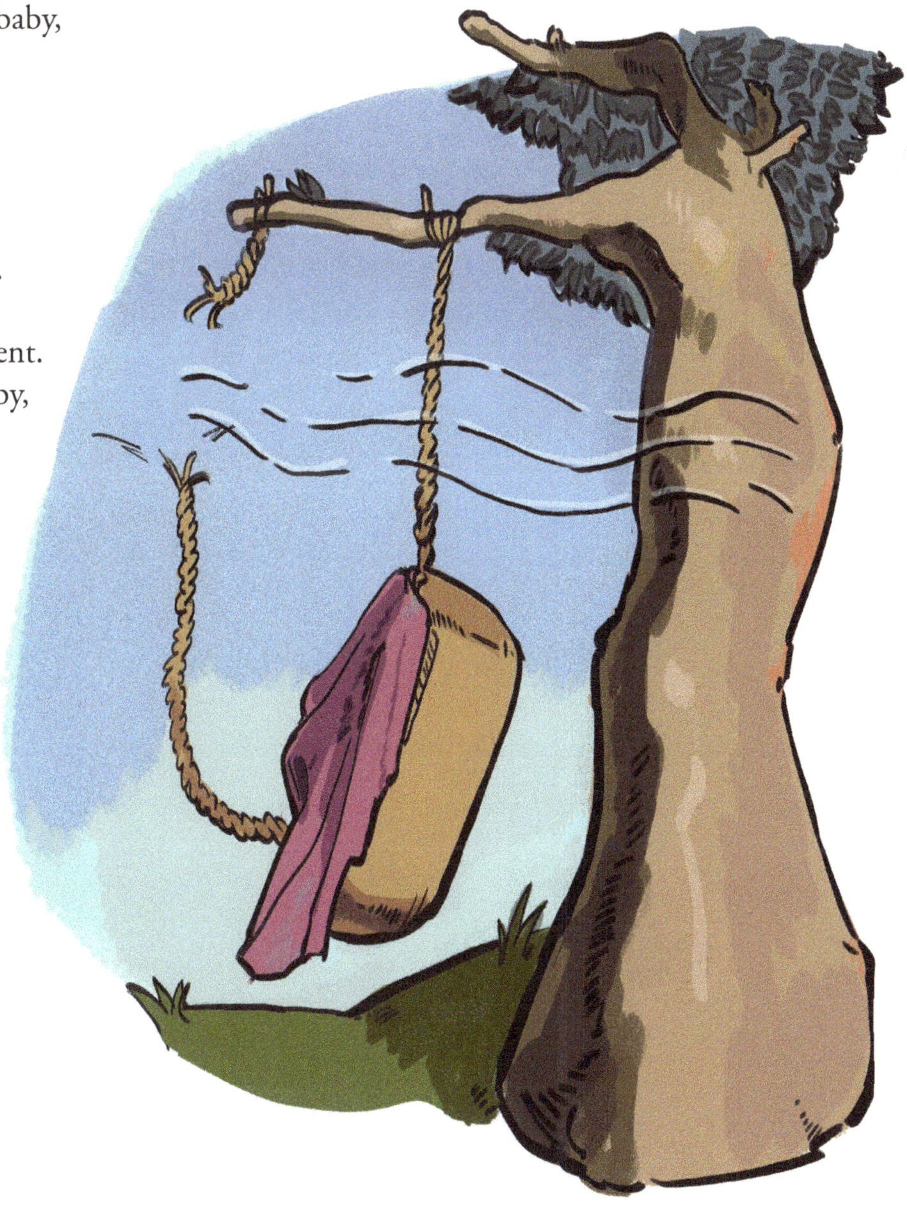

Moral of the Story

This morbid little rhyme has to do with damage to the insured's work product—in this case, the rope that is holding the cradle to the tree bough. When the rope, which was poorly made with old fibers, breaks and causes the accident, the policyholder is negligent, or responsible. The policy that would respond to this claim is a commercial general policy (CGL).

As discussed in *Humpty Dumpty* and *Jack and Jill*, the policyholder owes a duty to the claimant. In this instance, a business owes its client a safe product. Product liability insurance in the CGL policy is available for anyone in the supply chain of an item being sold, such as manufacturers, distributors, and retailers. If a product is defective or causes injury to a person, that person can then file a claim (or a lawsuit).

Businesses can also be held responsible for their completed operations—or work that is done away from their location or after the operations have been completed. These types of claims generally originate from contractors. An example would be an electrician who incorrectly wired the house, causing it to burn down. The job (wiring the house) was completed and was not performed at the electrician's business location (the jobsite was at the claimant's/client's home). The contractor incorrectly performed the work (not properly wiring the house) that caused damage (fire), thus there is negligence.

Businessowners should be aware of these kinds of risks and make sure they have adequate coverage for these types of claims.

Hark, Hark, the Dogs Do Bark

Hark, hark!
The dogs do bark,
The dogs are coming to town;
Some in tags,
Some in rags,
And some in velvet gowns.

Hark, hark!
The dogs do bark,
We think they are family;
Some are mutts,
Some are klutz,
And some are Collies.

Hark, hark!
The dogs do bark,
Laws say they are property;
Not worth much,
(They're out of touch!)
Valued at ACV.

Moral of the Story

This can easily be about cats as well as dogs. People love their pets, spending billions of dollars on vet care, pet supplies, and over-the-counter medicine every year. Unfortunately, U.S. laws treat animals as personal property and value them at "fair market value" or actual cash value.

This valuation method means there is no consideration for the human attachment or belief that pets are valued members of the family. The law sees no difference between Fluffy or Fido and the living room couch. This is especially true if the pet is not a pedigree or lacks special training.

A dog that sits on command does not fall into the "special training" category. A cat that obeys *any* command from a human should fall into "special training," but the author urges the cat's servant(s) to discuss this with an attorney before calling Good Morning America.

If the pet has been harmed (or, Fairy Godmother forbids, died) as a result of veterinarian malpractice, the owner must prove the vet improperly or negligently acted in her profession. The standards of negligence have been discussed in *Humpty Dumpty* and *Jack and Jill.*

Some states and courts are beginning to take into consideration the fact that pets have a special value, much like family photos—nothing quantifiable, but valuable nonetheless. There is some movement for emotional distress at the wrongful death of a pet due to veterinarian malpractice.

The vet's malpractice policy likely does not speak to this issue, and it would not be addressed in an insurance claim. The vet's insurance, except for malpractice, would apply to the building, in the case of hail or fire damage, and to liability exposures to human owners, in the case of a slip/trip and fall.

The Elves and the Shoemaker

It was a time of rapid inflation, and a shoemaker had become so poor that he could no longer afford supplies for his craft. He had only enough leather for one last pair of shoes, and if no one bought them, he and his wife would starve.

Determined to make a final go of his work before going to bed, he cut out the shoe pattern and laid it out on his workbench so he could begin work immediately upon waking in the morning.

The shoemaker got some sleep, woke with the sunrise, and went downstairs to his shop where opened the shutters, windows, and door. Coffee in hand, he sat down at his workbench. He looked down, amazed to see a finished pair of shoes sitting there. He picked them up and closely observed them. They were perfect and, if he admitted it to himself, nicer than he could have done. But he was also perplexed, because he had no idea how these shoes had come to be. His wife denied making them, chiding him that he knew the arthritis in her hands had prohibited her from sewing for the past few years.

Soon after, a customer came in and looked at the shoes. Because they were so well made, he offered to pay more than was customary. The shoemaker was thrilled, as this meant he would be able to purchase leather for two more pairs of shoes to be made the following day. Just as he did every night, he cut out the shoe patterns and prepared for the next day.

The next morning, the shoemaker went downstairs to his shop, opened the shutters, windows, and door, and sat at his workbench. He was amazed to see two pairs of shoes, finished, sitting there. This time, two customers were waiting outside when the shoemaker opened his door. They bought both pairs of shoes, which gave him enough money to purchase supplies for four pairs to be made the following day. Just as he did every night, he cut out the shoe patterns and prepared for the next day.

The shoemaker rushed downstairs the third morning and found four expertly crafted pairs of shoes. This time, more customers came who began to outbid each other for his shoes because they had heard of the shoemaker's quality and craftmanship.

And so, it came to pass that the old shoemaker saved enough money to become independent and feel comfortable again. However, it bothered him that these shoes continued to mysteriously appear and were better crafted than what he could do. He worried someone might accuse him of stealing, and if not that, he thought he should at least thank the person who was making these shoes for him.

"What do you think if we stayed up tonight to see who it is that makes such good quality shoes?" he inquired of his wife after supper.

His wife thought that was a good idea, so she cleared the table while he went about cutting out the patterns for all the shoes to be made for the following day. When he finished and set everything out, they turned out the light and crept into a corner of the dark workroom.

As the twelfth bell sounded in the church steeple, two elves, naked as the day they were born, approached the shoemaker's workbench. They sat down and quickly and quietly began to sew and hammer the leather into shoes. They did not take a break, but they hardly needed to, because they were so quick as to be finished within two hours. They looked at each other, winked, and then ran away.

The old shoemaker was astonished. Even when he'd been an apprentice, he could not work that quickly; but his wife was troubled.

"Those elves have made us rich, and they run around naked. What will people think? They will think we are cruel and uncaring. I will knit them some clothes, and you should make them some little shoes. We will ask that they wear them when they are working for us."

The shoemaker thought this was a good idea, and when everything was ready, the couple put the gifts together on the workbench and remained in the dark workroom to watch. Again, at midnight the elves came in. At first, they were confused, since there was no leather to be made into shoes. But they saw the tiny gifts. They opened them, tried on the clothes, and laughed in delight.

Since there was no work to be done, they left soon after.

For a few months the shoemaker continued buying leather and pre-cutting the shoes for the elves to make, secure in the knowledge they were warm and happy. But it came to pass that the shoemaker's wife was at the market one day when she saw another type of shoe—a heel that gave height to the wearer—therefore, it was called a "high heel" shoe.

The old shoemaker studied one of these high heels and learned how to make it. He wanted to sell the

new styled shoe, and so, like always, he cut out the leather and set out all the supplies for the elves. The shoemaker went downstairs to his shop the next morning, opened the shutters, windows, and door, and sat at his workbench.

He was dismayed to find only the old-style shoes made. That night, he repeated his steps to the same effect.

"Perhaps the elves don't know how to make the new style," suggested the wife, who was always wise. "You had to learn how to do it. You should show the elves."

The shoemaker thought this was a good idea, but he was not sure whether the elves would allow him to be there with them, since it was generally bad luck for an elf to see a human. So the old shoemaker made the high heel shoe in a series of steps laid out for the elves to see. He left them all the materials and went to sleep, secure in the knowledge that they could figure it out, and he would be able to sell the new shoes in the morning.

But when the shoemaker ran downstairs to his shop, he was again dismayed. The elves had tried to make the shoes, but they were clumsy and not very well made. The shoemaker could not sell these shoes.

The shoemaker wrote a note to the elves, specifically outlining what they needed to do to make the high heels correctly. He wrote out step-by-step instructions and drew pictures. He gave them more tools and more clothes and even more instructions.

The next morning the elves had made the high heels to the shoemaker's specifications. He was quite pleased and sold the high heels for double his normal price. Because the heels were so profitable, he expanded his business and bought more and more materials.

Until one day it came to pass that a customer's heels broke, causing her to break her leg. She went to the shoemaker and demanded to file a liability claim against him for his defective product.

"Madame," exclaimed the shoemaker, "These shoes are made by independent contractors. They are not my employees."

The woman insisted the fault was the shoemaker's, who insisted it was not. The woman sued for her medical expenses. The Fairy Godmother Supreme Court heard the case and found that the elves were the shoemaker's unpaid employees, which was quite a bad decision for the shoemaker, indeed. For the shoemaker had not declared to Mother Goose Insurance Mutual that he had employees. This dramatically increased his commercial general liability risk! Further, Mother Goose found the shoemaker had misrepresented the risk and voided his policy due to fraud.

The elves, upon learning they were employees, were overjoyed because they had begun to become quite disgruntled about not being paid. What's more, the shoemaker was increasingly demanding, and one elf's back had begun to hurt from leaning over the workbench all night. He hoped to have some health insurance, too, so he contacted the government of Fairytale Land about this.

Fairytale Land Tax Agency was not at all happy when they realized the shoemaker had not been paying wages or taxes, and was generally taking advantage of the poor elves. The shoemaker was hit with a host of fines, back taxes, and wages to pay. Further, the elf had also taken him to court, maintaining his back was injured as a result of his job, and, therefore, the shoemaker should pay his medical bills. Since there was no workers compensation coverage, the elf, as an employee, could sue his employer, the shoemaker.

All of these court costs, bills, insurance, taxes, wages, etc. ate into the old shoemaker's profits and earnings. The villagers heard how he treated his employees and began to boycott his shop. Meanwhile, the elves had quit, having been hired at a higher wage by a rival shoemaker. Because of all this and rapid inflation, the shoemaker had become so poor that he could no longer afford supplies for his craft. He only had enough leather for one last pair of shoes, and if no one bought them, he and his wife would starve…

Moral of the Story

If the businessowner tells the people who work for him what to wear, what to do, and how to do it, they are his employees, even if the owner gives them a 1099 form at the end of the tax year. The IRS has a test, which is beyond this story's purpose, to determine the difference between contractors and employees.

Misclassification of employees can lead to a host of issues, the least of which can be tax problems. Another key issue is that the person thought to be a contractor (who is now considered by the courts to be an employee) can seek workers compensation benefits from the business, or trigger insurance coverage for a negligent act.

Many states require businesses to have workers compensation and to pay for state unemployment insurance. Misclassification can also lead to underpayment of premiums because the insurer didn't account for all the risk involved. Or, it can result in the policy being cancelled for fraud.

The shoemaker turned the elves from contractors into employees when he began to control what they made and how they made it.

Homeowner policies, automatically cover domestic workers such as maids, gardeners, and nannies, but the coverage is very limited.

This story explains why the adjuster asks such intrusive questions regarding the business and requests a lot of information regarding bank statements and employee records. These requests may not seem relevant to the loss, but the adjuster is gathering information to ensure the first- or third-party claimant is paid in full.

Hansel and Gretel

Welcome to our weekly VA meeting. I see some old friends. BBW, how's it going? Queen Morganna, it's good to see you again. Nessierosa, so glad you could make it back.

"Schattenhexe, welcome to Villains Anonymous. I understand Judge Willowwitch has sent you to us?"

"Yes."

"Would you care to introduce yourself?"

"No." The assorted monsters, warlocks, and witches shifted in their seats uncomfortably and looked askance at the newcomer.

"Ah. Let me rephrase that. Since the Right Honorable Judge Willowwitch saw fit to allow you to grace us with your company, I'm afraid you must go through the program if I am to sign off on the paperwork proving your attendance," the Chair said apologetically.

A heavy sigh preceded an eyeroll. "Fine," the witch said. "Hello. I'm Schattenhexe, and I'm a Villain. I kidnap children and pump them full of candy and sweets before I eat them."

"Hi, Schattenhexe," came a monotone and unenthusiastic reply.

"Big Bad Wolf, I sense that Schattenhexe is not thrilled to be here. How have you been since we last saw you?"

"Hi, everyone, you know me. I'm BBW or Big Bad Wolf, and I'm a Villain," came the gruff introduction.

"Hi, BBW."

"Yeah, so, Schattenhexe, I don't know you or anything. I'll be honest, I was a little hesitant to come to a meeting like this the first time, but I realized that I needed to do something to address my...issues. See, I used to chase after those little pigs, Pete, RePete, and ReRun. I thought I could eat them.

"Before Pete, RePete, and ReRun, it was Puffy, Scruffy, and Fluffy. Before them it was Bacon, Hamlet, and Sausage and before them, Snout, Oink, and Wriggle and before that Porkchop, Ribeye, and Tenderloin."

Murmurs went around the circle as BBW began to noticeably salivate.

"My man, you've come far. Stay strong."

"Um, ur…it, it seems kind of silly now, but at the time, I couldn't help myself. I know I caused a lot of harm, and I want to make things right. That's why I'm here. Schattenhexe, I don't know much about you, but I'm glad I have the support of monsters like Nessierosa and evil stepmothers, like Queen Morgana, in this room. Thanks for allowing me to speak."

"Thanks, BBW," came another monotone reply from the circle.

"Thanks, BBW. Schattenhexe, what Big Bad Wolf didn't share—is it OK if I share your story, BBW?" The wolf nodded his agreement. "What Big Bad Wolf didn't share is how he'd value those little piglets.

"BBW viewed Scruffy as less valuable, because he was tough and not at all tender. Puffy was viewed as having some value, since he was softer. Although he had more tenderness, it was almost all fat, so he was less resilient than the other pigs. Fluffy was the most valuable, as her name indicates, because she has a certain level of comfort and luxury that was desirable…

"Yes, Nessierosa…"

"Aye, hi there! I'm Nessierosa, straight frae the depths o' Loch Ness, and I'm a Villain. Back in the day, I used tae reckon that huntin' was all about snappin' up as many fish as ye could. But as time passed, I came tae realize there's a deeper value at play.

Ye see, I had tae ponder on each fish, considerin' if it was worth the effort and energy tae nab it. It's just like what BBW was sayin' afore—I hope ye dinnae mind me repeatin' it, Schattenhexe—ye start assessin' what each pig, or in my case, fish, has been through.

How many bones they got, how much pickin' ye need tae do. Whether they're young and tender or auld and tougher, requirin' more time in the pot tae soften 'em up…"

"I know what you mean," an older woman interrupted.

"Your Majesty, you cannot interrupt…"

"Na, I was done. Ye go on ahead, Queen."

"Thank you, Nessierosa," the Chair conceded.

"Thank you, Chair," sniffed the monarch formerly known as Evil. "Hello, everyone. My name is Morganna, and I used to be known as the 'Evil Queen,'" Morganna used air quotes around "evil queen." "Although, I still maintain I am not a Villain."

The Chair cleared his throat and pointedly looked at Morganna while raising his eyebrow.

"I did terrible things. I would kick puppies and step on kittens' tails to hear them cry and whimper. I sent a huntsman to kill my stepdaughter, Snow White, and when that failed, I tried to poison her with an apple."

"That's rough, Morganna. I mean, I used to chase pigs and eat them and all, but that's cold, man."

"Aye, I've eaten a bonnie load o' fish in ma time, but I never once tried tae poison naebody. It just disnae sit right wi' me. We're predators o' the water, but we've got a code, ye ken? Poisonin' another bein' goes against it."

"BBW, Nessierosa, this is a judgment-free zone here. This is a safe space," the Chair gently chided. "Queen Morganna has shared with us before. We know she is not proud of what she did. But she's been seeking help, and through her, I have learned to value life more. As for Snow White, none of us can put a price on her life. As Nessierosa said, all life is unique.

"Thank you all for sharing your stories. Schattenhexe, I see that you've been listening carefully to everyone's stories, and I wonder if you would like to share your story with us tonight? Remember, we're all here to support each other, and there's no judgment in this room. If you're comfortable sharing, we would love to hear from you."

Moral of the Story

Adjusters consider several factors when valuing bodily injury claims. These factors include the severity of the injuries, the length of the recovery period, the medical treatment required, any permanent disabilities or scarring resulting from the injuries, and the impact the injuries have had on the claimant's daily life and ability to work.

Adjusters take into account objective elements, such as:

Medical expenses: The cost of medical treatment, including hospital stays, surgery, rehabilitation, and medication. Theoretically, the claimant is responsible for gathering all the medical bills and records for the adjuster to review so she can determine the value of the claim. In practice, the adjuster will send a medical authorization for the claimant to sign and return, and the adjuster will attempt to obtain the information. The claimant should be aware that if the adjuster cannot obtain the documents, the claimant must do so in order to resolve the claim.

Lost wages: This refers to income the injured person has lost due to being unable to work, as well as any potential future lost income. The adjuster will send an authorization for the claimant to sign so they can obtain the claimant's wage information from their employer. The claimant should also be prepared to submit a note from their doctor which requires them to be off work.

Future medical expenses: Any anticipated future medical costs associated with the injury. This is determined by a doctor who usually writes a report outlining the procedures needed going forward and their estimated costs.

Disability: The extent to which the injury has caused a permanent or temporary disability, and the impact this has on the injured person's life. This is determined by a doctor.

Adjusters also look at the subjective experiences of the claimant, such as pain and suffering, emotional distress, and the impact on their relationships with loved ones (known as *loss of consortium*). These can include:

Pain and suffering: The physical and emotional pain experienced as a result of the injury, including discomfort, inconvenience, and loss of enjoyment of life.

Comparative fault also plays a part in claims. In some cases, the injured person may have contributed to the accident or injury in some way. If so, this can affect the amount of compensation they receive. Fault determination is complex and depends on several factors such as the accident scenario, loss description, and laws. A broader explanation is beyond the scope of this book.

As members of VA discussed in the story, every case is unique, and there is no one-size-fits-all approach to valuing bodily injury claims. Negotiation of a bodily injury claim can be a complex process, and adjusters carefully consider all the relevant factors before making a determination about the appropriate compensation range.

Most claimants—and attorneys—do not understand that there is no settlement "figure," as in a set amount. Settlement in bodily injury claims comes in a range. Therefore, it is a misconception to think that if an adjuster settles at the bottom of the range, he or she has "low balled" the settlement. The claim value is like the speed limit. Most people don't remember this from their driver's test, but legal speed limits actually fall into a range. On the freeway, for example, the minimum speed (which may not be posted) can be 45 mph, while the maximum (which is posted) is 55 mph. Regardless of the posted speed limit, drivers are required to maintain a speed that is safe for the current road conditions. That's not only a speed range, but also taking individual aspects into consideration. The same effort goes into determining the value of a bodily injury.

Since the injury happened to themselves, it is understandably difficult for claimants to be dispassionate about their personal claim. The claimant can follow these steps to help them negotiate their claim:

- Gather all relevant evidence, which might include medical records, police reports, witness statements, and any other documentation that can help establish the extent of the injury and the liability of the other party.
- Establish a realistic demand, which is the amount of money the injured party believes is fair compensation for their injuries. This amount should take into account medical expenses, lost wages, and any other damages the injured party has suffered.
- Understand the insurance company's position. Adjusters will review the evidence and may offer a settlement that is lower than the claimant's demand. Listen to why they believe the settlement amount is fair and to negotiate based on this understanding.
- Negotiate in good faith, meaning that both parties should act honestly and with a willingness to reach a fair settlement. This means providing all relevant information and responding promptly to requests from the other party.
- Consider mediation if negotiations stall. A neutral third party can help facilitate communication between the parties and find a mutually acceptable resolution.
- Consult an attorney. If negotiations break down or if the injuries are severe, it may be necessary to consult an attorney. An experienced personal injury attorney can help navigate the negotiation process and ensure that the claimant's rights are protected.

Overall, the adjuster's goal is to arrive at a fair and reasonable settlement amount that adequately compensates the claimant for their losses and expenses, while also taking into consideration any applicable insurance policies, state laws, and other factors that may affect the final settlement amount.

First-Party Auto Claim Process

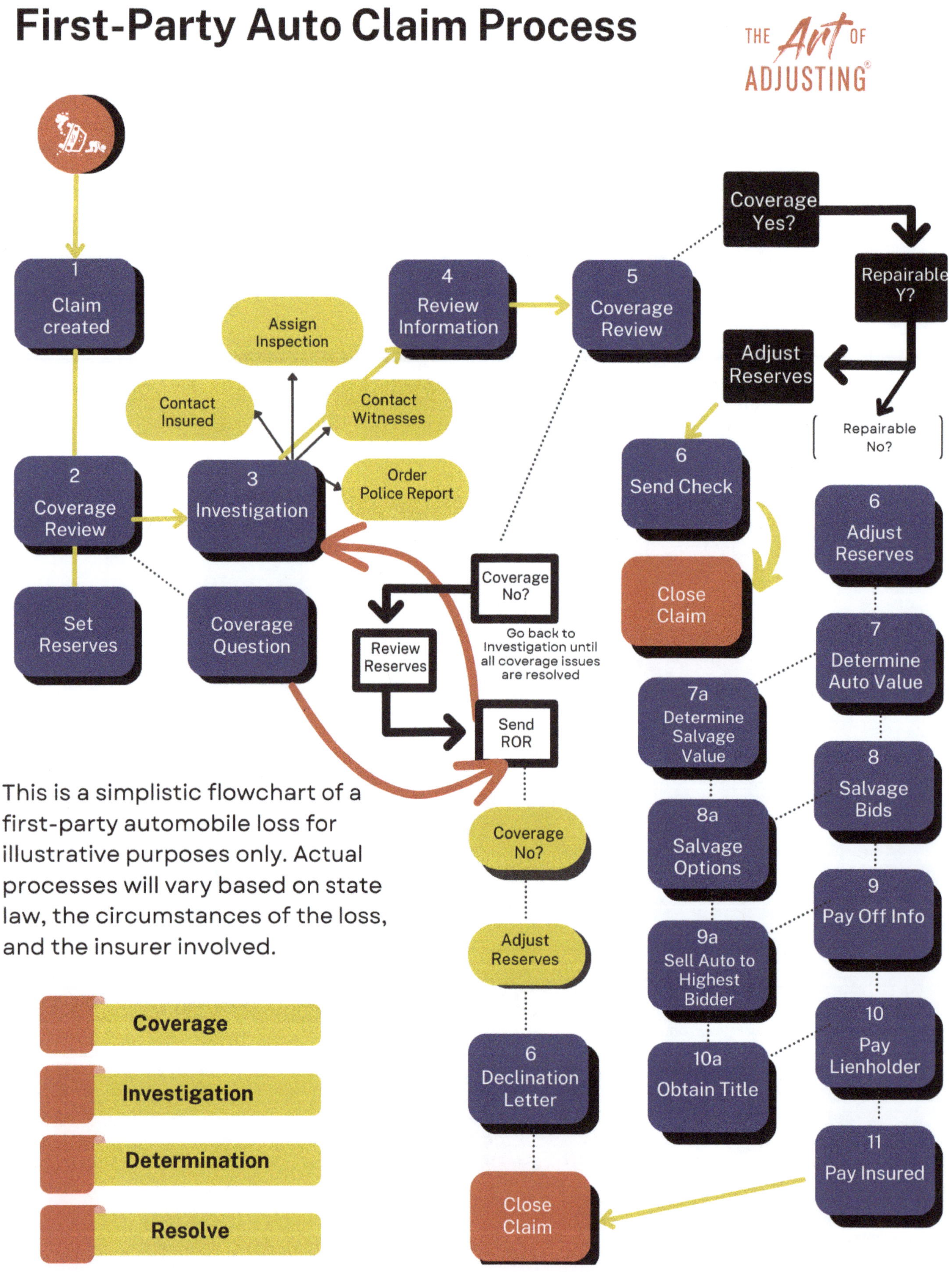

1 Claim created

2 Coverage Review

Set Reserves

Coverage Question

3 Investigation

Contact Insured

Assign Inspection

Contact Witnesses

Order Police Report

4 Review Information

5 Coverage Review

Coverage Yes?

Repairable Y?

Adjust Reserves

Repairable No?

6 Send Check

Close Claim

Coverage No?

Review Reserves

Send ROR

Go back to Investigation until all coverage issues are resolved

Coverage No?

Adjust Reserves

6 Declination Letter

Close Claim

6 Adjust Reserves

7 Determine Auto Value

7a Determine Salvage Value

8 Salvage Bids

8a Salvage Options

9 Pay Off Info

9a Sell Auto to Highest Bidder

10 Pay Lienholder

10a Obtain Title

11 Pay Insured

This is a simplistic flowchart of a first-party automobile loss for illustrative purposes only. Actual processes will vary based on state law, the circumstances of the loss, and the insurer involved.

Coverage

Investigation

Determination

Resolve

Old King Cole

Old King Cole was a merry ol' soul,
And a merry ol' soul was he;
He called for a fête, and he called for his glass,
And he called for his doctors three.

He loved to dance and move his feet,
And throw parties that couldn't be beat.
But one night, as he danced with glee,
He twisted his back and couldn't break free.
In his merry dance, he stepped on Mary's toes,
His partner stumbled and fell on her nose;
She cried in pain, with tears in her eyes,
And King Cole realized it wasn't wise.

Old King Cole needed medical care,
For his health was not so fare;
He looked to his policies for some aid,
To cover the bills he had made.

But when the bills came, he began to fret,
For his wallet was feeling the debt;
He turned to his homeowners and auto plans,
To see if they could lend a hand.

He checked his policies, and to his relief,
Homeowners covered Mary's grief;
She received care without any strife,
And was back on her feet and enjoying life.

But when it came to King Cole's back,
His homeowners policy had a lack;
No MedPay coverage to ease his pain,
His wallet felt the medical strain.

Old King Cole drove to the doctor's place,
To get treatment for his back's twisted case;
But on the way, he faced a scare,
As a car hit him from the rear.

His auto policy had coverage in place,
For an insured's injuries in such a case;
King Cole was relieved and let out a sigh,
As he knew his medical bills wouldn't be sky-high.

The other driver's policy paid for the car's wreck,
And King Cole's auto policy covered his medical check;
With his auto and homeowners plans on his side,
King Cole could rest easy and let his worries subside.

So, Old King Cole was a happy ole soul,
For his auto policy covered him whole;
He could focus on feeling right as rain,
Not on how to pay for his and Mary's pains.

Moral of the Story

Poor ol' King Cole just wanted to have a good time at his party when he injured his back, but these kinds of things happen as one ages. This rhyme covers the two types of medical payments (MedPay) coverages available to an insured: one on the homeowner policy and one on the auto. Fortunately, both coverages are available, regardless of fault.

Homeowner Policy

MedPay coverage in homeowner policies typically cover injuries sustained by others while on the insured's property. This coverage is intended to provide quick and easy compensation for minor injuries that occur on the property, without requiring a lengthy claims process or legal action. MedPay typically has a relatively low limit in homeowner policies, often in the range of $1,000 to $5,000, and does not cover bodily injuries sustained by the insured themselves such as a sprained back.

Auto Policy

On the other hand, MedPay coverage in auto insurance policies is designed to cover medical expenses incurred by the insured and their passengers in the event of an accident, regardless of who is at fault. Like homeowner MedPay, this coverage is intended to provide quick and easy compensation for minor injuries sustained in an accident, without requiring a lengthy claims process or legal action. Auto MedPay typically has a higher limit than a homeowner policy, often in the range of $5,000 to $10,000 or more, and may cover a wider range of medical expenses.

The auto policy may also have another coverage available for the insured: Personal Injury Protection (PIP), which provides more comprehensive coverage for medical expenses and other related expenses than MedPay.

While MedPay provides coverage for medical expenses regardless of fault, it may have a lower limit and covers only medical expenses. PIP, on the other hand, characteristically has a higher limit and can cover a wider range of expenses, such as lost wages, rehabilitation expenses, and funeral expenses. Additionally, PIP coverage can be mandatory in no-fault states, where drivers are required to carry PIP coverage as a part of their auto insurance policy. In no-fault states, each driver's auto insurance company pays for their own policyholder's medical expenses, regardless of who was at fault for the accident.[2]

Insureds may be able to obtain both PIP and MedPay coverage depending on their state and the policy language. Some states, such as Arkansas, South Dakota, Texas, and Virginia, offer the ability to have both PIP and MedPay. Having these two types of coverages, which are subtly different in what they pay for, may be ideal.

People who have health insurance are often shocked by the high cost of medical treatment. Ambulance rides may be rather affordable at approximately $500, depending on the level of care needed and the distance between the accident location and the hospital. Of course, if additional treatment in the ambulance is needed (e.g., medicine, bandages, triage, or oxygen) those costs go up. Ambulances are, for

2 There are specific instances, in no-fault states, when liability reverts to its more traditional roles. These instances are not discussed in this book, but insureds and claimants should be aware of them. For example, if injuries involved in the loss exceed a certain dollar amount, the injured party may be able to file a lawsuit against the at-fault driver if their medical expenses and other damages pierce that monetary threshold.

whatever reason, not "in network," which has nothing to do with a homeowner or auto MedPay coverage (being "in network" is strictly a health insurance issue). But not being "in network" means that there are no contract rates, and the ambulance company can charge whatever it wants. Therefore, it is possible (and the author has seen it happen many a time) for the ambulance cost to be more than $1,000 for a single trip. For the homeowner MedPay coverage, this one invoice could use up the entire limit. Emergency room visits are generally five times more expensive, which would deplete the auto MedPay limit.

Many do not think about these coverages, either for themselves or for their guests, because they think their health insurance covers this. Health insurance, as a general rule, will ***not*** cover auto accidents—the reasons are varied and complex and beyond the scope of this book. Health insurance can cover accidents that happen at the house, but when the health insurer learns the accident occurred because of someone else's negligence, it will seek reimbursement (subrogation) from the at-fault party. See *Sleeping Beauty* for a discussion on subrogation.

If a claimant is injured in a liability claim (whether auto or homeowner), that liability claim is not settled until the claimant has completed treatment. This could be a week after the loss, or three years after the loss. This also means the medical provider is not receiving money for treatment of the claimant. One reason health care providers dislike treating property and auto casualty victims is because they are not paid promptly. A great deal of pressure is exerted on the injured party who cannot pay the medical invoices until they receive payment on their claim, which doesn't happen until they complete treatment; and likewise, the at-fault insurer will not pay until treatment is completed. It is a vicious circle.

The low limits for both homeowner and auto coverage and the high cost of medical treatment are excellent reasons insureds should give serious consideration to increasing said limits of coverage, since it may serve as a stop-gap measure against the onslaught of collection letters.

If Wishes Were Horses

If wishes were covered autos,
And every car was insured,
We'd all be driving worry-free,
From accidents, we'd be assured.

But alas, a "covered auto"
Has a definition alive.
It's the car named on your policy,
That you're allowed to drive.

If your covered auto is damaged,
And is in the repair shop for days,
Your policy may provide a substitute,
To help you go about your ways.

But remember, a substitute vehicle
Is usually only provided in these cases
When your covered auto's being repaired,
Or when it's lost, stolen, or displaced.

But alas, a rental car
May not be covered by your plan,
So it's wise to consider extras,
That the rental company can scan.

The collision damage waiver,
Can help you save your cash.
It covers the cost of damages,
If your rental takes a bash.

Additional insurance,
Can offer coverage for theft,
And other mishaps that may occur,
While you're on your vay-cay quest.

Your personal auto policy,
May not cover a "substitute" ride,
So buying that extra coverage,
May save you from taking a slide.

So make sure you know your policy,
And what's covered under its scope.
It'll save you stress and headache,
And give you peace of mind and hope.

Moral of the Story

This nursery rhyme imparts an important lesson on personal auto policies and rental cars. Most people immediately turn down the collision waiver offered when they rent a vehicle for their vacations or as an "extra" car for when relatives are in town.

It is vital to know and understand what is and isn't covered under an auto policy. Though your auto policy may cover your personal vehicle, it may not extend to rental cars or "substitute" vehicles. The standard policy definition of a covered auto is the one that is listed on the declarations page, or a substitute

vehicle because the covered auto is being repaired, is damaged, or is lost (as in stolen). A rental for any other reason, say a business trip out of town, is not covered under a standard auto policy.

Some drivers will not take the proffered coverage because they used their credit card to pay for the rental and believe this offers protection against damage. This could be a dangerous belief, however, since the rental agreement grants the company the right to charge the card in the event of damage to the vehicle. True, the charge could be contested, but that would likely result in a headache and a lot of work. Further, if the card does provide coverage for a rental, the policy might state that it is in excess of any other insurance, while the rental company might state it is in excess of the card, while the personal auto insurance might state there is no coverage because the rental unit is not a "covered auto" vehicle by definition.

Short answer? It might be wise to purchase the additional insurance offered by rental companies. Rental companies offer a variety of coverages for their vehicles, and the collision coverage isn't the only one that might be of interest to the rental driver.

Many rental agreements, in the fine print, will make the renter responsible for the diminished value of the car. Diminished value is the concept that a vehicle, after it has been involved in an accident, is worth less, even though it has been repaired. Most policies do not cover diminished value, since standard policy language states coverage is for direct damage to the vehicle. The carriers believe diminished value is an *indirect* loss—something that results *from* the damage to the vehicle.

Standard auto policies will pay the reasonable cost to repair the damages or replace the totaled auto. The rental agreement, however, may mandate that the renter pay the "full value" of the vehicle, which presumably would be the reasonable value. But in reading the fine print, you might learn that the rental company determines the "full value." The rental company will also require the renter to pay for the downtime it sustains—this is the time in which the company cannot rent the vehicle because it is in the shop being repaired (or the time it takes until the company buys a new car to replace the damaged one).

By taking the time to understand the definitions and coverage of the policy, you can avoid headaches and financial burdens in the event of a rental vehicle accident or theft.

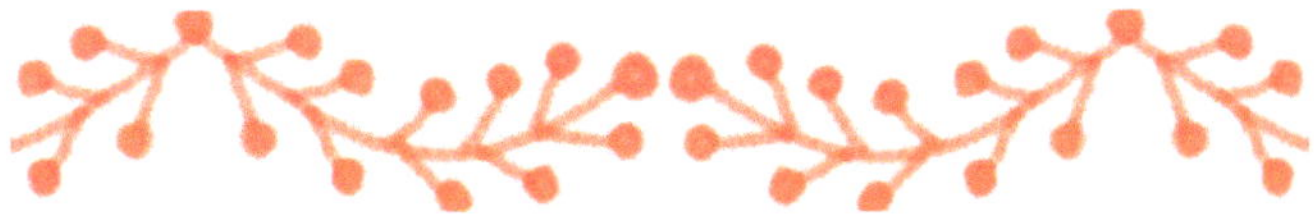

Bearskin
?

A young man once enlisted as a soldier, and he was the bravest of the brave whenever there was a war, and there was often war in the part of the world where he resided. As long as the wars lasted, the young man was able to earn his room and board. One day, the two fighting kingdoms made peace because their son and daughter fell in love and married. Since there was no more war, the young, brave soldier was dismissed.

The young man no longer had a way to earn his keep; the only skill he knew was waging war. His parents were long dead—having been casualties of the war—so he went to his younger brother's house to ask him and his wife to support him until the prince and princess began to fight, as all newlyweds are wont to do.

His younger brother, however, was ungrateful, even though he had not had to go to war because his older brother had gone in his stead. The younger brother said, "What can you do? Can you grow crops?"

Of course, the hero could not grow crops. He was a killer, not a grower.

"So, be off with you. I have no use for you."

The young, brave man turned to his sister-in-law, who was hardhearted. She asked, "What can you do? Can you raise sheep and goats and cows?"

Of course, the hero could not grow

animals. He was a killer, not a rancher.

"So, be off with you. I have no use for you."

The soldier's sole possession was his gun, which he shouldered, as he left his brother's house and went out into the world. And so it came to pass that he came to a large ***heath*** which had, right in the middle of it, evergreen trees arranged in a perfect circle. Filled with self-pity, he went to the ***copse***, sat down, and thought about his fate.

"My younger brother and his wife are right," he thought, "I can only kill things. Other than that, I have no trade. I shall surely starve."

Suddenly he heard a rustling sound. The brave young man looked up to see a man who had one human leg and one with a horse's hoof. Despite this, he looked quite stately in his green jacket.

"I know what you need," said the man. "You need a purpose, and you will have more money and property than you can squander, even if you gave a castle away each day. But first you must know, I only give this gift to the bravest of the brave. I don't waste the gift and I will know if you are fearless."

"Sir, I am a soldier. I do not know fear."

"All right. Look behind you."

The soldier turned around and saw a large, snarling, hungry, mamma bear running toward him. The brave young man crouched in the grass until the large, snarling, hungry, mamma bear was almost on top of him, and then he jumped up in front of her, threw up his arms to make himself appear bigger, and roared with all his might.

The mamma bear was so taken aback that someone had the ***temerity*** to yell at her, she stood stock still for what seemed like an eternity before sniffing and turning around with her head held high as she lumbered back to her den with her cubs.

"Ah, very good," said the strange man. "You are, indeed, brave, but there is one more condition you will have to fulfill."

The soldier, who now ***sussed*** the identity of the man before him, said "If I fulfill this condition, I will keep my soul, otherwise I'll have nothing to do with your deal."

"Very well," the Devil agreed. "For the next seven years, you are neither to bathe, comb your beard and hair, cut your nails, nor say the Lord's prayer. I will give you a jacket and a cloak which you must wear during this time. If you die during these seven years, your soul is mine. If you stay alive, you will be free, and rich as well, for the rest of your life. And your soul will remain yours."

The young, brave man thought about his desperate situation. Having faced death so often before, he decided to risk it now as well, so he entered into the agreement with the Devil.

The Devil removed his green jacket and gave it to the soldier, saying, "Reach into this pocket when you want money. You will pull out a handful of gold coins."

Then he removed a hide from his back and said, "This shall be your cloak, and your bed as well, for you are to sleep on it. You may not lie in any other bed. Because of your clothing, you shall you be called Bearskin."

With that statement, the devil disappeared.

Thinking he might as well start the seven years right away, the young, brave man put on the jacket, immediately reached into the pocket, and found that the promise was really true. Then he put on the bearskin and went forth into the world. He did whatever he pleased, partaking in activities that did him good and was generous with his money.

In the first year, his appearance was still suitable, but as the first year turned into the second, he began to look like a monster. His beard blended with his bearskin cloak; his hair stood on end, caked with mud.

Children said that if someone planted a seed in his hair, that seed would grow! Women fainted when they saw him. Men were known to devolve into coughing fits from his smell alone. His fingernails grew like claws, so much so that it was hard for him to hold a cup from which to drink. Despite this, he was still able to give money to the poor to pray that he might not die during the seven years, and because he paid well for everything, he always found shelter.

In the fourth year of his curse, Bearskin arrived an inn. The innkeeper would not let him enter, refusing even to let him have a place in the stable because he was afraid that Bearskin would frighten the horses. However, when Bearskin reached into his pocket and pulled out a handful of gold coins, the innkeeper's greed caused his heart to soften. The innkeeper made Bearskin swear that he would hide himself from the townsfolk and inn guests, lest the inn should get a bad name. Bearskin took the oath, and he rested in the stables for the evening.

As the fourth year passed into the fifth, Bearskin was sitting alone one evening in the woods, wishing with all his heart that time would speed up and that the seven years would be over. He heard weeping down the path a way. He had a compassionate heart, so Bearskin walked toward the sound and saw an old man crying unconsolably, striking his hands together above his head. Bearskin went nearer, but the man jumped to his feet and tried to run away.

"Wait!" called Bearskin, "I mean you no harm. I heard you weeping and thought I may be able to help."

Hearing the human voice coming from a monster confused the man, yet he did stop and did not immediately run away. After a spell, the old man revealed the cause of his grief. The man had inherited some money, so, he'd stopped working. Then he had three daughters who were growing up, but they needed new dresses and shoes. Who knew that children were so expensive? And so it came to pass that slowly but surely the old man had lost his wealth. He was now too old to work, and it seemed he and his daughters would starve. He was so poor that he could not pay the innkeeper. He had snuck out of the inn without paying his bill. He was to be sent to prison, and what would happen to his girls now?

"Ah, well, if that is your only problem," Bearskin smiled, "I have money enough. Take this to pay your debt."

He put a bag full of gold into the poor man's pocket. When the old man saw that he he'd been freed from all his troubles, he did not know how to show his gratitude.

"You are a kind man. You should not be left to wander out in the cold. My daughters are all miracles of beauty. Choose one of them for your wife. When she hears what you have done for me, she will surely not refuse you. You do look a little strange, to be sure, but she will put you in order again."

This pleased Bearskin well, and he went with the old man.

When the oldest daughter saw him, she was so terrified at his face that she screamed and fainted.

The second one stood still and looked at him from head to foot, but then she said, "The shaved bear that you attempted to pass off as a man last year pleased me far better. At least it was wearing a hussar's fur and white gloves. I will not marry this thing."

The youngest one, however, said, "He must be a good man to have helped you out of your trouble. If you promised him a bride for doing that, your word must be kept. I will marry him."

Because Bearskin was so filthy, the man and his soon-to-be-wed daughter did not see how her kindness had brought joy to his heart and tears to his eyes. Bearskin took a ring from his finger—which was a trial in and of itself, given the fact that his long fingernail had to pass through the ring—broke it in two, and writing his name on her half and her name on his, gave the youngest daughter her half of the ring.

"I must complete this trial; I have two more years. Keep this ring safe, for I will come for you when my time is up. If I do not return at that time, you are free, for I shall be dead. But ask God to preserve my life."

The poor bride-to-be dressed herself entirely in black, and when she thought about her future bridegroom, tears came to her eyes. From her sisters, she received nothing but contempt and scorn. The youngest daughter said nothing and did not allow them irritate her. Bearskin, however, traveled about the world from one place to another, doing good wherever he could, and giving generously to the poor, that they might pray for him.

Finally, at dawn on the last day of the seven years, he went once more out to the heath and seated himself beneath the circle of evergreens. Before long, the wind began to howl, and the devil stood before him, angry because he had never once lost a bet. He threw Bearskin's old jacket to him and demanded the return of his own green jacket.

"Wait a moment, if you please," answered Bearskin. "First, you have to clean me up."

Whether the devil wanted to or not, he had to fetch water and wash off Bearskin, comb his hair, and cut his nails. After this, he again looked like a brave soldier and was much better looking than he had ever been before.

When the devil was safely gone, Bearskin was quite lighthearted. He went into the town, purchased a splendid velvet jacket, seated himself in a carriage drawn by four white horses, and drove to his bride's house. No one recognized him. The father took him for a distinguished colonel and led him into the room where his daughters were sitting. He was given a seat between the two oldest ones. They poured wine for him, served him the finest things to eat, and thought they had never seen a more handsome man in all the world.

The bride-to-be, however, sat across from him in her black dress without raising her eyes or speaking a word. Finally, he asked the father if he would give him one of his daughters for a wife, whereupon the two oldest ones jumped up and ran into their bedrooms to put on splendid dresses, for each of them thought she was the chosen one.

As soon as he was alone with his bride-to-be, the stranger brought out his half of the ring and dropped it into a glass of wine, which he handed across the table to her. She took the wine, but when she had drunk it and found his half of the ring lying at the bottom, her heart began to pound. She took the other half of the ring, which she wore on a ribbon around her neck, put them together, and saw that the two pieces matched perfectly.

"Yes, it is true. I am your betrothed, whom you know as Bearskin. I have completed my trial and am now human again."

He went to her, embraced her, and gave her a kiss. In the meantime, the two sisters came back in full dress. When they saw that the youngest sister had captured the heart of the handsome man and learned that he was Bearskin, they became enraged. The eldest sequestered herself in a convent, and the middle married the hussar-man-bear.

But only the youngest, with her sweetness, married the real thing.

Moral of the Story

Readers will, no doubt, wonder what a man wandering about Fairytale Land neither bathing nor shaving for seven years has to do with automobile insurance or auto claims. This fable is used to discuss the theory of "matching" repaired areas to the non-damaged areas. The soldier is still the same person as he was before the deal with the Devil; he was restored to himself once the seven years passed. During the period of the seven years, the young man was a horrible, grotesque-looking being, but he was, in essence, the same person.

The man is a car which has been in an accident. The accident is the seven years in which the man can neither bathe nor shave. The car is almost unrecognizable in the event of a particularly bad accident.

However, it's good as new once the car has been repaired.

Automobile losses and the parts that are used to repair the vehicles are a subject that riles people up. It is based on a fundamental misunderstanding of auto insurance and confusing it with property insurance. Logically, policyholders know these are two different kinds of insurance which covers different types of belongings. Auto insurance covers cars; property insurance covers homes and possessions; liability insurance covers bodily or personal injury.

With property damage coverage, the insured has the ability, for an additional premium, to receive payment for the replacement of the damaged item, which will, ostensibly, be more than the depreciated value of the item which the insured originally had, and which is now damaged. Auto insurance does not have replacement cost coverage for car parts, putting aside the carriers who offer "replacement cost" for an insured's total loss.

The damage estimate describes, line by line, how the body shop will repair the auto. In it, the vehicle owner will see a series of letters or acronyms. There are three categories of auto parts:

1. New or Original Equipment Manufacturer (OEM)
2. Like, Kind, and Quality (LKQ)
3. After-Market

Almost everyone wants new, or OEM, parts on their car, and they are upset when they do not receive them. The insured and the third-party claimant are allowed to have the body shop put OEM parts on their vehicle, but the carrier may not pay for it. The claimant (whether first- or third-party) will owe the difference between the estimate and any additional, non-covered, charges.

In the standard personal auto policy, there is no valuation or endorsement for new parts. The carrier will pay the "reasonable" costs to repair. Reasonableness is discussed in *Rumpelstiltskin*. Briefly, though, it is what an average person would or would not do; or what they would or would not pay.

In general, vehicles which are less than three years will receive OEM parts. LKQ parts can be considered to be the "actual cash value" equivalent of the auto policy. This will replace a part that is damaged on the claimant's car with another part that is similar.

For example, if a 2019 Mini Cooper's hood is damaged, the carrier will allow an LKQ part from another 2019 Mini Cooper. Sometimes a 2019 Mini hood cannot be located, and if a 2018 Mini's hood has the same specs, then the claimant would receive a 2018 Mini Cooper's hood. These parts are obtained from salvage yards, or other vehicles which cannot be repaired, but still have usefulness in parting the vehicle out—as in the case of the Mini's hood.

After-Market parts are the equivalent to generic brands of food at the grocery store. The parts are probably made by the OEM, in the same factory as the OEM part, but the After-Market part lacks the brand name which means that they can compete on price. There is always the possibility that the After-Market part will not be fully compatible with the car, especially if made by another manufacture, which the car owner may not know beforehand.

Many people dislike strongly After-Market parts, believing they are inferior. If the reader uses generic drugs, that is the After-Market equivalent of the drug world; if one buys generic ground beef helper or chips or sodas, then these are the After-Market equivalents of food shopping.

There are pros and cons to each. Naturally, OEM and LKQ parts are more expensive and have a longer lifespan because they are the original parts. But After-Market parts are more readily available (followed closely by LKQ parts, which have the benefit of straddling both worlds) and are cheaper. Body shops are still, at the time of writing, experiencing the backlog and scarcity of parts which makes repairs longer, in which case, it may behoove the claimant to use an After-Market part if feasible.

Ultimately, it is up to vehicle owners what kind of parts they wish to use. Owners must be aware that the carrier will only pay what's reasonable, and if the owners choose another type of part, the owner will be responsible for paying the difference.

People are no doubt familiar with the argument that if a vehicle is damaged, the entire car should be painted because it'd be "impossible" to match the paint. This comes from the theory that the sun, road grime, and wear and tear have faded the original paint. It is not reasonable to paint an entire vehicle because the rear quarter panel of the auto was damaged. A skilled painter can feather the new paint into the old and the car will be good as new. Likewise the young solider was the same man underneath all his filth and grime; so, too, is the newly repaired vehicle.

As a side note, the issue of matching original sections of a belonging to new also appears in property claims. Policyholders often want the entire roof or floor replaced if one section is damaged. It's not reasonable to replace the entire roof if only a part is damaged; it is not reasonable to replace the entire flooring, for example, because the same type of material is used in every room. It is reasonable to replace or repair an entire section until there is a visual break, referred to as a "line of sight" in insurance terminology. In other words, the insurer may replace a slope of the roof, because the other slope cannot be seen at the same time as the first slope; or the insurer may replace one room of the flooring because there is a door which breaks the line of sight. As always, these rules and regulations depend on the policy and the state where the loss occurred.

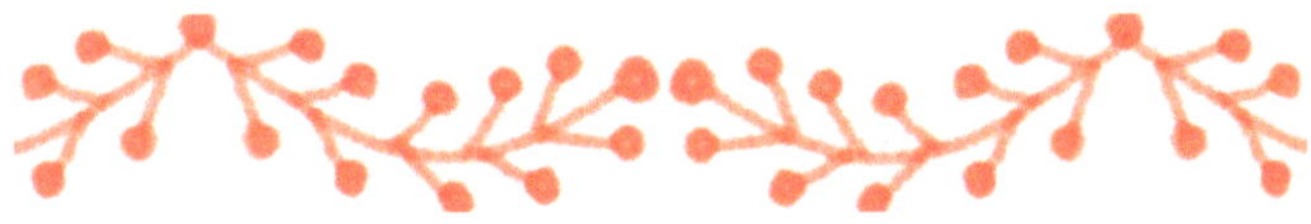

Ring Around the Rosie

Ring around the chassis,
A pocket full of woesies.
Crash! Bam! Crash! Bam!
We all fall down!

Diminished goes the value,
Repairs are not the issue.
Shiny! New! Shiny! New!
The price goes down!

Price difference between
Prior and mended it seems
That's it! The loss!
We write the check!

Moral of the Story

Contrary to popular belief, *Ring Around the Rosie* is not about the Black Death. It's about insurance companies using different methods to determine the diminished value of a vehicle that has been in an accident.

"Diminished value" is a term used in the automobile and insurance industries to describe the reduction in value of a vehicle after it has been involved in an accident, even if it has been fully repaired. Essentially, the idea is that a vehicle that has been in an accident and repaired will never be worth as much as a similar vehicle that has not been in an accident, all else being equal.

Inherent Diminished Value, which is the automobile's loss of value once its repairs are completed, is the most frequent claim of this type. The reason for this is that buyers of used cars are often wary of purchasing a car that has been in an accident, even if it has been fully repaired, because they are concerned about potential underlying damage that may not have been visible or fully fixed. As a result, they are typically willing to pay less for a car that has an accident history than they would for an equivalent car with no history of any accidents.

The amount of the diminished value can vary depending on several factors, such as the extent of the damage, the age and condition of the vehicle prior to the accident, and the type of vehicle. In some cases, the diminished value can be significant, especially for high-end or luxury vehicles.

Insurance companies may offer diminished value claims to help compensate car owners for the reduction in value of their vehicle after an accident. However, the process for making such claims and determining the amount of the claim can be complex and may vary by state and by insurance company.

Here are some of the most common methods for determining the amount of the claim:

- **Formula method:** This method involves using a formula to calculate the diminished value, based on factors such as the age and condition of the vehicle, the extent of damage it sustained, and the type of repairs performed.
- **Market research method:** This method involves researching the market value of similar vehicles in the same condition before and after an accident. The difference in value is then used to determine the diminished value of the vehicle.
- **Appraisal method:** This method involves hiring an appraiser to assess the vehicle and provide an estimate of its diminished value based on factors such as the vehicle's make and model, mileage, condition, and the extent of damage.
- **Claim history method:** This method involves reviewing the insurance company's claim history for similar vehicles that have been in accidents and calculating the average diminished value paid out for those claims.

Insurance companies may use a combination of these methods to determine the diminished value of a vehicle. Additionally, the process can vary depending on the state or region, and the terms and conditions of the insurance policy.

Some policies may not reimburse the vehicle owner for diminished value since the repairs are supposed to be done in a workman-like manner to the manufacturer's specifications. The reasoning goes that if poor repairs were done on the vehicle, that would not be the carrier's responsibility—the fault would lie with the body shop that repaired the vehicle. Of course, many states and courts disagree. Vehicle owners are encouraged to discuss the issue with the adjuster, their agent, or an attorney.

Mary Had a Little Lamb

Mary had a little lamb,
Little lamb, little lamb.
Mary had a little lamb,
Its fleece was white as snow;
And everywhere that Mary went
Mary went, Mary went,
And everywhere that Mary went
The lamb was sure to go.

The lamb was acting up one day
Up one day, up one day.
The lamb was acting up one day,
And drove into a tree;
Mary's car got scratched up bad,
Scratched up bad, scratched up bad.
Mary's car got scratched up bad,
And that was a sight to see.

Mary's lamb was feeling bold,
Feeling bold, feeling bold.
Mary's lamb was feeling bold.
And ate the upholstery.
The fabric torn, the stuffing strewn,
Stuffing strewn, stuffing strewn,
A comprehensive loss was soon,
And that was a sight to see.

Moral of the Story

Comprehensive and collision coverage are both types of auto insurance coverage that protect against damage to a vehicle, but they cover different types of damage.

Collision coverage pays for damage to a vehicle when it is involved in a, well, collision with another object or vehicle. This can include accidents with other vehicles, as well as crashes with stationary objects like trees or guardrails. Collision coverage typically covers damage to the vehicle, regardless of who is at fault in the accident.

Comprehensive coverage, on the other hand, covers damage to the vehicle from other incidents, such as theft, vandalism, fire, lambs eating upholstery, or natural disasters. It can also cover damage caused by hitting an animal, such as a deer or a bird. Comprehensive coverage may also include coverage for broken windows and damage from falling objects, flying debris, or even flying monkeys.

Auto insurance coverage, such as collision and comprehensive coverage, is normally optional, because it's not a legal requirement in most states. However, liability insurance, which covers damages and injuries caused by a driver to others in an accident, is mandatory by law in every state except for New Hampshire.

Both comprehensive and collision coverage are optional but may be required if the car is leased or financed. Collision and comprehensive coverage are usually recommended but not compulsory since they offer additional protection for a vehicle. They can be particularly useful for new or expensive cars, since they help cover the cost of repairs or replacement if the car is damaged or totaled in an accident or another covered event. However, collision and comprehensive coverage are often more expensive than liability insurance, and some drivers may decide to forgo this additional coverage to reduce their insurance premiums.

Owners should weigh the costs and benefits of collision and comprehensive coverage before deciding whether to include them in an auto insurance policy. It is a popular idea not to have comprehensive or collision coverage on older model vehicles. While it may be tempting to forego the coverages on an older model vehicle to save money on insurance premiums, it could be a bad idea for several reasons.

First, older vehicles may be more susceptible to damage from non-collision incidents such as theft, vandalism, or natural disasters. Comprehensive coverage can help cover the cost of repairs or replacement in these cases, which could be expensive without insurance coverage.

Second, even if an older vehicle is not worth much on the open market, collision coverage can still be beneficial in an at-fault accident. Without collision coverage, you would be responsible for paying for your vehicle's repairs or replacement out of pocket.

Finally, while older vehicles may have a lower overall value than newer models, repairs can still be costly. Collision coverage can help cover the cost of repairs to the vehicle in the event of an accident, which could be a significant expense without insurance coverage.

In summary, collision coverage protects against damage caused by collisions, while comprehensive coverage protects against damage caused by non-collision incidents, and it may be wise to keep the coverage despite the alleged savings in insurance premiums for older cars.

The Practical Bride

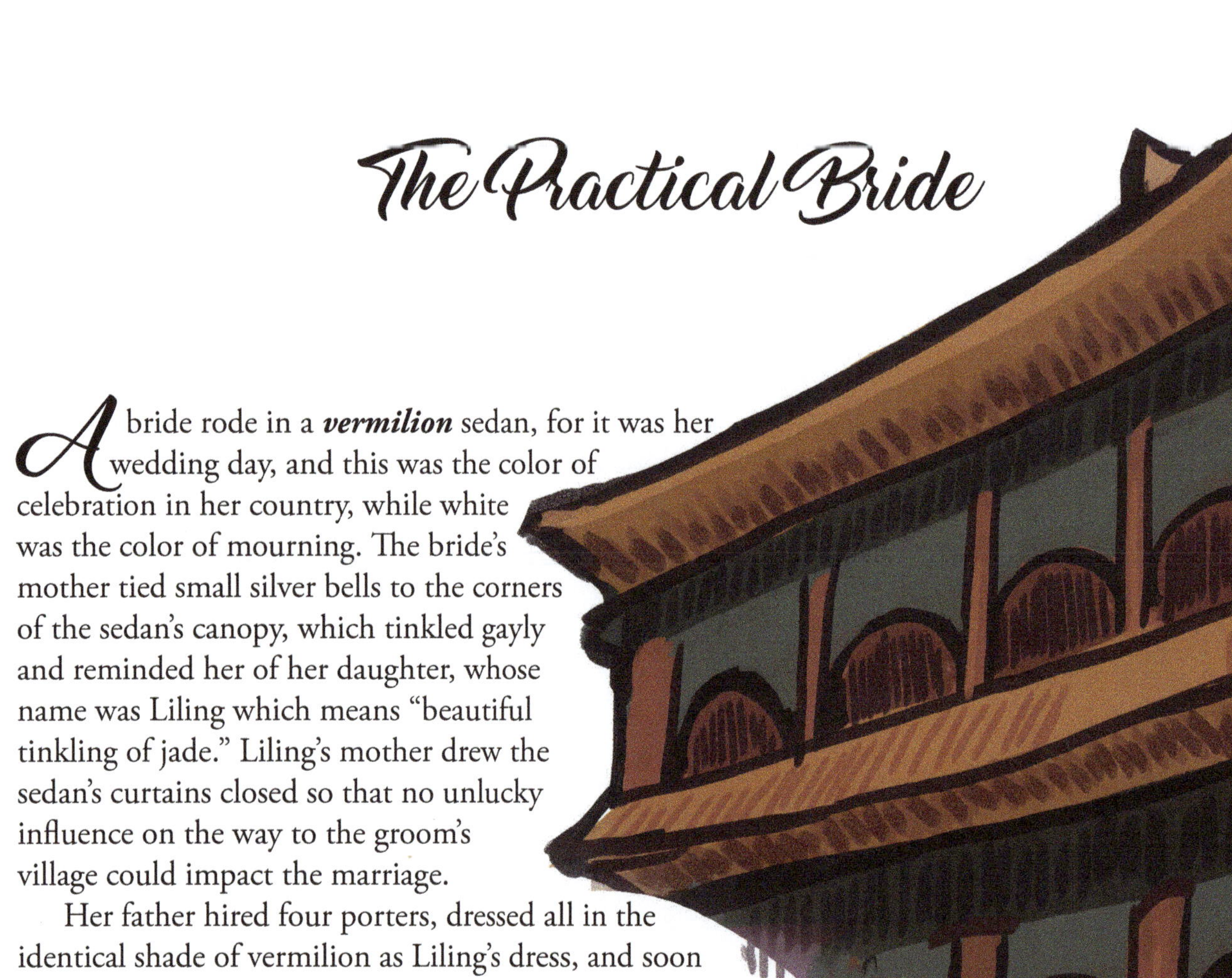

A bride rode in a ***vermilion*** sedan, for it was her wedding day, and this was the color of celebration in her country, while white was the color of mourning. The bride's mother tied small silver bells to the corners of the sedan's canopy, which tinkled gayly and reminded her of her daughter, whose name was Liling which means "beautiful tinkling of jade." Liling's mother drew the sedan's curtains closed so that no unlucky influence on the way to the groom's village could impact the marriage.

Her father hired four porters, dressed all in the identical shade of vermilion as Liling's dress, and soon they jogged along the road carrying the bride from her father's house to her bridegroom's home in the next village, Lingxiu.

Despite the curtains on all four sides of the sedan which hid the passenger within, everyone knew that Liling was going to her new home. She was quite happy, as her Aunt Jin-Li and Cousin Jun-Li lived in Lingxiu, so she already knew people in her husband's village. Farmers and townspeople stood outside their doors, waving and calling out congratulations and felicitations as her sedan chair passed.

As the sun reached its apex, a loud rip came from the interior of the sedan, quickly followed by an indignant umph. The gayly tinkling bells continued for a few paces, but one of the rear porters said to one of the front porters, "Hey, Xiaolong, why does this sedan feel so light?"

"I don't know, Baozi. Why?"

"Because Liling just fell out!"

Shifu, the other front porter, who felt the sedan wobble and thought Baozi and Xiaolong were not pulling their weight, said, "Oh, you're a funny guy, eh?" He dropped his side of the pole, stopped jogging, and Zhangzi ran smack into the back of him.

"Why I oughtta…"

Shifu fell and his legs tangled in the sedan curtains, ripping them from the canopy.

As Xiaolong, Baozi, Zhangzi, and Shifu began arguing anew over who was at fault for dropping Liling—none of them realizing that the bottom of the chair had fallen out.

"Did you check the chair before we started?"

"Nobody told me to."

The bride gingerly came to her knees and rose from the ground. Not a strand of hair, not a single ornament of her elaborate headdress was out of place.

"Well, it was bound to break! It's the rope that held the cradle after all."

"Liling's father should've bought a better chair."

The bride walked to the shady side of the road and sat on a rock, waiting for the porters to begin repairs.

"He could've sent two chairs as a precaution."

"You run and tell Liling's father to send another chair. We will wait here."

"No, you run to tell the groom. We're more than halfway to Lingxiu, so the groom is responsible now."

So the porters continued to bicker, and no repairs were begun.

"But it will be dark by the time I get back."

"And if it rains, where can we go for shelter?"

"Oh, what's to be done?"

Out of patience with the nincompoops, Liling commandeered the situation. She ripped the canopy from the top of the sedan, took her hairpin to make holes in it, then carefully threaded the canopy on the poles to fashion a skirt from the poles to the ground. She stepped between the poles where the chair had been, closed the curtains once again, and ordered Xiaolong, Baozi, Zhangzi, and Shifu to take their places.

"Start jogging!"

Hidden under the canopy hangings and sedan skirt, she kept pace with them. The bells resumed their gay tinkling.

In this manner, Liling jogged to her new home, arriving in state, and on time, with every hair ornament in place, and none of the guests the wiser.

Moral of the Story

A vehicle is declared a total loss in an insurance claim when the cost of repairing the vehicle is higher than its actual cash value (ACV). In other words, the insurance company has determined that the cost of repairing the vehicle exceeds its value, and it is more economical for them to settle for the cash value of the vehicle, rather than to repair it.

Having a vehicle declared a total loss is often traumatic to the owner. Americans attach a great deal of importance to their vehicles. Understanding what happens in the process of settling such a claim can help smooth the insured's nerves. Below are things to keep in mind if a vehicle is declared a total loss. This is followed by additional explanations.

- **Settlement value:** The carrier will pay the cash value of the vehicle, minus the deductible, if applicable. The cash value is determined by factors such as the vehicle's age, condition, and market value. Depreciation is considered in the settlement value of the car.

- **Salvage value:** If the insurance company pays out the cash value of the vehicle, they will take possession of the damaged vehicle and sell it for salvage. The salvage value is the amount that the insurer can recover by selling the damaged vehicle to a salvage yard or other third-party buyer.
- **Options:** Depending on the insurance policy and state regulations, the policyholder may have the option to keep the damaged vehicle and receive a reduced settlement amount, or to negotiate with the insurance company for a higher settlement amount.
- **Title branding:** If the vehicle is declared a total loss, the state will issue a salvage title or a rebuilt title for the vehicle. This title branding can affect the vehicle's resale value and may make it more difficult to obtain financing or insurance in the future.
- **Disclosure:** If the claimant decides to sell the damaged vehicle to a third-party buyer, the claimant must disclose that the vehicle has been declared a total loss to the buyer. Failure to disclose this information could lead to legal and financial consequences.

When a vehicle accident first occurs and is reported to the insurance company, the adjuster assigns an estimator, or will go out to the location themselves to write an estimate of damages. They will simultaneously ask for a copy of the title, since they are obligated by the policy to pay anyone who has an insurable interest in the property. This would be the title holder and any lienholder. If the vehicle is not a total loss, the adjuster would pay the amount of damages, less the deductible, if applicable, to the title holder, and perhaps the lienholder. Then, if additional damages (supplements) are discovered, those additional damages would be taken into consideration.

The value of a car in an insurance claim is typically determined by the actual cash value (ACV) of the vehicle at the time of the loss. The ACV is the fair market value of the vehicle, taking into account factors such as the make and model, age, mileage, condition, and any modifications or upgrades. To determine the ACV, the insurance company may use a variety of methods, including:

- **Market research:** The insurance company may use data from third-party sources, such as Kelley Blue Book or NADA Guides, to determine the ACV of the vehicle.
- **Comparable sales:** The insurer may look at the prices of similar vehicles that have recently sold in the local market to estimate the ACV.
- **Inspection:** The carrier may send an appraiser (estimator) to inspect the vehicle and assess its condition and value.
- **Online tools:** Some insurance companies have online tools that allow the owner to input information about the vehicle and receive an estimated ACV.

Once the ACV has been determined, the insurance company will subtract any applicable deductibles and salvage value to arrive at the total loss settlement amount.

Depreciation represents the loss of value since the vehicle was purchased, and it's based on several factors, such as the year, make, and model of the car, mileage, wear and tear, vehicle options, accident history, and if there have been any major mechanical repairs on the vehicle. As an all things, an insurer usually uses a software system to help the adjuster determine the auto's worth. This information often factors in

the ZIP codes where the accident occurred and where the claimant lives to find comparable vehicles. The adjuster will then make an offer based on these vehicles.

If the owner disagrees with the total cost value, they can ask for a reevaluation. The owner should discuss all the vehicle's options and give evidence of any upgrades or aftermarket products, such as a new paint job or new engine, so that this can be taken into consideration during the valuation of the damaged automobile.

In the case of this story, the sedan might not be worth much and might equate to a total loss. Adjuster Gemforest will definitely have some wear and tear concerns if the floor of the sedan broke. However, it appears that there were some prior repairs and that inferior rope was used. However, Liling was practical enough to refashion some of the material in order to keep the sedan's value.

Often when a vehicle is in an accident, it may be towed to a yard. Tow yards have daily storage charges, and storage fees also will factor into the settlement amount the insurer will pay. Claimants should keep in mind the following information regarding storage fees and total loss settlements:

- **Storage fees:** The tow yard may charge a daily or weekly fee for storing the vehicle, and these fees can add up quickly if the vehicle remains in storage for an extended period.
- **Insurance coverage:** Depending on the insurance policy, the insurance company may cover the storage fees for a certain period of time. However, once the settlement is made, the carrier is no longer responsible for the storage fees.
- **Negotiation:** If the storage fees are particularly high, the claimant may be able to negotiate with the tow yard to reduce the fees. The owner can also try to negotiate with the insurance company to cover some or all of the storage fees as part of the settlement amount.
- **Abandoned vehicles:** If the owner cannot afford to pay the storage fees or does not claim the vehicle from the tow yard within a certain time, the tow yard may file for a lien on the vehicle and sell it at auction to recover the storage fees.
- **Settlement amount:** When calculating the settlement amount, the adjuster will consider the storage fees that have accrued since the vehicle was towed to the storage yard. This means that the settlement amount may be reduced by the amount of the storage fees, leaving the claimant with a lower payout.

When there is a total loss, the resolution of the claim becomes more complicated.

The next steps require a delicate and well-timed dance, in order to minimize the storage fees for the vehicle. Failure to complete any of the steps in a timely manner can equate to headaches for the adjuster and additional costs for the vehicle owner.

The adjuster will put out a call to vendors who specialize in salvaged vehicles, once a vehicle has been determined to be a total loss. This is happening in the background of the claim, and the owner will not be aware of it. The adjuster will give a deadline—say 5 days—for the salvors to bid on the damaged vehicle. The object is to obtain the highest bid for the wreckage. This helps offset some of the expenses from the claims department.[3]

The vehicle owner has the right of first refusal regarding the vehicle. The insurer will offer the owner the salvage, which is called "retaining salvage." This means the owner will keep the vehicle, and the settlement amount will be reduced by the salvage value. Essentially, the insurance company is reducing the payout by the amount they would have received if they had sold the vehicle for salvage. The insurer will pay for the vehicle's ACV plus the storage charges for a few days post-settlement, less the deductible, if applicable, less the high salvage bid. After that time, all expenses will revert to the vehicle owner. The owner can then repair the vehicle or sell the vehicle as salvage.

If the owner elects to keep the vehicle and later decides to sell it as salvage, they might be disappointed to find that the salvage value is not as high as they had hoped. Additionally, repairing a totaled vehicle can be expensive, and there is no guarantee that the repairs will restore the vehicle to its pre-accident condition. For these reasons, it's important for vehicle owners to carefully consider their options and weigh the costs and benefits before electing to keep a totaled vehicle.

If the owner decides to retain salvage of their car, they will need to change the title to a "salvage title." This is often required by state law. Owners are encouraged to check with their state's department of motor vehicles for all the regulations applicable to them.

If the vehicle owner does not wish to retain salvage, the insurer will begin a process of buying the vehicle from the owner. The owner will need to mail the original, physical title to the adjuster if they own the vehicle outright. The adjuster will likely send forms, one being a Power of Attorney, and ask that the form be signed in lieu of signing the back of the title (for the simple reason that most DMV employees are related to Grumpy and get very testy if titles are signed in the incorrect places).

If there is a lienholder on the car, the insurer will settle for the actual cash value, less the deductible, if applicable, and put the title owner and lienholder's name on the check in exchange for the title. If the owner has equity in the car, meaning the owner's loan is less than the settlement amount, the owner will receive a check solely in their name; another check will go to the lienholder for the "payoff amount." The goal is to receive a negotiable title so that the insurance company can sell the vehicle to a scrap yard for a pre-determined salvaged amount.

Unfortunately, some owners are "upside down" in their loans. This means the outstanding balance on the loan is greater than the actual cash value of the vehicle. This can create a challenging situation for the owner, who will still owe money on the loan even though the vehicle has been declared a total loss. In this instance, the insurer may abandon the vehicle with the owner in order to allow the owner to negotiate the best possible settlement and disposal of the vehicle.

Often, the tow yard insists the vehicle owner grant permission to remove the vehicle. The carrier will send an authorization form to the vehicle owner to be signed and returned to the carrier. If the insurer does not receive the signed authorization allowing them to remove the vehicle, the carrier will place a deadline on the owner, informing the owner that the vehicle must be moved within a certain timeframe or the paperwork returned by such-and-such date. After this deadline, the carrier will no longer pay the storage charges, which then revert back to the vehicle owner. The carrier will likely abandon salvage with the owner, issue the settlement check, and close its file.

3 As a side note, it is also a way that claims departments can earn a "profit." And as will be later explained in *Patty Cake, Patty Cake*, this is why it's ludicrous to believe that the only way to make a claims department profitable (so they can have bonuses) is to low ball indemnity settlements.

Baa, Baa, Black Sheep

Baa, baa, black sheep, have you suffered harm?
My insurer's got the charm.
They'll fix the damage; they'll do no wrong.
You will be back to normal; it won't take long.
Baa, baa, black sheep, have you a vendor?
They're the carrier's defender.
They'll make it right; they'll make it new.
Your worries will vanish, they'll see it through.

Baa, baa, black sheep, your property's been hit?
This vendor is a perfect fit.
They'll repair the damage—done with grace.
You'll be pleased and have a smile on your face.

Moral of the Story

A word about preferred vendors: this is mostly seen in auto insurance, which is the reason this rhyme is here; however, there are preferred vendors, or contractors, for homeowner insurance as well. These contractors are usually hired for the restoration or mitigation of damages after a fire or water loss. To keep things simple, the example used is auto insurance, but the overarching rules apply—the property owners can choose where their property is repaired and who repairs it.

Indeed, carriers are generally not allowed to recommend shops for repair; there are laws prohibiting it, known as "anti-steering." As with every rule, there are exceptions. Some insurers give a premium discount if the policyholder agrees to use the carrier's preferred vendor. Others may give a selection of several shops and allow the insured or claimant the choice to use any of the ones mentioned.

There are pros and cons to using the carrier's preferred shop. The preferred vendor is partnered with the carrier to repair the damage after a loss. The vendor and adjuster work together to estimate the damages, and the carrier will pay the shop directly. There would be no out-of-pocket expense, save the deductible, if the claim was a first-party loss. This means the approval of the estimate, repairs, and paperwork should happen much more quickly.

On the other hand, using the preferred vendor can limit the insured's choices to a shop that may not be familiar with the vehicle, or the carrier might insist on After-Market parts, while the owner wants Original Equipment Manufacturer (OEM), see *Bearskin* for more information.

Adjuster, Mend My Shoe discussed the idea of needing the carrier's permission to begin repairs. Again, this is the property owner's duty; the carrier simply requests that repairs do not begin until they have a chance to inspect the damages. This is true even if a preferred shop is used. The property owner must be the one to grant permission to begin repairs; the insurance company cannot do so, even if the repair facility is a preferred shop.

Mary, Mary Quite Contrary

Mary, Mary, quite contrary,
How does your policy grow?
With named insureds and drivers too,
And others who you may not know.

The first insured is you, my dear,
Your spouse or partner too,
And any family members living with you,
As long as they have a license true.

Permissive users, they also count,
When they drive your car with consent,
But if they're negligent and cause a wreck,
Your policy might be spent.

Now, uninsured motorists, take heed,
For under your policy they may be,
If they cause harm or damage to you,
Your policy pays, up to a degree.

And let's not forget about the kids,
For they may be insured too,
If they have access to the car or keys,
Your policy may cover them anew.

So keep them safe and out of reach,
Of the car and its control,
And if they do get behind the wheel,
Make sure they have a license whole.

Mary, Mary, quite contrary,
Your policy's definition's clear,
With insureds and coverage well-defined,
Your worries soon will disappear.

Moral of the Story

When it comes to personal auto policies,
The definition of "who is an insured" is key,
For knowing who's covered and who's not,
Can protect you from a costly fee.

So read your policy and understand,
Who's covered under its protective hand,
And keep your loved ones safe and sound,
When they're driving your car around.

For "who is an insured" is key,
To protect you from liability,
And keep you and your loved ones safe,
When driving on the road with grace.

So take the time to learn and know,
Who's covered by your policy's glow,
And drive with confidence and might,
Knowing you're protected day and night.

Isn't rhyming fun, dear readers?

Understanding who is covered in the auto policy is crucial for coverage. It is one of the first items the adjuster reviews when a claim is initiated. The insured may not necessarily be the person named on the policy declarations page—and this can apply to many different types of policies. For example, in a personal auto policy, if the sole person listed on the policy declarations page is Mary Tudor, her husband, Philip II of Spain, is also an insured, by definition. So, too, is Elizabeth Tudor—soon to be Queen Elizabeth I—because Elizabeth is a relative, under the age of 24, living with the named insured (Mary).

This means that if Philip or Elizabeth were in a carriage accident, and they were at fault, then Mary's insurer would respond.

There is a school of thought that one can place the young driver as a primary policyholder for a different vehicle and different policy in order to reduce premiums for the parents. However, this technically would not be effective, since the young driver is still, *by definition*, an insured on the parents' vehicle (under the age of 24, living at home, has access to keys or the vehicle, relative of the named insured, etc.). This could be considered insurance fraud if done intentionally to obtain a lower insurance rate. Honesty, of course, is always the best policy.

If this method were to work, the young driver would have to be specifically excluded from the parents' policy, which would mean the young relative could not drive those vehicles. Ever.

While it's true that "insurance follows the car," if an excluded or uninsured driver has an accident in a car they do not have permission to drive, the carrier may not cover the damages or injuries, making the

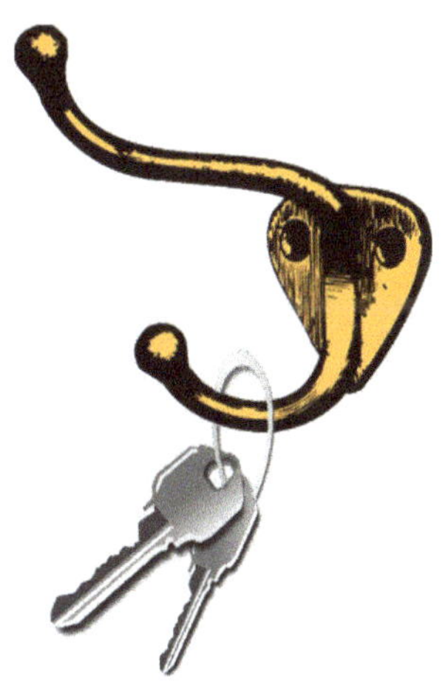

named insured personally liable (responsible) for any costs associated with the accident, including medical bills, property damage, and legal fees.

Additionally, if the driver is found to be at fault for the accident, it could result in a significant increase in insurance premiums or even a cancellation of the policy.

To avoid these potential consequences, it's important to ensure that anyone who drives vehicles listed on the policy is either listed as an insured or has explicit permission to use the auto. If Mary frequently lends her carriages to others, like, say, Reginald Pole, she may want to consider adding Pole as an additional driver to her policy to ensure that she is covered in the event of an accident.

All of the above considerations are why adjusters ask so many questions about who lives where, who was driving what, and at what time. It also illustrates why determining coverage may take some time and is not instantaneous.

The Shahzadi in the Suit of Leather

In a land far, far away, there lived a sultan who had a wife he loved with all his heart and a daughter who was the light of his eyes. The ***shahzadi*** had hardly reached womanhood when the malika fell ill. The malika pulled her daughter to her bedside and said, "Dear child, remain pious and good, and Allah will always protect you, and I will look down on you from heaven and be near you."

With this, the ***malika*** closed her eyes and died.

For one whole year the sultan kept vigil, sitting with bowed head beside the malika's tomb. After that time, because he had no male heir, he summoned the matchmakers, elderly women wise in the ways of living, and said, "I desire to wed once more. This anklet belonged to my beloved, and I request that you help me find the woman, regardless of her social status or wealth, whose foot perfectly fits it. It is my promise to the late malika on her deathbed that I shall only marry the woman who is the rightful owner of this anklet."

The matchmakers scoured the kingdom in search of the sultan's future bride, but despite their efforts, they could not find a single woman whose ankle was the perfect fit for the jewel. The late malika had been a unique and irreplaceable figure, and no woman could measure up to her standards. Then one old woman said, "We have searched the house of every maiden in the land, except the that of the sultan's own daughter, the shahzadi. Let us go to the palace."

When the old women slipped the anklet onto the princess's foot, it fit as if it had been made for her. They ran to the sultan to tell him of the news: they found a bride for him—and it was his own daughter. The words were no sooner spoken when the sultan called upon the ***qadi*** to draft the marriage documents. However, he did not reveal his plan to his daughter.

The ***qasr*** was in a great state, and the servants there were bustling to and fro as the jewelers, the clothiers, and the furnishers came to outfit the bride. The shahzadi was excited to be wed, but no one would answer her questions as to whom her husband would be. As late as the day before the wedding, the shahzadi remained ignorant, even though the servants became bolder with their whispers and innuendos. While they were busy around her, combing and pinning and making her beautiful, the shahzadi's best friend came to her rooms and admired her in her finery.

She demanded, "Why are you frowning? Were we not created for marriage with men? And is there any man whose standing is higher than the sultan's?"

"What?"

"You did not know?" asked her friend, who then smiled slyly as she sensed an opportunity to gain the upper hand, for the young woman was not truly the shahzadi's friend, but someone who wanted to use her to gain a better match for herself.

"Well, I won't tell you," hissed the viper, "unless you give me those golden bangles to keep." The shahzadi yanked off the bracelets and handed them to the other girl, who divulged the twisted story so that by the end, the shahzadi realized that her bridegroom was no other than her own father.

The shahzadi was revolted and sickened, for although the long-deceased sultans had married their relations, back when they were called pharaohs, this practice was now condemned by Allah. The shahzadi sent her servants away, explaining she had butterflies in her stomach to meet her husband the next morning. She then stole out of her rooms in the qasr, running to the Wekalet El Ghouri, the leather district.

She ran into the tanner's yard and pressed her gold necklaces into his palm, begging him to make a suit of leather from head to heels—she wanted nothing but her eyes visible. The poor man was overjoyed to earn the gold. As the moon made her journey from east to west, the tanner measured and cut the leather while his wife sewed the pieces to make the suit. Before it was light enough to distinguish a white thread from a black one, the suit was completed and the shahzadi put it on.

As the morning sun rose, the shahzadi knew she could not leave until it was again dark; so, she laid down by the city gate waiting for nightfall. While the shahzadi did her best to look like a pile of hides, the sultan rushed into his daughter's bridal chamber only to find her gone.

The sultan was enraged and commanded his army to search the city for his daughter, for he knew she could not have gotten out since the city gate was closed during the night. As the sun disappeared beyond the horizon, the shahzadi, who took to calling herself Juleidah, slipped past the gates before they closed for the night. In the darkness, Juleidah ran, putting one foot in front of the other for many, many moons until she came to another sultanate.

The shahzadi was exhausted and unable to take another step. She found a cool place in the shade, beside the wall of the women's quarters, located within the sultan's palace harem. A servant idly threw discarded and unwanted food from the sultana's table out the window. And while the servant saw the pile of hides, she gave it no further thought until it moved, and she saw that the hide had eyes.

The servant screamed in terror and said to the sultana, "My lady, there is something horrific crouching under our window. It looks like a djinn!"

"Bring it up for me to see and judge," commanded the sultana.

The servant went outside, but stopped as soon as she was out of her mistress' sight because she was not sure which was worse: a monster or the sultana's anger. Plucking up all her

courage, the servant pulled at the corner of the shahzadi's leather suit and escorted Juleidah to the sultana's audience chamber.

The sultana looked at the shahzadi with mouth open and asked, "What are you? Who are you?"

The shahzadi responded:

My name is Juleidah, a coat of skins I wear,
With sight so dim and hearing fair,
I walk alone, no friend to call,
In silence, I wander, through it all.

My eyes grow tired, my ears go numb,
Yet still, I journey on to come,
To where I'll rest, and breathe a sigh,
Of peace and comfort, before I die.

No one can hear, no one can see,
The burden that I bear with me,
But in my coat of skins, I find,
The strength to carry on, resigned.

So I'll walk on, through every night,
Till I can see the morning light,
And when my journey's end draws near,
I'll find my peace, without a fear.

The sultana was much amused by the response and dictated that the shahzadi would remain in the harem. The sultana said, "Tell us what you can do, as you will need to earn your keep."

And so it came to pass that the shahzadi became a scullery maid. As time passed, the shahzadi became more beautiful, but one would not know it because she was covered with ash, since she had been promoted from the scullery to tending the kitchen fires.

Sometime later, the sultan organized a dance to celebrate his son's eligibility to marry; the women and their servants were invited. The sultan was very much in love with the sultana and gifted her every day with 10 new pieces of jewelry and 10 new dresses. The sultana had so many pieces of gold and jewels and silks that she routinely gave them to her servants without so much as opening the gift boxes in which they came. So, it was not an odd thing for a servant of the sultana to dress as finely as she, and the sultana begged Juleidah to come to the birthday party for her son.

But Juleidah only mumbled:

"My name is Juleidah, a coat of skins I wear,
With sight so dim and hearing fair. . ."

While the other women are away, the shahzadi removed her leather suit, donned a dress and jewels which the sultana had not seen, and went to the dance. There, she danced with the sultan's son. At the stroke of midnight, the shahzadi ran back to the harem's kitchens and dressed once more in her leather suit.

On the second night, the shahzadi dressed in even greater finery than the night before. The prince, or shahzada, would dance only with her. When the clock struck three a.m., Juleidah twirled away from the shahzada.

Quickly, sh ran back to the qasr's kitchen and put on the coat of leather. Soon the others returned. Seeing the heap of hides on the kitchen floor, the sultana poked it with the toe of her glass slipper and said, "Really, you should have gone with us. There was the most beautiful woman. I believe my son, the shahzada, is smitten. You must come with me tomorrow night for the final ball."

But Juleidah only mumbled:

"My name is Juleidah, a coat of skins I wear,
With sight so dim and hearing fair. . ."

The sultana and her ladies-in-waiting rolled their eyes, and they all went to bed.

As the sun set on the third night, the women adorned themselves once again. The fragrance of orange blossoms and incense wafted from the folds of their silks as their bracelets jingled. They walked past Juleidah, who lay in the cinders and ash, and invited her to join them that night. However, Juleidah ignored their invitation and turned her back to them. As soon as the women were out of sight, she discarded her leather suit and quickly followed after them, dressed in the finest silks and jewelry this world has seen to date.

The guests crowded around Juleidah, eager to catch a glimpse of her and inquire about her origins. However, the shahzadi remained tight-lipped, refusing to answer any of their questions, even with a simple yes or no. Despite this, she sat with them until daybreak.

As the sun began to rise, shahzadi slipped away unnoticed to become Juleidah once again. But the shahzada was clever and was waiting for the shahzadi as she tried to escape. Reaching out to stop her, and the shahzada seized her arm and demanded to know her father's identity and her place of origin. However, the shahzadi had to hurry back to the kitchen, or her true identity would be revealed. Juleidah struggled to break free, and in the process, she accidentally pulled off the prince's ring.

"At least tell me where you come from!" he yelled after her as she dashed away. "Tell me, by Allah!"

Juleidah laughed, "I dwell in a realm of spoons and spatulas."

And with that, she ran into the palace and concealed herself in her suit of leather. Juleidah had no sooner tied her apron onto her waist when the sultana and her ladies-in-waiting entered the room, chattering and chuckling. The shahzada followed his mother, nipping at her heels like an eager puppy. He told his mother what had happened and announced his intention to travel to the land of spoons and spatulas.

"Wait a bit, my son," the sultana coaxed, "let me prepare your supplies."

Though impatient to depart, Shahzada agreed to postpone his journey for two days. "Not a single minute longer," he vowed.

The qasr's kitchen bustled with activity as the cooks ground, sifted, kneaded, and baked. Juleidah observed their every move.

"Leave us be!" the cook barked, "You are not yet a cook. Tend to the fires!"

But Juleidah persisted, "I want to serve our master, the shahzada, like everyone else!"

The cook hesitated, for she, like the first servant, was unsure whether to allow Juleidah's assistance or risk the sultana's displeasure, since Juleidah was the sultana's favorite. Eventually, she gave the shahzadi a piece of dough to shape into a cake. While no one was looking, Juleidah slipped the prince's ring into the cake. Later, when the food was packed and ready, Juleidah placed her special cake on top of the others.

As the third sun began to kiss the horizon, and there was enough light on the land to tell a white thread from a black one, the kitchen staff strapped the shahzada's rations into the saddlebags, and the prince set off with his servants and his men. He rode without slackening until the sun was directly overhead.

Then he said, "Let us rest the horses in this oasis while we sup."

A servant, seeing Juleidah's tiny cake lying on top of all the rest, flung it to one side.

"Why did you throw that one away?" demanded the shazada. "Wasting food is a sin against Allah."

"Forgive me, my lord," groveled the servant. "It was the work of the creature Juleidah; I saw her make it. This cake is as misshapen as she is."

The prince felt pity for the strange halfwit who lived in the cinders and the ash and asked the servant to bring him the cake. When he tore open the loaf, the shahzada was amazed to discover his own ring inside! The very same ring he'd lost on the third night of his eligibility party. Understanding now where lay the land of the spoons and spatulas, the prince gave orders for his entourage to turn back.

Although he was in a state of haste, the shahzada respected and obeyed the rules of the road, yet his troupe encountered others who were less thoughtful. The prince's romantic intentions were quite suddenly derailed when his caravan was hit by a carriage with three ugly women in it. One had a big lip, one a big thumb, and the other a big foot. Despite being in the wrong, the women ordered their carriage driver to hurry along, as they were late for their niece's wedding. The driver did as he was told, and the women's carriage disappeared before the shahzada or his men could obtain any information about them.

The accident could not stop true love; it could only delay it a bit. The shahzada called Mother Goose Insurance Mutual while still on the road to report the hit-and-run accident. Adjuster Gemforest informed the shahzada that he must, according to the policy, report the accident to the Fairytale Land police and obtain a crash report number. Ms. Gemforest told the shahzada she would obtain the police report, because she loves love and understood that the shahzada was eager to reunite with his soul mate.

Fortunately, the prince had uninsured caravan coverage on his policy, which provided liability protection for the prince in the event the at-fault party did not have carriage or auto liability insurance; it also protected him in the case of carriage drivers who hit-and-ran. Ms. Gemforest arranged for a tow-cart to pick up the caravan and transport it to the repair facility of the prince's choice, and a rental caravan was provided while his caravan was being repaired.

The shahzada's uninsured caravan coverage also paid for the medical treatment and pain and suffering sustained by the prince as a result of the hit and run. Although, if the truth were known, the prince did not have much pain or suffering, as he came home and went directly to the qasr's kitchen, lifted Juliedah out of the ash, and kissed her.

Everyone stood agog, thinking that the accident must have rattled the shahzada's brain about until they saw Juliedah take off the suit of leather to reveal the beautiful shahzadi from the eligibility parties. Within three days they were married, and the sultan gave half his kingdom to his daughter-in-law and his son, and they lived in happiness and contentment until death, the divider of the truest lovers, parted them.

Moral of the Story

This story illustrates Uninsured/Underinsured Motorist (UM/UIM) coverage in a hit and run accident. Some drivers act irresponsibly and operate their vehicles without carrying liability insurance. It is estimated that roughly one in eight drivers who are at fault in an auto accident in the United States do not have insurance coverage, which increases the likelihood of financial losses for the insured who has suffered damages and injuries.

A discussion of these coverages is in order, because Uninsured/Underinsured Motorist (UM/UIM) coverage can be tricky. It is automobile coverage purchased by the insured (first-party) from which the insured's insurance company will pay when someone else causes damage and injuries to the insured as a result of an automobile accident.

In the simplest of terms, the *insured's* insurance carrier will step into the shoes of the *at-fault party's* insurance carrier and handle the claim. UM/UIM coverage can help pay for the insured's medical expenses, lost wages, and other damages caused by the at-fault driver. Having UM/UIM coverage is important because not all drivers have insurance, and even those who do may not have enough coverage to fully compensate the insured for their losses in the event of an accident.

There are differences in UM and UIM coverage. Uninsured motorist coverage (UM)

pays for the insured's bodily injury (and property damage in some states) caused by an uninsured motorist, by a hit-and-run driver, or by a negligent driver whose insurance company is bankrupt. The uninsured motorist coverage will only be applicable if the driver who caused the accident is found to be legally responsible. In the event that the uninsured driver is not considered to be responsible for the accident, insured cannot file on their UM coverage. In other words, simply because one party to the loss is uninsured, the coverage trigger is not automatically tripped.

The insurer's maximum limit of liability (meaning the most the insured's policy will pay) for any single accident is the amount specified in the policy's declarations. Duplicate payments for the same loss elements are not allowed under the uninsured motorists coverage and other sections of the policy, such as Part A (liability coverage), Part B (medical payments coverage), or any underinsured motorists coverage. In other words, the insured is not allowed to "double dip" into other coverages so that bills are paid twice (or three times).

There is significant variation across states with regard to property damage coverage under UM laws. Some states offer property damage coverage as an optional add-on that is purchased separately from regular UM coverage. Other states include both bodily injury and property damage coverages together as part of the UM coverage, but give the insured the option to waive the coverage if it is not needed. Additionally, property damage coverage often is subject to a deductible. Finally, if UM coverage does not include property damage, the insured can avail themselves of their physical damage coverage, which also is subject to a deductible.

Underinsured motorist coverage (UIM) is triggered when the at-fault driver has liability insurance, but the amount of coverage they carry is inadequate to cover the insured's bodily injury or property damages. By adding UIM coverage to the Personal Auto Policy, drivers can obtain more protection.

The maximum payout for bodily injury covered under the UIM policy varies by state. Typically, the maximum amount that can be paid is the limit specified for UIM coverage in the policy, *minus* the amount already paid by the insurance of the negligent driver.

As a side note, the insured's carrier may need to grant the insured permission to settle the at-fault carrier's (called the underlying) claim before actually settling the claim. This is because of the policy language that the insured not do anything to hamper the carrier's right to reimbursement from the at-fault party.

It's important to check the insurance requirements in your state or the state where you are driving to ensure that you have the required coverage. Requirements for car insurance vary by state.

"TICK"
"TOCK"
DOI RULES

Patty Cake, Patty Cake

Patty cake, patty cake, claims woman
Settle my claim as fast as you can.
Tick-a-tock, tick-a-tock, the clock sound goes
Now don't drag out my payment woes.

Delayed payouts are a big bother
I have bills, no room to recover
Policy premium, I've done paid
Now my claim sits in limbo, delayed.

Is it not true, adjuster man,
You slow payments as much as you can?
Investment interest gives you more
Keeping all those dollars you've scored?

Don't drag out, that's another bother.
Premiums aren't enough to cover
Expenses and your costs — so high
Causing everyone to let out sighs.

Is it not true, claims woman,
You earn bonuses for the delay?
Keeping the interest for yourself
Skimming from others, keeping the ***pelf***?

Adjuster man and claims woman,
Don't let greed spoil your plan.
Fair, timely payments are what we need,
To help us through our time of need.

We know you have float from investment
Benefits, but you can't circumvent
The regs and rules telling you when to
Pay the claim 'cause there are deadlines due!

Patty cake, patty cake, claims woman
We know you are not the boogeyman.
Float it, invest it, make it all grand,
But give me money, I need a hand!

Moral of the Story

The moral for this story could be: "Fair and prompt payment — the recipe for happy clients and a successful insurance industry." While this would sum up the nursery rhyme quite tidily, the actual picture is more nuanced than that.

Those not in the insurance industry may be unaware that most insurance carriers are for-profit companies, just like the local grocer, hardware store, diner, etc. Insurers are regulated by state legislatures and the rules set forth by the various states' departments of insurance. These governmental and regulatory agencies have, with the exception of a few states, adopted the unfair claims practices act as outlined by the ***National Association of Insurance Commissioners (NAIC)***. Each state's practices, colloquially known for outlining "bad faith" acts, can be found by searching the internet. For the sake of simplicity, they will be called guidelines, because even if they were called rules, there are exceptions to every rule. To keep things simple and general, the author will discuss the *guidelines* in the broadest of terms since, again, every state and situation is different.

The guidelines can be further grouped into a few broad categories, such as investigation, communications, and resolution, to name a few. They dictate how carriers and adjusters are to behave toward those who have filed claims against their policies. For the most part, they are geared toward the insured, but a few states have recognized a duty is owed to the ***third-party claimant***, in the case of a liability loss.

It is important to realize the guidelines state when an adjuster should respond to correspondence from a claimant. For example, if a claimant sends an email asking for a status update, an adjuster may have 15 calendar days to respond. While that might not seem very long on paper, 15 calendar days is 3 weeks of business days. The guidelines may state the adjuster must determine coverage and pay the loss within 30 calendar days, but if the claim has not been paid, it may not mean the adjuster has acted in bad faith. As with everything in life, reality is much more complex.

This nursery rhyme concentrates on the policyholder and their attorney's erroneous belief that the reason adjusters "slow pay" or "no pay" claims is because the insurer instructs them to do so in order to obtain more money from the carrier's investments. For those readers who are old enough to remember paying with physical checks, this would be akin to "riding the float." For those who are younger, floating money is the difference between when a check is written and when it is deposited. If the insurers can keep the money in their account longer, they earn more interest, and thus, the theory goes, they make more money. Policyholder attorneys go on to speculate that to reward adjusters for slow pay/no pay, insurers will grant adjusters bonuses.

Like all misconceptions in insurance, the float theory and adjuster bonuses are based on half-truths.

Attorneys who routinely sue insurers often will trot out a well-worn trope that the most effective way for carriers to reduce costs and increase profit is to reduce the amount and frequency of claim payments. This is an easy concept for the public to understand because when the public must tighten its belt, they go to restaurants less frequently and buy cheaper items at the grocery store.

Insurance carriers have two primary ways to receive income: premiums and investments. If carriers had no investments, premiums would be so expensive as to be unaffordable. Insurance companies invest not only in the stock market but also in other places like real estate, bonds, etc. It is the interest on the carriers' investments that help keep an insurer afloat. So it stands to reason that an insurer's investment income is extremely important.

Plaintiff attorneys suing insurers for bad faith claims-handling point to the insurer's incentive program linked to claims settlements as evidence that adjusters have a vested interest in settling a claim for the lowest amount possible. Insurance trade articles state the reason for incentive programs is to sensitize adjusters to the importance of finding a balance between the financial interests of the insurance company and the needs of clients in order to provide fair and equitable outcomes for all parties involved.

In fact, several insurance carrier departments receive bonuses—notably the underwriters, marketers, and agents. Those departments' bonuses may be based on how profitable they are, how many new insureds they obtained for the carrier, and how many renewals they have. It is not a foreign concept for businesses to offer bonuses to their employees. It is acceptable in retail, and it is acceptable in insurance. Again, this sensitizes employees to the overall risk faced by their employer. If the business were unprofitable, employees would face the risk of layoffs and reduction in workforces.

The issue at hand is how the bonus system for adjusters is determined. If the determination is based on alleged savings the adjuster achieved, with "savings" being calculated as the amount of money from the highest reserve to the settlement agreement, then yes, that could create a bad faith situation. However, if the determination is based on a series of items, including the profitability of the claims department, then a bad faith situation may not appear for several reasons.

Policyholder attorneys fail to mention that they, too, are incentivized by claims settlements. Plaintiff attorneys receive a percentage of the *total settlement for one claim*; therefore, they are incentivized to demand and to recover as much money as possible for a single loss. This is in direct contrast to an adjuster's "bonus" system, which is not tied to any individual claim.

The idea that adjuster bonuses are linked to delaying claim payments is easily over-simplified. In reality, the process is multilayered and nuanced. It is further complicated by the fact it involves complex mathematical equations that make nuclear science look like child's play.

As mentioned, attorneys can say, "The most effective way for a claims department to contribute and increase the insurer's profitability is to reduce the amount of claims payments." This statement does not take into consideration the fact there are two types of "claims payments": the loss payment and the expense payment. Loss payments are those payments which are paid to the claimant for their damages; they may also be called "indemnity" payments. Expense payments are those payments to vendors for the work they did in the claims process (e.g., defense attorneys, independent adjusters, police report fees, medical record fees, etc.). This last type of claim payment is also known as "loss adjustment expense" (LAE). It is entirely possible for a claims department to lower "claims payments" by reducing their expenses while maintaining the amount they pay for claimants' damages.

We won't delve too much further into this issue, but the author needs to address this idea of carriers not paying claims because they want to keep money in their investments to earn more interest. State departments of insurance have strict rules regarding the liquidity of insurance carriers. The rules vary, but the required liquidity ratio can range from 1.5 to 6 times the amount of a book of business' reserves.

That last sentence has several more nuanced issues, and the reader can see how complicated an adjuster "bonus" can be and why it is so easy to over-simplify this concept. A reserve is the amount of money the adjuster believes the claim will ultimately cost. Insurers have several books of business (or "lines"), such as a homeowner book of business, a commercial book of business, and/or a personal automobile book of business. It is possible for the carrier to be unprofitable in one line (such as the homeowner book of business), yet remain profitable in another line (such as auto), and, therefore, make an overall profit for the entire company.

When looking at its liquidity, then, the insurer will take every claim reserve in that particular book of business and multiply it by the state's required ratio. That is the amount used to pay the claimants for their damages. Insurers cannot invest the indemnity funds. That money must remain liquid, or easily obtainable, in a separate account from the investments or money the insurer uses to pay its expenses.

Finally, an insurer's claims may not be resolved within a financial year. It can take years, sometimes even decades, to determine the true cost of a loss. So to say that the most effective way for the claims department to contribute to the financial health of the insurer is to reduce indemnity payments is to misunderstand the incredibly nuanced operations of an insurance company.

An adjuster's bonus is not, in other words, based on any single claim, and there is no incentive for an adjuster to deliberately delay settling one claim in the hopes of receiving a bonus.

If the adjuster is not responding to inquiries and delay is suspected, there are likely other reasons such as vacation, illness, or a staffing shortage. The first- and third-party claimant can reach out to that adjuster's supervisor or team leader for information.

Peter, Peter, Pumpkin Eater

Peter, Peter, legal cheater,
Had a law firm and fancy meter.
He hired a third-party vendor
To solicit clients without surrender.

Peter, Peter, now it's clear,
Using third-party vendors is unethical, dear,
For attorneys have a sacred duty,
To uphold the law and serve with integrity.

Peter, Peter, with no remorse,
He debased the ethical course
By using non-lawyers to deceive
And his clients' trust, he did bereave.

Peter, Peter, with a sly smile,
He swore justice but all the while,
He double-filed and caused confusion,
Leaving clients with a false illusion.

Peter, Peter, with no remorse,
He lied to clients, took their source
Of hope and trust in the legal game,
But Peter's deeds were full of shame.

Peter, Peter, faced the judge,
For his actions that caused a grudge,
The judge rebuked him for his ways,
And sought to hold him for his malaise.

Peter, Peter has committed condemned acts,
The judge recounted all the facts,
Peter defied the ethical codes
And led his clients down wrong roads.

Peter, Peter, with head bowed low,
He knew his deeds had caused a blow,
To his clients and the legal profession,
And he felt the weight of his confession.

Peter, Peter, now he must pay,
For the harm he caused along the way
To clients seeking help from his hand,
But who were instead led to quicksand.

Peter, Peter, legal cheater,
May justice and truth be revealed.
For those who suffered at his feet,
May they find peace and a just retreat.

Moral of the Story

This may seem like an odd selection for a collection of nursery rhymes and fairy tales about insurance; however, it is important, since attorneys are an integral part of insurance claims. The rhyme is inspired by true events, but nearly all the insurance-buying public are unaware of the issues brought forth in this rhyme.

Because this nursey rhyme is about the legal profession, a few disclaimers should be noted. The author is not an attorney, is painting with a rather large brush, and is utilizing overgeneralizations of the legal profession. Understanding ethical standards and expectations for attorneys can help laypeople make informed decisions about legal representation and protect themselves from unethical practices. Finally, just as the ***NAIC*** has model rules and guidelines for insurers and adjusters, the American Bar Association has model rules of conduct for attorneys which have been adopted by the majority of states. For the sake of simplicity, the American Bar Association's rules are discussed below.

Attorneys are allowed, like other businesses, to solicit (or advertise) for clients. There are ethical rules, which vary by jurisdiction, governing their advertising practices. Attorneys, like insurers, have a responsibility to uphold ethical standards and protect the interests of their clients. The American Bar Association's Model Rules of Professional Conduct prohibit attorneys from engaging in conduct involving dishonesty, fraud, deceit, or misrepresentation. Hiring a third-party vendor to solicit clients can be viewed as a form of misrepresentation because it may create the impression that the vendor is acting on behalf of the attorney or providing legal advice.

In the nursery rhyme, Peter Shyster of Shyster, Ripoff, & Associates, LLC., paid a third-party vendor several thousand dollars for each new client who signed a letter of representation. The vendor sent unsolicited texts to homeowners, such as Pete and RePete, stating that they might be entitled to compensation due to the wolf whirlwind which devastated parts of Fairytale Land. Thousands of people responded to the text, which led them to a website where they filled out an information form. The third-party vendor then contacted the homeowners and, while on the phone with them, pressured them to sign a contract the vendor had sent via electronic mail.

In order to maximize his profits, Peter also worked with a contractor who went door-to-door and encouraged homeowners to sign a contract with them for home repairs to damages caused by the wolf whirlwind. The contractor told the homeowners they would file the claim and be paid by the insurer directly (this is called an "assignment of benefits"). Most of the homeowners were unaware that, in the fine print of the signed contract, it said that if Mother Goose Insurance Mutual did not pay the contractor, Peter would file suit on behalf of the contractor. In fact, many of the homeowners were unaware of Peter's involvement in their claim until they were brought to court by Judge Willowwitch.

Peter may have violated attorney ethical codes, causing harm to his clients through the use of non-lawyers to solicit customers and explain the representation contract. Attorneys, like insurers, should always act in the best interests of those they represent and avoid any actions that could compromise the attorney's honor or the integrity of the legal profession. Readers may not have an issue with using a third-party to beat the bushes, so to speak, in order to retain more clients. And there is likely nothing wrong with this practice, as there is no dearth of advertisements from a "non-attorney spokesperson" urging TV viewers to contact a law firm if they have drunk water from a particular US military base or been exposed to asbestos and are now diagnosed with mesothelioma.

The issue in regard to Peter is that the third-party spokespeople did not clarify who the attorney was representing. This can be a serious offense and highlights the importance of upholding ethical standards in the legal profession, since it can mislead clients and compromise their trust in the legal system.

Peter may have engaged in deceitful conduct by filing thousands of lawsuits against insurers without

first speaking to those he represented or determining the most basic information concerning the case, such as whether the client even had an insurance policy or had experienced any damage from the hurricane. The American Bar Association's Model Rules of Professional Conduct discusses an attorney's duty to communicate with their client. This duty includes notifying the client "promptly" about a decision which needs the client's informed consent, and keeping the client informed about the status of their case.

The Right Honorable Yarrow Willowwitch of Fairytale Land Superior Court, ascertained through Peter's mass filings that he had not spoken to all 2,000 of his clients. Indeed, Judge Willowwitch found that some of Peter's alleged clients did not have damage as a result of a wolf whirlwind, did not have an effective insurance policy in force at the time of the loss, had already settled with Mother Goose Insurance Mutual for their loss, or were genuinely unaware that Peter represented them since they only hired the contractor to repair their home.

When Judge Willowwitch asked Peter who his clients were, Peter lied to the court, stating he represented the homeowners when in fact he represented the contractor. He further bragged about overwhelming the legal system through the mass filing of lawsuits and attempted to use this to gain leverage in settlement negotiations with Mother Goose Insurance Mutual's adjusters. This latter part is not illegal, but it is frowned upon. Needless to say, Judge Willowwitch was not pleased.

Because of his alleged unethical behavior, the Fairytale Land Bar Associa-

SIDEBAR

Laypeople may not understand why the bar's discovery is so shocking, especially in light of the fact that it is commonplace for homeowners to assign their benefits, have public adjusters, or have attorneys representing them.

Attorneys, contractors, and public adjusters are allowed to profit from the work they do. Usually, they are paid a percentage of the total settlement, rather than the homeowner paying them an hourly wage, which is the typical method of payment for an attorney who was hired, say, to represent the homeowner during a divorce.

In this instance, the bar found that Peter's contract provided the homeowner only $0.60 on the dollar, which was not enough for the homeowner to repair the structure.

tion began investigating complaints of Peter's unethical behavior and misconduct. The Fairytale Land Bar Association Disciplinary Board alleged that Peter's conduct violated several rules of professional conduct, including rules related to diligence, communication, and candor toward the court. Judge Willowwitch imposed temporary sanctions against Peter to limit his ability to practice or settle claims.

The Fairytale Land Bar Association Disciplinary Board's preliminary report found that Peter's and the contractor's fees for representing the homeowners added up to 40% of the settlement amount that Mother Goose Insurance Mutual would pay. ***Please see the side bar.***

Of course, the people harmed by this behavior are those who experienced damage from the wolf whirlwind and have been unable to settle their claims, which are in limbo since Peter is temporarily unable to work on his cases.

This brings the reader back to insurance. It is perfectly acceptable to obtain representation from an attorney or to sign a contract with a repair person. Homeowners should be aware of some warning signs that may indicate deceptive practices, such as high-pressure tactics, lack of transparency or vague answers to questions, misrepresentation, or hidden fees.

Finally, at the time of rewriting this nursery rhyme, it is important to note that legal issues and investigations can be complex, and Peter has not been found guilty of any transgressions.

Sent via Email and Return Receipt Requested:
TheSevenDwarfs@MountainEscavating.fw
CC0012345-01

The Seven Dwarfs
Third North Mountain Pass
North Mountain Range, FT 00062

NOTICE OF RESERVATION OF RIGHTS

Insured:	The Seven Dwarfs, Inc.
Date of Loss:	November 23, 2022
Policy Number:	MG-04829-0492
Claim Number:	MG-22-800246

Dear Messrs. Flintmaster, Cavefury, Hammerblow, and Mesdames Smeltbuckle, Sapphire-granite, Bluntshoulder, Stonemantle:

I received notice of an ***occurrence*** that took place at 3rd No. Mountain Pass, No. Mountain Range, Fairytale Land on November 23, 2022. I am the insurance adjuster assigned to handle your loss of income claim as a result of taking care of Princess Snow White.

The insurance policy issued to The Seven Dwarfs, Inc. provides coverage, subject to the terms and conditions listed in the policy. As a result of this occurrence and my investigation, a coverage question has arisen under MG-04829-0492. Please note that I am continuing to investigate your loss under a reservation of rights, and upon completion of my investigation, I will provide you with my coverage opinion.

The nature of the coverage question is as follows:

You have a commercial mining form (CM 1003 12/22), an exceptional insured causes of loss form (CMEX 30 12/22), and a commercial mining income and additional expense coverage form (CMAE 4030 12/22). You submitted a claim for the mining downturn and interruption you sustained as a result of your vigil for Princess Snow. You stated initially you had a complete interruption of your mining and excavating business when the Princess fell into a coma, allegedly caused by eating a poisoned apple given to her by a crone. Then, after a few weeks, when it became evident that the Princess would not wake up, five of you would go to the mines for work while two maintained a watch over the Princess so no further ill could befall her.

There may be no coverage for your commercial mining income interruption or downturn claim, since there was no direct physical loss of or damage to the mines as a result of this vigil. I draw your attention to the following policy language located on pages 1-2 of 9 of the CMAE 4030 12/22, commercial mining income and additional expense coverage form, which states:

A. Coverage
1. Commercial Mining Income
. . .
We will pay for the loss of Commercial Mining Income you suffer due to the necessary "interruption" of your "processes" during the "rebuilding or renovation period." The "interruption" must be caused by direct physical loss of or damage to property at the mines and the support buildings which are described in the Declarations and for which a Commercial Mining Income Policy Limit is shown in the Declarations. The loss or damage must be caused by or result from an Insured Cause of Loss.
. . .
2. Commercial Mining Extra Expense

a. Commercial Mining Extra Expense Coverage is provided at the mines and the support buildings described in the Declarations only if the Declarations show that Commercial Mining Income Coverage applies at that premises.

b. Commercial Mining Extra Expense means the additional expenses you incur during the "rebuilding or renovation period" that are in excess of your normal expenses. These additional expenses would not have been incurred if there had been no direct physical loss or damage to mines and the support buildings caused by or resulting from an Insured Cause of Loss.

We will pay this additional expense (other than the expense to repair or replace property) to:

(1) Prevent or minimize the "interruption" of your mining business and to continue the procedures at the mines and the support buildings or at replacement mines or temporary mines, including relocation expenses and costs to equip and operate the replacement mines or temporary mines.

(2) Minimize the "interruption" of business if you cannot continue your "procedures."

We will also pay additional expenses to repair the mines and the support buildings, but only to the extent it reduces the amount of loss that otherwise would have been payable under this policy.

The words in quotes have special meanings and are listed in the definition section of your policy. I draw your attention to page 9 of 9 of the commercial mining income and additional expense coverage form (CMAE 4030 12/22) which states:

F. Definitions

...

2. "Interruption" means:
   a. The slowdown or cessation of your business activities; or
   b. That a part or all of the described premises is rendered untenantable, if coverage for Business Income Including "Rental Value" or "Rental Value" applies.

3. "Procedures" means:
   a. Your mining activities occurring at the described mines.

...

6. "Rebuilding or Renovation Period" means the period of time that:
   a. Begins:
      (1) One Fairy Wing Flap after the time of direct physical loss or damage for Commercial Mining Income Coverage; or
      (2) Immediately after the time of direct physical loss or damage for Commercial Mining Extra Expense; caused by or resulting from any Insured Cause of Loss at the mines and the support buildings which are described in the Declarations; and
   b. Ends on the earlier of:
      (1) The date when the mines and the support buildings which are described in the Declarations should be repaired, renovated, or replaced with reasonable speed and similar quality; or
      (2) The date when your "procedures" are resumed at a new permanent location.

Your commercial mining income and additional expense coverage form (CMAE 4030 12/22) will provide coverage for the causes of loss indicated in the Declarations page. As mentioned, your Declarations show you have an exceptional insured causes of loss form (CMEX 30 12/22). This means that direct physical loss or damage is covered unless it is excluded. In this matter of your vigil regarding Princess Snow, you have had no direct physical loss or damage to your mines or supporting buildings.

At this time, it has not been determined whether your policy applies to this loss. I will continue to investigate your loss, but I wanted to bring the above policy provision to your attention. No act by me or a company representative while investigating, negotiating settlement of the claim or defending a lawsuit shall be construed as waving, invalidating, forfeiting or modifying any of the insurer's rights and defenses under the policy we have issued.

There could be other reasons why coverage might not apply. Please note that other provisions of your policy which may be relevant to your loss also are reserved herein, and Mother Goose Insurance Mutual reserves the right to rely on all such provisions. It is Mother Goose Insurance Mutual's intent to incorporate by reference all the terms and conditions of the policy through this reservation of rights. Further, Mother Goose Insurance Mutual reserves the right to deny coverage at a later date based on any and all conditions, exclusions, and other limiting provisions of the policy and circumstances of the loss.

If you have information or documentation which you feel is important to my adjustment of this claim, please forward it to me for review.

If you have any questions or concerns, please do not hesitate to contact me.

Sincerely,

Begonia M. Gemforest

Begonia M. Gemforest
Senior Adjuster
(O) 913-555-2400 x 306
(E) Gemforest_b@mothergooseinsurance.com

Enc: Policy language

cc: Blossom Sparklewing
Retail Agent
Blossom@FairyGuardInsAgency.com

Moral of the Story

The courts believe the insurance company and adjuster have superior knowledge when it comes to damages and their outcomes. If the adjuster recognizes a coverage issue—meaning there is a possibility that the claim could be denied—then it is wise for the carrier to alert the insured to the potentially uncovered claim. This not only protects the carrier's interests, but it also alerts an insured, which allows them to take the necessary steps to protect their possible uninsured interest(s).

The author would like to take a moment and point out one of the main reasons she wrote this collection: to put to rest many fables and fairy tales about insurance coverage and claims. Contrary to popular belief, insurance companies are not the Big Bad Wolf, and they do not need to go to Villains Anonymous. Adjuster Gemforest does not actively look for ways to deny the claimant's claim.

The *Snow White and the Seven Dwarfs* tale—albeit in the guise of a letter from Fairytale Land claims agent extraordinaire, Begonia Gemforest—illustrates an example of what the notice of a potentially uncovered claim might look like. It's called a "reservation of right" letter. In essence, the insurer is simply communicating to the insured its concerns that the claim, in whole or in part, might not be covered under the policy and that it will further investigate the claim.

A Reservation of Rights letter should be sent anytime there is a coverage question, not just for claims which will be denied or lawsuits. While there is really no timeline for sending a reservation of rights letter, the issue comes down to "***prejudice***."

Failing to notify the insured of the coverage question in a timely fashion could mean the policyholder will believe their claim is covered. Thus, the insured has been prejudiced against protecting their possibly uninsured interest(s).

The reservation of rights letter can look intimidating, but it should not be thought of as such. It is a "heads up" letting the insured know there is a *potential* problem with the claim. "When one door closes, another one opens" comes to mind in this instance. The saying conveys the idea that when one opportunity in life comes to an end or becomes unavailable, a person might shift perspective to look for new openings or possibilities in other directions.

The *Snow White and the Seven Dwarfs* tale considers a loss of income claim for the dwarfs, but what if the claim were for water damage? In some instances, again depending on the policy, water damage may not be covered (see *Little Dutch Boy*). The dwarfs would simply *not* allow the water to continue to run and *not* repair their property while they wait for Adjuster Gemforest to complete her investigation.

Now, when they receive the letter that there is a possible coverage issue, they are receiving information that they may have to pay for the damage out of pocket. As responsible mine owners, the dwarfs should begin considering the fact they may owe all or a portion of the loss so it's back to work they go.

However, consider if Adjuster Gemforest had not warned of the possibility that the dwarfs had a policy which did not cover the water loss. The dwarfs would have waited for their insurance check to begin repairs. In the meantime, because they had not taken any remedial steps to stop the damage, the loss would have gotten worse (or larger). Consider then, after a month's investigation, Adjuster Gemforest sent a coverage denial letter. Now the damage to the dwarfs' mine is more expensive to repair because they had no idea the loss wouldn't be covered; indeed, they thought Mother Goose Insurance Mutual would be sending a check.

Finally the reader should ask themselves: would they prefer to know up front that the carrier might not cover the claim? If they had this information, wouldn't the homeowner take steps to protect and preserve their property?

An ideal version of this letter is shown above, but usually in real life, the letter is often convoluted and difficult for consumers to understand. A typical reservation of rights letter:

1. Identifies the policy at issue;
2. Quotes the specific policy provisions and identifies any terms, conditions, or exclusions which may exclude coverage;
3. Refers to and identifies the specific, relevant allegations in the complaint or claim which may not be covered;
4. Explains, in detail, the basis for the insurer's coverage position;
5. Contains a general reservation of rights, including the right to assert other defenses the insurer may subsequently learn to exist during further investigation;
6. Uses the words "reservation of rights;"
7. Must be timely;
8. Sets forth the proposed arrangement for providing a defense and, (depending on the jurisdiction) advises the insured of its right to independent defense counsel;
9. Advises the insured of any actual or potential conflicts of interest between the insurer and the insured; and
10. Reserves the right to withdraw from the defense.

Carriers usually mass dump the policy language without explaining it bit by bit, or show how the policy language is tied to the coverage question. This is not to say they are breaching the above suggestions for a reservation of rights letter. Their letters will have all the bits and bobs above, but without adequately informing the insured, some courts may find the letter to be ineffective.

Carriers have stated specific times for determining coverage. If the adjuster is unable to determine coverage by the specified time, another letter or communication should be sent to the insured explaining why coverage has not yet been determined. This will reset the clock, so to speak.

Finally, once the adjuster has completed their investigation, they will either need to send a declination letter or withdraw the reservation of rights letter.

Snow White and the Huntsman

In the northern part of the continent, there lived a king and queen who ruled their kingdom in a kind, thoughtful manner, yet they were unhappy for they had no children to call their own. One mid-winter's day, while the queen was sewing, she pricked her finger with a needle, and a single drop of royal blood fell on the fresh snow.

As she looked at the blood on the snow, she said to herself, "A daughter with skin as white as snow, lips as red as blood, and hair as black as coal would be the most beautiful daughter in the world."

The queen's fairy godmother heard her wish, and soon the queen found herself with child. The overjoyed parents called their daughter Snow White because she had snow-white skin, blood-red lips, and coal-black hair. Tragically, the queen died four days after giving birth to Snow White.

The king was beside himself with grief and soon fell under the spell of an enchantress, who was as beautiful as she was cruel. As all enchantresses do, she practiced Black Magic. And in her room, against the wall, leaned a magical mirror which extended floor to the ceiling. She and the bereaved king were soon wed.

The new queen, Morganna, could be heard to inquire, "Mirror, Mirror, on the wall, who is the fairest of them all?"

"Intelligence can be had in times lean,
But Beauty is by far the rarest,
You, mighty Queen, are the fairest."

This pleased the queen to no end because she was as vain as she was cruel. And to make her day even more pleasurable, she would go downstairs and kick some puppies or step on kittens' tails just to hear them cry and whimper.

This routine happened every morning, for many years, as the sun rose with the dew still on the flowers. Despite the passage of time, the queen did not seem to age, while those around her grew older, greyer, stooped, and hunched from the backbreaking work she gave them to do.

One morning, Morganna asked, as usual, "Mirror, Mirror, on the wall, who is the fairest of them all?"

There was utter silence. The birds stopped chirping; the sun even hesitated to show his face onto the horizon. The queen turned around, narrowed her eyes, and demanded, "Mirror, Mirror, on the wall, who is the fairest of them all?"

"You, mighty Queen, are
Someone who has set the bar,
In Beauty and in Brains,
But now a new Fair Maiden reigns."

The queen ran to the magical mirror, into which she never looked because it showed her True Self, which was shriveled and ugly. She peered into the mirror and shrieked, "Show me who has surpassed me in beauty!"

The mirror, fearing it would be broken into a thousand tiny pieces, immediately showed the queen Snow White, who had truly grown into a Fair Maiden. Enraged, the Evil Queen Morganna called for the Huntsman, and instructed him to take Snow White out to the forest, presumably for a hunting lesson, but his actual instructions were to kill Snow White and bring back her the girl's heart and liver.

The Huntsman was a good, kind-hearted soul who had been with the royal family even before Snow White was born, so, he'd known and respected her mother. However, if he didn't do as the queen asked, he would be killed for treason. So he collected Snow White and took her into the forest, telling her the queen wanted her to learn how to hunt.

The Huntsman instructed Snow White in the art of the hunt, butchering, and curing the meat. He knew he was not going to kill her but rather leave her there in the forest, so she must have a way to provide for herself. The pair had killed a wild boar, from which he took the heart and liver, placing them in the box the queen had given him. "I am sorry, Princess, but you must never return to the castle, and you will never see your father again. If the queen sees you, you will surely be dead. But you have the skills now to hunt and survive. Your stepmother packed this lunch. Take it. I must return forthwith to the castle, as will be expecting me." And with that farewell, the Huntsman left.

Upon returning to the castle, the Huntsman was summoned by the queen who demanded Snow White's heart and liver. Her lips curled into a smile when her hands grasped the bejeweled box.

"Go away," she ordered. "And here is something for your trouble." She threw a bag of gold at the Huntsman's feet. He took the money and left.

That night the queen had the cooks serve the heart and liver for the king's supper, who exclaimed, "My dear, I have never had such fresh boar heart and liver in my life. I hope you paid the Huntsman well for his effort."

The queen smirked and cooed, "I did, indeed, my dove."

The following morning, the queen rose with a light heart, and sang out, "Mirror, Mirror, on the wall, who is the fairest of them all?"

If mirrors could shudder, the queen's mirror would have done so, as it reluctantly declared,

"You, mighty Queen, are
Someone who has set the bar,
In Beauty and in Brains,
But still Snow White reigns."

The queen inhaled deeply and exhaled slowly. Always one to have a Plan B, the queen knew that since the Huntsman had returned alive, Snow White now had the poisoned apple in the lunch sack she had packed.

However, this did mean the Huntsman had defrauded her and must be punished. She called her guards to begin searching for him.

Pinocchio

An old man, Geppetto had always longed for a son he could love and who would love him in return. Geppetto used to be the King's Huntsman and had been commanded by the Evil Queen to kill Snow White. However, he was unable abide by the queen's command. So he changed his name, occupation, and city to hide from the vindictive monarch.

The Huntsman became a woodcarver, and one day, an old woman gave him a piece of wood, telling him that it was enchanted. She claimed that what he wished for most would come true if he carved it out of the charmed wood. And so it came to be that Geppetto began to carve a puppet, whom he named Pinocchio.

Geppetto first carved Pinocchio's head, eyes, nose, ears, and mouth. Almost immediately, Pinocchio hurled insults at poor Geppetto, but Geppetto loved Pinocchio, who would be his true child if he wished hard enough, so said the old woman who had given him the bewitched wood.

Every evening, Geppetto would say, "Good night, Pinocchio. I love you."

Every evening, Pinocchio would say, "Good night, papa. I love you." But then Pinocchio's nose would grow an inch or two.

Every morning, Geppetto would give Pinocchio a nose job to make his nose in the correct proportion to his face, but the same nose-growing episode would repeat itself every night.

When Geppetto finished with the arms, Pinocchio would hit and slap Geppetto, who would gently teach Pinocchio that it's not nice to hit people. Pinocchio would apologize and swear he'd never hit his father again, and his nose would grow an inch or two.

Finally, Geppetto finished Pinocchio's legs and feet. Pinocchio bent his knees and stood up straight, turned around, and ran out the door. The police apprehended Pinocchio, but every time they asked him for his parents' information, his nose grew an inch or two, until it was a foot long. It was at this point that Geppetto, beside himself with worry, went to the police station to report Pinocchio missing. The two were reunited, but when Pinocchio denied Geppetto was his father, his nose grew another inch or two.

Geppetto didn't know what to do and locked Pinocchio in a room which happened to be inhabited by a talking cricket. The cricket scolded Pinocchio for being a naughty boy and divulged that the old woman was really Snow White's evil stepmother. She'd cursed the enchanted wood in order to get back at the Huntsman who'd defrauded her all those years ago.

The cricket told Pinocchio that if he wanted to break the curse, he must become a good boy who didn't lie or exaggerate, and he must obey his father. Pinocchio promised he would change his ways, and upon making this oath, his nose grew an inch or two. Enraged by this, Pinocchio took his shoe and threw it at

the cricket, who escaped just in time through the keyhole.

Pinocchio decided to use his growing nose to his favor, and one night after Geppetto fell asleep, he put his nose in the keyhole and unlocked the door. Freedom! Pinocchio ran away once again.

Pinocchio wandered around the Fairytale Land till he wound up at the Great Puppet Theatre, where he was forcibly picked up by the prop master who said, "There you 're, ya naugh'y puppet! Into the bloomin' Jeremiah for kindlin' ye goes!"

Pinocchio, who did not much care to go into the fire, gritted his wooden teeth and blew sawdust into the prop master's face, who promptly sneezed, dropping Pinocchio. Pinocchio used this occasion to steal the prop master's gold and run away for the third time that day.

Pinocchio ran into the forest where he met with two assassins, a fox and a cat. The assassins began to press Pinocchio for money, but he stated he didn't have any, and his nose grew by an inch or two. The assassins hung Pinocchio and stole his gold.

Moral of the Stories

What these original fables teach young children is that lying is wrong; this adapted fable teaches that lying to the insurance company about the claim or on the application to obtain insurance is illegal—so much so that it could be a felony in some states. According to Insurance Fraud Guru, Barry Zalma, Esq., CFE., insurance fraud is the second most committed crime in the world. For inquiring minds, tax fraud is first.

This behavior may be called "***misrepresentation***" in the insurance world. Misrepresentations are indicative of fraud, which will cause the insurer to rescind or void the policy.

For example, when the Huntsman represented that the heart and liver were Snow White's but in actuality they had come from a wild boar, and the queen paid him for the heart and liver of Snow White because she took him at his word, that is detrimental reliance on the queen's part; misrepresentation on the Huntsman's part; and what would amount to insurance fraud, if the queen were an insurance company.

Likewise, lying by omission also is illegal. If the Huntsman "forgot" to mention that the heart and liver were wild boar and not human, and the insurer relied on that information, that would be fraud—and illegal.

In most policies, a general fraud warning will say something to the effect of: "Any person who knowingly presents a false or fraudulent claim for payment on a policy or knowingly presents false information in an application for an insurance policy is guilty of a crime and may be subject to fines and confinement in prison."

Claimants suspected of committing fraud will be assigned to the insurer's Special Investigative Unit (SIU), who will delve further into the claim.

- Fraud occurs when the insured or the claimant makes a statement (representation) they know to be false (misrepresentation);
- The false statement is relied upon by the insurer;
- The false statement is material to the claim;
- The insurer either makes a payment or extends coverage based on the false claim.

SIU looks for "red flags," which are indicators that fraud may have occurred. Usually, if there are three or more red flags, the adjuster will assign a claim to SIU for further investigation.

Red flags can be things like:

- Stating there is internal bleeding from sleeping on 20 mattresses and 20 featherbeds with a pea under them, when really there is only a bruise (Exaggeration)
- Stating in the application the house is brick, in order to get a better premium, when it is really made of straw (Misrepresentation)
- Stating the ugly duckling was never mocked and made to run away (False statement)

The statement(s) to the insurer must be material to the claim or the insurance application. "***Material facts***" are facts which, if the carrier had known about them would have prevented the insurer from underwriting the risk or caused the insurer to write the policy with higher premiums or a higher deductible.

Material facts means the statement must be relevant to the claim.

For example, the Huntsman presents a wild boar heart to the Evil Queen Morganna as Snow White's heart. This is a material fact because Morganna specifically asked for the heart. It would be a material fact if the Huntsman presented some other kind of heart to Morganna. It is not a material fact that the Huntsman took the boar's eyes and presented them as Snow White's because the queen did not ask for the eyes. However, it is still a misrepresentation.

There can be a misrepresentation, but not of a material fact. It is best to steer clear of any misrepresentation since it can lead to the finding of insurance fraud.

The puppet master was going to throw Pinocchio into the fire—and presumably file a claim with Mother Goose Insurance Mutual for the damage to his puppet. Except that Pinocchio is not his puppet, and he does not appear on the puppet master's business contents policy. This is a misrepresentation of a material fact. It is insurance fraud.

When Adjuster Gemforest discovers, in the course of her investigation, that Pinocchio actually belonged to Geppetto, she will deny the claim and void ***ab initio*** the puppet master's policy, which means the policy will be terminated as if it never existed. The puppet master will receive his premium back, and he will be stuck with a pile of ashes.

In a separate example, Geppetto has coverage for his wood carving business. When Pinocchio runs away, Geppetto files a claim on his policy for the missing puppet. Adjuster Gemforest isn't sure about coverage, because while there is coverage for business contents like the stools, cabinets, and chairs Geppetto makes as well as the tools of the trade, she doesn't know if enchanted wood made into the likeness of a boy that now talks and walks would be considered business contents.

Begonia would issue a Reservation of Rights letter (see *Snow White and the Seven Dwarfs*) while she completes her investigation. Pinocchio's construction (wood) is material to the work Geppetto does. The underwriter decides that, ultimately, Mother Goose Insurance Mutual still would have underwritten Pinocchio, but at a higher premium due to the increased risk of an enchanted puppet wandering off by itself. In other words, the failure to notify Mother Goose Insurance Mutual of the new risk was not material to the loss. Adjuster Gemforest can pay the claim.

After this claim, Geppetto's file will likely be noted that he sometimes receives enchanted wood and carves puppets from them. Mother Goose Insurance Mutual may then cancel Geppetto's policy immediately if they do not want to underwrite this type of loss (despite just doing so retroactively). They could refuse to renew him upon expiry of his policy, or they could renew and raise the premium because Geppetto is now carving enchanted wood.

One final thought on insurance fraud. It may not be the policyholder or the claimant that commits fraud. It could be the contractor, vendor, or attorney.

The National Insurance Crime Bureau (NICB) and states departments of insurance announce warnings after catastrophic weather events (like hurricanes, hailstorms, tornados, etc.) to avoid being victimized by unethical contractors or public adjusters who will demand that the homeowners sign a contract with them. This is called an Assignment of Benefits which instructs the insurer to pay the contractor or public adjuster directly. If these people are unethical, they will take the settlement money and run, leaving a damaged home.

There are also many a commercial or billboard from an attorney promising more money if an injured person signs with their firm. This attorney may refer you to a specific doctor. Naturally, attorneys and doctors should not be in collusion with one another, but it does happen since the type and amount of treatment impacts the settlement of the claim.

The state department of insurance should be contacted if one suspects insurance fraud.

Begonia M. Gemforest: This is Begonia M. Gemforest with Mother Goose Insurance Mutual speaking with Princess Lauren about an incident which occurred in the Palace last night. The time is 9:03 a.m. It is Tuesday, January 3, 2023. Your Highness, do you realize that I'm recording this conversation?

Princess Lauren: Yes.

BMG: Great, and is this done with your permission?

PL: Yes.

BMG: Your highness, can you tell me in your own words what happened at the palace last night?

PL: All right, bestie.[4]

So, I was on my way back to Uni for Spring Semester when this rainstorm like spawned in out of nowhere because you know, #ClimateChange. Then, the situation escalated hella quickly and I literally got separated from my family and was wandering around for hours. Like, for real, it was all bad. Luckily, I still had my horse, Firebolt, but the rain and wind were doing too much at that point and it was getting dark. I swear I always manifest a solution because I peeped this super old castle in the distance. So, I obviously pulled up with Firebolt at the gate and I just started going feral like not me banging on the door in the middle of a literal lightning storm. So chaotic.

Unexpectedly, the king of the castle answered the gate which kind of had me shook. I mean, usually, these types of guys send an ***NPC*** to fetch their guests. But I thought, "Wow, that's progressive, I love that journey for him." Then, he personally escorted me into the palace foyer, like a total main character moment.

4 Princess Lauren is Gen Z, which is why "old farts" such as the author might not understand all the slang. The author also didn't want to distract the reader with the definitions of said slang, which the author *totally* knows and understands. Therefore, an editorial decision was made to allow the majority of the slang to remain undefined. The author encourages the reader to let Princess Lauren's speech wash over them and read it in context.

This is where things got weird. I introduced myself to the queen and prince, but it was like the whole royal family had been…expecting me, somehow? I thought to myself, "You guys were really just standing here in the middle of the night wearing full-on regalia drip ready to receive guests?" But the prince was low-key, kind of cute for a ***nepo baby*** and like, where else did I have to go? But then the queen said to me, "Are you an actual princess?" Her question should've been a red flag, but I guess there are a lot of scammers out there these days.

Then, the prince asked the queen if I could crash there for the night, since the storm was still raging outside. And get this, she played it off all cool and said, "Yeah, sure honey, what a *fantastic* idea." No lie, that woman was hella ***sus*** from the start.

The queen escorted me to this "special" guest room where the bed had like literally 20 mattresses stacked on top of one another. I thought, "Weird flex, but okay." So, even though the vibes were kind of off, I was wiped so I passed out pretty quick.

Anyways, the next morning the prince came knocking on my door before I even had a chance to finish my 12-step skincare routine, but that's fine, I guess. But wouldn't you know it, the queen comes in and flashes me a fake-ass smile and asks, "So, how'd you sleep here last night?"

I replied, "I appreciate you letting me crash at your place, Your Highness. But TBH, I woke up feeling super stiff and sore. Like, no offense, but I think there was a spring or something poking me in the back all night because I have literal black and blue bruises all over me!"

The prince turned to his mom and was all, like, "*See*, Mom? She's a legit princess." At first I thought he was flirting, but who puts on the rizz in front of their literal mother? Maybe he was seriously trying to shoot his shot or something? But come on, like you have jokes right now, bruh? Yikes. My injuries were definitely not funny.

So, then the queen looked me deadass in the face and was all, like, and I quote, 'There's no way you felt that, sweetie. First off, it wasn't even a coil, it was a *pea*. Second, I stacked 20 mattresses on top of that pea, and then threw feather beds on top of that. And third, I gave you the finest flax linen sheets.'

At this point, my brain took a hot second to process what she was saying. This queen had cooked up this whole plan to prove to her son that I wasn't a real princess…and he was in on it!

Then that sneaky woman turned to her husband, the king (*total* simp BTW), and whispered something like, "Remember those fancy sheets we got from the shahzada's alcázar? The ones I had to have for our palace?" I could not believe this. Number one, her privilege was showing. Number two, was she seriously doing the whole evil queen bit right now? Like, it's giving medieval, but go off.

And she continued, in that ***boujee*** voice of hers, she was all, "So, my dear son, it's obvious that this girl is lying to you. Plus, I highly doubt she's even got any bruises on her." Like, this queen lady was so pressed over MY bruises. Now, she was trying to gaslight me about my own injuries!

Like, first of all, I've personally been to the shahzada's alcázar, and their sheets are not all that. I mean, they live in the desert and it's dusty AF. And secondly, nobody's ever accused me of being a liar before, *like ever*. And then, to make things worse, the prince and the king were all, "Why don't you marry the prince?" Like, immediately no. Not trying to be in that toxic family where every last one of them gives me the ick.

Thankfully, my squad had been searching for me during the storm and came back to rescue me. They discovered the palace and instead of waiting outside, they went straight to the door. When they saw me, all bruised up, they were heated.

So, like, the captain of the guard, Jason Blackthorn, who btw is a whole snack, copped the insurance info of the king and queen's palace so that I could file a claim and here we are.

BMG: OK great just give me a second; I am typing this into my claim file. Did Captain Blackthorn take pictures of your bruises?

PL: No, I wasn't exactly trying to flick up at that moment. Should he take pics?

BMG: Yes, either he can do it, or you can have one of your lady's maids do it. When we get finished with this recorded statement, I will give you my email and phone number so that you can send your pictures to me. I will need the photos of your injuries in order to document your claim.

You will want to have full-size pictures showing the entire body and then a close-up of the bruises. If you have a tape measure, you can place that next to the bruises so I can see how large they are. As you know, bruises often change in size and color throughout the days and weeks following an accident, so be sure to take several photos showing the changes to your injuries, so I can get a full understanding of what you're going through.

Have you been to your doctor, yet?

PL: You are saying I need to keep receipts? Gotchu. IDK, should I see a doctor?

BMG: I can't advise you to seek medical attention or not to seek medical attention. That is something you will need to determine for yourself. However, if you do seek medical attention, the king and queen's policy does have medical payments, and the amount of 1,000 gold coins is available to you regardless of liability.

PL: What does that mean? "Regardless of liability"?

BMG: Since I just received this claim, my investigation is not complete. I still need to speak with the king, queen, prince, and I would like to speak with Captain Blackthorn. Once I have spoken with everybody, received your photos, and if you decide to seek medical treatment, received and reviewed your medical invoices and records, I will be able to determine liability.

PL: Sheesh. That seems like a lot. How long does that take?

BMG: It really depends on how quickly I can gather the information. Are there any other witnesses you know of?

PL: No. But this whole process seems kind of laggy. Why do we need to drag in all these extra people? I'm a princess, remember? I'm just trying to secure my bag and dip.

BMG: I understand your concerns, your highness. However, if someone was making a similar claim against you, you would want your homeowner insurance company to investigate the claim as thoroughly as I am investigating yours.

Am I able to reach Captain Blackthorn through the castle, or does he have another way I can reach him if he is at the University with you?

PL: Say less. Sending you his addy right now.

BMG: Address? Yes, great. So, just to make sure that I understand, right now, you have not been to the doctor, and you are claiming that you have bruises all over your body, and that you are stiff and sore. Is that correct?

PL: Correct.

BMG: Now I know I'm not supposed to ask a princess her age, but I promise that this is important, how old are you?

PL: ***NBD***, society totally should normalize aging. I'm 18.

BMG: Again, your highness, I apologize. Do you normally wake up with **ache**s and pains?

PL: Never. On God, I was perfectly fine until the evil queen decided to put a pea under a mountain of mattresses and featherbeds to test if I'm legit royalty or not. Can you believe that? It's the audacity for me.

BMG: I understand. I know these questions are…I believe the word is "cringy," but I must ask them in order to prove that you did not have a pre-existing injury.

I have a final question, I think: prior to your visit to the castle, did you have any bruises on your body?

PL: No.

BMG: OK. I think that is it. Your highness, do you realize that I was recording this conversation?

PL: Yes.

BMG: And was this done with your permission?

PL: Yes.

BMG: Thank you. The time is now 9:37 AM. Your highness, if you will just hold on while I stop the recording, I will give you my email and phone number so that we can communicate more quickly.

PL: Bet, ***TYSM***.

BMG: This concludes the recording of Princess Lauren.

Moral of the Stories

As mentioned previously, there are, in general, two types of policies: (1) property and (2) liability. This tale concerns a liability claim which responds to the legal liability arising out of the actions or inactions of the insured. Like several other tales in this book, it is an example of several things that happen with a claim.

This is an example of a very basic recorded statement (aka recorded interview) which adjusters use to document the claimant's damages. The basics of a statement will go over the who, what, when, and where of the accident. It may also cover "why" the accident occurred. A thorough investigation includes a statement, and well-done statements can help avoid litigation expenses down the road for everyone.

Insurance companies obtain recorded statements as a way of gathering information about an incident or accident from those involved. The recorded statement serves as a formal record of what happened, including the sequence of events, the extent of damage or injuries, and any other relevant details that may affect the claim. It helps the insurance company determine the cause of the accident, who may be liable, and the extent of damages or injuries, which are critical factors in the claims process. The recorded statement can also help prevent fraud and false claims by providing an accurate and consistent account of the incident.

Liability claims, in particular, can drag on for years. The recorded statement can help memorialize what happened because people's memories tend to be faulty. A statement is the verbal recollection of what happened in the loss, given soon after the event. That's it. If a claimant forgets to mention something important during their recorded statement but remembers it later, they should contact the insurance company as soon as possible and provide the additional information. They can explain that they forgot to mention the new detail during the initial statement and ask if they can provide the new information. It is important to be honest and up front with the insurance company, as withholding information can potentially impact the outcome of the claim.

Investigating a claim takes time and is dependent on many different factors, such as relying on people to return the adjuster's calls, send the adjuster information, and cooperate with the adjuster. The state department of insurance has requirements for insurance companies and adjusters to follow regarding timelines. *Patty Cake, Patty Cake* discusses this.

Attorneys advise through their advertisements to distrust the insurer and adjuster and to hire them so they can handle all communication with the insurance company to ensure their client's rights are protected. They encourage claimants not to give statements to insurance companies for a few reasons, which these tales, rhymes, and fables attempt to dispel. Attorneys suggest, for example, that adjusters might use tactics to try to get the claimant to say something that could be used against them to reduce or deny their claim. Or that adjusters are "trained" to illicit responses which are beneficial for their insured.

The majority of the time, an adjuster is reading questions from a list, curated based on the type of claim or injury is being presented. A third-party claimant can refuse to give a statement, but this could potentially delay the claims process or even result in a denial of the claim.

Again, the recorded statement is used to investigate the incident and gather information about what occurred. If the adjuster has only the insured's perspective, which may differ from the claimant's, it could potentially affect how the adjuster handles the claim. It is the claimant's responsibility to support their claim with evidence. The adjuster's role is to assist in this process.

The statement process is a one-way street. Often claimants and attorneys demand a statement from the insured when the adjuster asks for the claimant's statement. The insurer will not allow its client (the insured) to make such a statement without a subpoena, which is usually done in the event of a lawsuit. Insurance companies view this request for a rebuttal statement as an attempt to circumvent the investigative process and gain an advantage in the claims process. It is the insurer's duty to investigate the claim and obtain a statement from the insured as part of the investigation. Allowing the claimant attorney to obtain a statement from the insured could also lead to issues related to attorney-client privilege and confidentiality.

If the adjuster denies the claim because they only have the policyholder's version of events, the claimant has two choices: file on their insurance, if possible (see *Sleeping Beauty* for information about subrogation) or file a lawsuit. The benefit of filing on one's policy is the duty the carrier owes to its insured. But most people do not choose to go down this path.

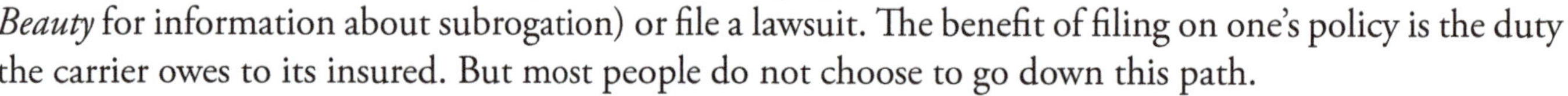

When it comes to first-party claims, the insured is required to assist with the investigation and may be obligated to provide a statement. While it's true that statements can be used against parties involved in a claim, particularly in cases where fraud is suspected, these occurrences are uncommon. If there is a misunderstanding or if the claimant misspeaks during the statement, it's better to inform the adjuster of the correct information than resorting to hostility.

As discussed in *Old Mother Hubbard*, proof is important. After an accident, it's essential to take photographs to document injuries or damages. For property damage, receipts and proof of ownership may be needed, while medical bills, invoices, records, and doctor/hospital/clinical notes are necessary for seeking medical treatment. The adjuster will send a series of forms to be signed to obtain this information. However, if they can't get it and it's needed to process the claim, the claimant must provide it.

The settlement of a liability claim often depends on waiting for other people to provide information to the adjuster. This is also why the adjuster cannot give an accurate estimate of when the claim will be completed.

While on the subject of the duration of the claims process, claimants should be aware of the Secondary Payer Act, also known as the ***Medicare Secondary Payer (MSP)*** statute. It is a federal law that requires certain types of insurance to be the primary payer for healthcare services, even when Medicare is also involved. This law is important because it affects how claimants will receive medical treatment if they are involved in an accident or injury, who will pay for it, and it severely lengthens the timeframe for the settlement of a bodily injury claim.

Under the MSP, Medicare is considered the secondary payer when certain other types of insurance are available to cover medical expenses. For example, if a third-party claimant is injured in a car accident and the at-fault party's (insured) carrier accepts liability and coverage, the auto insurer is required to pay for the medical treatment first. Medicare will only cover medical expenses that are not covered by the at-fault (insured) auto insurance policy.

If Medicare mistakenly pays for an auto related injury, the at-fault carrier must reimburse Medicare. Failure to comply with the MSP can result in significant financial penalties for the insurance company such as a $1,000/day fine for every day it is not in compliance. Due to these stiff penalties, the adjuster will confirm the "Big 5" of the claimant, which is (1) first name, (2) last name, (3) date of birth, (4) social security number, and (5) gender. Medicare will also want to know the date of the loss so they can compare their medical bills with the at-fault carrier's. This information-gathering process can delay the time it takes to settle a bodily injury claim by several months.

Additionally, the MSP can also affect the settlement or judgment amount in a personal injury lawsuit. If the claimant's medical expenses have already been paid by another insurance company, that amount cannot be included in the settlement or judgment amount. This can significantly reduce the amount of money the claimant receives in compensation.

Overall, claimants should be aware of the MSP and how it might affect their medical treatment and claim settlement. They may wish to consult with an attorney who is familiar with the MSP and can help them navigate the complex regulations and requirements involved.

Brothers Grimm News

Grimm.news

FEBRUARY 10, 2024 | GODMOTHER-APPROVED NEWS | 1 SILVER PIECE

LOCAL CHICKEN CAUSES PANIC AMONG RESIDENTS: SKY FALLING, OR JUST A FALSE ALARM?

TATIANA TALESPINNER
LOCAL DESK

Residents of Enchanted Hollow's quiet suburbs were thrown into a state of panic earlier today when a young chicken, later identified as Chicken Little, began running along Goldfinch Street shouting, "The sky is falling! The sky is falling!"

Because the event occurred in the suburban portion of Goldfinch Street, it wasn't immediately remedied due to confusion over jurisdictional authority. The Fairy Godmother Task Force was originally dispatched to the scene until it was determined that the Enchanted Enforcers had jurisdiction.

"I couldn't believe my ears when I heard that chicken shouting about the sky falling," recounts Mabel Bluebird. "I've lived in Enchanted Hollow for more than 50 years, and I've never seen anything like it. I knew something had to be done, so I called the Fairy Godmother Task Force right away."

Mrs. Bluebird, a retired schoolteacher and longtime resident of Enchanted Hollow, was out for her morning walk when she heard Chicken Little's cries of the sky falling.

The Task Force arrived on scene minutes later. Upon arriving, they quickly secured the area; it was the Enforcers who determined there was no immediate danger. According to witnesses at the scene, Little had been testing a new device he recently invented when he became convinced that the sky was falling. His invention was meant to measure the weight and density of objects in the air.

The incident caused widespread panic and disruption, with many residents reportedly barricading themselves in their homes.

Little and Bushytail prior to the Enforcers arriving; photo by Bluebird

A rabbit who identified himself as Thistle Hoppsworth and a childhood friend of Little said, "I was just walking by when I saw Chicken running around in a panic. Now, he's been a bit high strung since childhood, but this was different. He was shouting that the sky was falling and that we were all in danger. I didn't know what to make of it at first, but I could tell he was genuinely scared."

Little believed that the machine malfunctioned causing the sky to collapse in on itself when in actuality he was just hit with an acorn. The Enchanted Enforcers soon discovered the acorn was dropped by noted acorn collector, Nutmeg Bushytail, at her residence 43 Red Oak, Goldfinch St.

According to Sergeant Detective Inspector Lily Greenleaf, "We take all reports seriously, no matter how outlandish they may seem at first. Our job is to keep the citizens of Enchanted Hollow safe, and we'll do whatever it takes to ensure their well-being."

Greenleaf, a seasoned detective who rose rapidly through the Enchanted Enforcers, busted the puppeteer fraud ring last year but not, unfortunately, before the young (Little cont. on p. 2)

Sergeant Detective Inspector Lily Greenleaf, Enforcer photo

LITTLE CONT. FROM PAGE 1

Pinocchio tragically died. Greenleaf assessed the situation, finding no evidence of any objects falling from the sky.

After a thorough investigation, she determined that the commotion was caused by Bushytail dropping a rare Golden Acorn she was attempting to store at her home until she could transport it to a museum.

"I feel just awful, and I hope that everyone is safe and sound," Bushytail said to reporters.

In a statement to the press, Mayor Willowbranch, first cousin twice removed of Judge Willowwitch, expressed relief that the situation had been resolved without incident.

"Thankfully, no one was hurt during the incident," stated the mayor. "I would like to assure the residents of Enchanted Hollow that we take their safety very seriously and are working closely with local authorities to investigate the matter."

The incident has sparked widespread debate on social media, with some users expressing concern about Little's mental state, others concerned about valuables being stored near their homes, and some questioning whether there may be a deeper meaning behind Little's warnings.

For now, Little is being held at a local hospital, where he is reportedly being treated for shock. The authorities are urging residents to remain calm and carry on with their daily activities, assuring them there is no reason to believe the sky is in fact falling.

We continue to watch this story for developments.

CULTURE VULTURE

Fae-Ree Rapport
Culture Desk

At the New Year Festival, Jun-Li Searches for Love

As the Year of the Rabbit drew to a close, thousands of people from all over the kingdom flocked to the New Year Festival in search of fortune, happiness, and love. Among the attendees was Jun-Li, the young and ambitious daughter of First Wife, Jin-Li, from Lingxiu.

One former beau, who declined to be named, stated Miss Li was "unattractive and lazy." Another stated on condition of anonymity that Mrs. Li was unloving and cruel and he did not want her for a mother-in-law.
(Culture cont. p. 6)

Jin-Li seen speaking to her daughter, Jun-Li; staff photo

BOOK LOOKS

Perry N. Quillscribe
Culture Desk

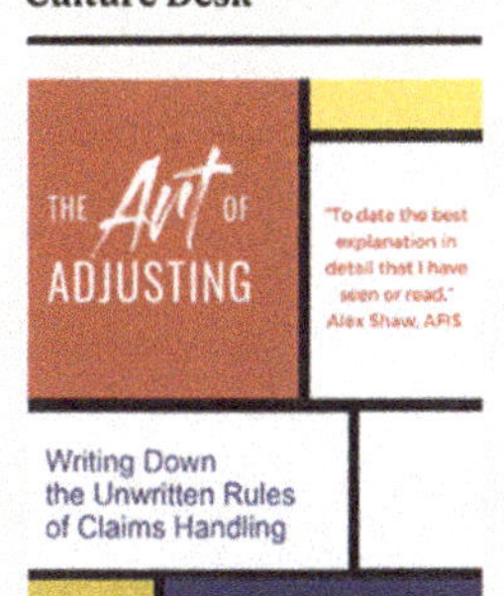

'The Art of Adjusting' Review: Mastering the Claim Game

An Insider's Guide to Elevating Claims Handling Skills and Tackling Industry Hurdles with Grace and Expertise

As a non-adjuster venturing into this realm, I was captivated by Roberts' insightful foray into the nuances of claims handling. This is not merely a guide; it's a masterclass for mid-career adjusters seeking to refine their skills and navigate the oft-tricky waters of their profession. While my usual beat at Brothers Grimm News has more to do with
(Book cont. p. 6)

WEATHER

Today:

The northern kingdoms will have snow with accumulation of 4" to 6" by nightfall.

The sun continues to pummel the southeastern area with temps so high camels won't want to work.

This drastic temperature contrast is stirring up the notorious Wolf Whirlwind storms across the rest of Fairytale Land. Expect swirling winds, sporadic frog showers, and flying carpet traffic jams.

BROTHERS GRIMM NEWS MORAL OF THE STORY

Dear Bros. Grimm:

The incident with Chicken Little serves as a cautionary tale against catastrophizing every little bump in the road, or on the head. While it's understandable to be shaken up by unexpected events, such as a fire, wolf whirlwind, or auto accident, it's important to realize that ads from personal injury attorneys boasting about their multi-million-dollar settlements may not be all they're cracked up to be.

Insurance policies are contracts that outline the specific terms and conditions under which the insurer will pay claims. The insurer is not obligated to pay in every possible scenario, but only for those that are covered by the policy. Policyholders must read and understand their insurance policies to know what is and isn't covered. Likewise, plaintiff attorneys should be truthful and ethical in their advertising. Claimants should be aware that these advertisements are designed to attract new clients for the law firm.

Attorneys often highlight that their initial consultations and services come at no up-front cost to policyholders. Little do their clients understand that their contingency fees and expenses will ultimately come out of any settlement recovered. This may leave policyholders and claimants with less money than they anticipated to repair damages.

Of course, there are benefits of seeking legal counsel for insurance claims. Consulting with an attorney on insurance claims can have several benefits for claimants, including:

- **Understanding rights:** An attorney can help the claimants understand the insurance policy and their rights under the policy.
- **Maximizing recovery:** An attorney can help claimants identify all the damages they are entitled to under their claim and negotiate with the insurance company to ensure that they receive a fair settlement.
- **Leveling the playing field:** Insurance companies have teams of attorneys (called panel counsel) working for them. Hiring an attorney can help claimants level the playing field and have someone on their side who is familiar with the insurance industry and can advocate for their interests.
- **Reducing stress:** Dealing with an insurance claim can be stressful and time-consuming. Hiring an attorney can help claimants focus on their recovery and let someone else handle the legal aspects of the claim.
- **Potentially avoiding litigation:** In some cases, having an attorney negotiate on behalf of the claimant can help the parties reach a settlement without the need for litigation.

Many claimants seek attorneys because they are unhappy with the handling of their claim. There is, however, a free service by the departments of insurance (DOI). It is most useful for first-party claimants since the policyholder is the person with whom the carrier has a legal contract (the policy). The departments of insurance can review the claim in some instances, encourage mediation or arbitration, or provide information about how to move the claim forward toward resolution. They also investigate complaints about carriers from the public. While third-party claimants can also lodge complaints about carriers, adjusters, or claims handling, and can still receive free advice from the departments of insurance, the services are mostly for policyholders.

Sincerely,

Begonia M. Gemforest

Morals Index

Glossary

A

Ab Initio: A Latin term meaning "from the beginning." See *Snow White and the Huntsman* and *Pinocchio.*

Agreed Estimate of Repairs: The estimate of the amount of damage and the cost of the repairs which are agreed upon by the insurance carrier and the owner's contractor of choice. See *Adjuster, Mend My Shoe.*

Agreed Value: When the carrier and the policyholder agree on the value of the item being insured. See *There Was an Old Woman Who Lived in a Shoe.*

Anti-Concurrent Causation: A loss is not covered when it is the result of two or more risks/perils/causes of loss, and one of those risks/perils/causes of loss is excluded in the policy. See *Little Dutch Boy.*

Appraisal: A dispute resolution method outlined in property policies which can help the property owner and carrier agree on the amount of damages to the structure. See *Sleeping Beauty.*

Arbitration: A method for resolving contested claims. It is similar to litigation in that a judge is present and will render a judgment and award. Insurance companies often participate in "inter-company arbitration" when they are unable to agree on settlement or subrogation. It is different from "mediation." See *Sleeping Beauty.*

At-Fault: The person who is liable, or responsible, for the accident. If the at-fault person has insurance, that carrier is known as the "at-fault carrier." See *Sleeping Beauty.*

Attractive Nuisance: Something that may not be particularly dangerous in and of itself, but may hold a particular interest to a child. The interesting thing should be kept out of the reach of children. See *Goldilocks and the Three Bears.*

Bad Faith: An act describing deliberately unfair conduct by a person or business. It is usually leveled against insurers. It is the opposite of good faith. See *Sleeping Beauty* and *Adjuster, Mend My Shoe.*

Boujee: Gen Z slang for "someone who overindulges in luxuries." It is generally used in a derogatory manner. Pronounced: BOO-jee. See *The Princess and the Pea.*

Cause of Loss: A peril or what causes the accident. Examples are fire, lightning, and smoke. See *Three Blind Mice.*

Claimant: A person making a claim on the insurance policy. The claimant can be either a first-party claimant or a third-party claimant. Pronounced: CLAIM-ant. See *Three Blind Mice.*

Claims-Made Policy: A type of policy which requires that losses are reported to the carrier during the policy period, even if the loss occurred before the policy began. This is different from an "occurrence policy." See *Sleeping Beauty.*

Co-Insurance: The concept that the insured will pay a pro-rata portion of the loss if that person is not adequately insured-to-value. See *There Was an Old Woman Who Lived in a Shoe.*

Copse: A grove of trees. Pronounced like "cops" as in the police officers of the Fairy Godmother Task Force. See *Bearskin.*

Deductible: The portion of the claim the insured will pay prior to receiving any money from the insurance carrier. See *The Three Little Pigs.*

Diary: A system for tracking the status of a claim. See *Sleeping Beauty.*

Djinn: Genie. As in three wishes. Lives in a bottle. Pronounced: Gin, as in the drink. See *How the Camel Got His Hump.*

Drop Down Coverage: A feature of the umbrella policy in which the umbrella policy will "drop down" to insure a loss that is not covered by the underlying policy. See *It's Raining, It's Pouring.*

Endorsement: Wording in a policy that changes, either by adding or deleting, coverage in an insurance policy. See *Three Blind Mice.*

Examination Under Oath (EUO): A legal proceeding in which a person is asked to answer questions while under oath, typically as part of an insurance claim investigation. See *How the Camel Got His Hump.*

Exception to the Exclusion: Wording in the exclusion that adds coverage back to the policy. It is found in the exclusion language. See *Three Blind Mice* and *Little Dutch Boy.*

Excess Policy: Policy that has higher limits than the underlying policy. It is usually a following form unlike the umbrella policy. See *It's Raining, It's Pouring.*

Exclusion: Wording in a policy that solely deletes coverage. See *Three Blind Mice.*

Fabulist: A person who composes or tells tales. Pronounced: FAB-you-list. See *Introduction.*

Fixtures: Property attached to a building, such as light sconces, cabinets, ceiling fans. Once installed, they become part of the building. See *The Magpie's Nest.*

Following Form: A type of excess policy that follows the terms and conditions of the underlying policy. See *It's Raining, It's Pouring.*

First-Party Claimant: Insured or policyholder. The insured will make a claim against their policy; therefore, they are a claimant. They are not to be confused with a Third-Party Claimant. See *Sleeping Beauty.*

G

Good Faith Claims Handling: The concept that insurance companies must treat insureds fairly. See *Adjuster, Mend My Shoe* and *Rumpelstiltskin.*

Hazard: Something that increases the likelihood of a peril or loss. It is different from "risk" which is the probability of a loss. It is also different from "peril" which is the cause of the loss or accident. See *The Magpie's Nest.*

Heath: Uncultivated area of land. It rhymes with "Keith." See *Bearskin.*

Hookah: A pipe with a long, flexible tube attached to a bowl with water. The smoke is pulled through the bowl. Pronounced: HOO-kah. See *The Historic Fart.*

Hussar: Horse mounted soldiers. Pronounced: HUS-zar See *Bearskin.*

I

Indaba: A conference to discuss a serious topic. Pronounced: in-DA-bah. See *How the Camel Got His Hump.*

Insurance-to-Value (ITV): Concept used in insurance which aims to ensure that the policy limit for a property accurately reflects its current value. It is particularly relevant in property insurance, such as homeowner insurance or commercial property insurance. See *There Was an Old Woman Who Lived in a Shoe.*

Jeremiah: Cockney slang for "fire." See *Pinocchio.*

Juleidah: Shahzadi's name. Pronounced: JULE-lah-DUH. See *The Shahzadi in the Suit of Leather.*

Liability: Responsibility. Pronounced: Lie-uh-BILL-uh-TEE. See *Humpty Dumpty* and *Jack and Jill.*

M

Made Whole: A concept in subrogation which refers to the idea that an insured should not be left in a worse financial position after a loss is reimbursed by the at-fault carrier. See *Sleeping Beauty.*

Malika: Arabic for queen. Pronounced: muh-LEE-kuh. See *The Shahzadi in the Suit of Leather.*

Material Fact: A critical piece of information or fact which, if the carrier had known about it, would have prevented the insurer from underwriting the risk or caused the insurer to write the policy with higher premiums or a higher deductible. See *Snow White and the Huntsman* and *Pinocchio.*

Medicare Secondary Payer (MSP): A federal law that requires certain types of insurance to be the primary payer for healthcare services, even when Medicare is also involved. See *The Princess and the Pea.*

Mediation: A method for resolving contested claims. It is a type of negotiation where a mediator, or independent third-party, will attempt to bring the two sides together for an agreed settlement. It is different than "arbitration." See *Sleeping Beauty.*

Misrepresentation: False statement meant to mislead or conceal facts. If the misrepresentation is relied upon by the carrier, the carrier may cancel the policy. See *Snow White and the Huntsman* and *Pinocchio.*

N

NBD: Gen Z slang for "no big deal." See *The Princess and the Pea.*

NPC: Gen Z slang for "Non-Player Character." These are characters in video games who are not controlled by the player of the game. It can also refer to an unimportant person. See *The Princess and the Pea.*

National Association of Insurance Commissioners (NAIC): The association of all the states, territories, and possessions of the US insurance commissioners. See *Patty Cake, Patty Cake.*

Negligence: Fault. Liability. Failure of care. See *Humpty Dumpty* and *Jack and Jill.*

Nepo Baby: Gen Z for a child of a famous person. See *The Princess and the Pea.*

Occurrence: An accident, loss, or damage due to a covered peril or because the insured is legally liable for the cause of the accident. See *Snow White and the Seven Dwarfs.*

Occurrence Policy: A type of policy which covers loss or damage which occurred during the policy period. It is different than a "claims-made policy" which can provide coverage for losses or damage that occurred prior to the beginning of the policy dates. See *Sleeping Beauty.*

Pelf: Archaic term for money. It could be where English get the word "pilfer." Or the author could be making that up. Pronounced: "Elf" with a "p" in front of it. See *Patty Cake, Patty Cake.*

Peril: The cause of the loss or claim. It is different from "risk" which is the probability of a loss and "hazard" which is something that increases the likelihood of a loss. Examples are water, hail, wind, and ice. See *Three Blind Mice.*

Permutation: Lots of different ways to organize something. Pronounced: PER-mu-TAY-shun. See *Suvannahamsa-Jataka.*

Policyholder Release: A legal document which acts in the same manner as a release for a third-party claimant indicating the insured may no longer seek additional payments for the loss in question. It is usually used in the instance of suspicious claims. See *How the Camel Got His Hump.*

Prejudice: Act that can harm or impair a decision. See *Snow White and the Seven Dwarfs.*

Premium: The rate the insured pays for the insurance policy. See *The Three Little Pigs.*

Proof of Loss: A formal statement used in property claims which serves as evidence of the loss incurred by the policyholder and includes a detailed description of the loss or damage, the date and cause of the loss, and the amount of the claim being made. It is different from a "release." See *How the Camel Got His Hump.*

Qadi: A judge. Pronounced: KAH-dee. See *The Shahzadi in the Suit of Leather.*

Qasr: Palace or castle. Pronounced: KAS-ir. See *The Shahzadi in the Suit of Leather.*

Rajah: A prince or a king of India. Pronounced: RAH-juh. See *The Historic Fart.*

Rampion: Green stuff to put in salads. Supposed to be good for you. Pronounced: RAM-pee-un. Rhymes with "onion." See *Rapunzel.*

Reasonableness: Fairness; what the average person would or would not do in a similar situation. See *Rumpelstiltskin.*

Recorded Statement (aka Recorded Interview or R/S): An investigation tool used by adjusters to obtain the persons who have been in a loss recollection of events. The statement is recorded to preserve the facts since memories tend to fade over time. See *Sleeping Beauty* and *The Princess and the Pea.*

Release: A legal document used in liability losses. The release will be signed by the third-party claimant (or their representatives) stating that in exchange for an item (usually money), the claimant will not pursue any future claims, additional damages, or sue the at-fault party (the insured) related to the same injury in the future. It is different from a "proof of loss." See *How the Camel Got His Hump.*

Remedial: Steps taken to correct a deficiency. Pronounced: re-MEE-dee-ul. See *Snow White and the Seven Dwarfs.*

Reporting Form: A type of property policy endorsement in which the insured will report their inventory monthly or quarterly. The carrier will adjust the premiums based on the report from the insured. The goal is to minimize over- and under-insurance. See *There Was an Old Woman Who Lived in a Shoe.*

Reservation of Rights (ROR): A letter carriers send to policyholders alerting them to the fact there is a question regarding coverage. See *Snow White and the Seven Dwarfs.*

Retroactive Date: A specific date in the insurance policy which denotes the beginning of the coverage period for losses which occurred before the policy was issued. See *Sleeping Beauty.*

Risk: The possibility of loss or damage to persons or property. It is different from "hazard" which is something that causes the likelihood of a loss and from "peril" which is the cause of the loss. See *Three Blind Mice.*

S

Shahzadi: Arabic for princess. Pronounced: shah-ZAH-dee See *The Shahzadi in the Suit of Leather.*

Snack (as in "a whole snack"): Gen Z slang for "cute." See *The Princess and the Pea.*

Special Investigation Unit (SIU): A division in the insurance company which investigates insurance fraud. See *Snow White and the Huntsman* and *Pinocchio.*

Stand Alone Policy: A type of excess policy that has its own policy provisions and conditions. This could lead to gaps in coverage. See *It's Raining, It's Pouring.*

Statute of Limitations (aka Prescription Period): A time limit for filing a claim or a lawsuit based on the sustained loss or damage. The limitations are specified by the policy and state laws. See *Sleeping Beauty.*

Strictly Liable: Legal theory that the insured is responsible for a loss or damages even if they were not at fault for the accident. It is liability without regard to fault and usually seen in defective or dangerous situations or when children are involved. See *Goldilocks and the Three Bears.*

Sublimit: A special limit in a policy which places a lower policy amount on specific items such as money, jewelry, and silverware. See *Jack and the Beanstalk.*

Subrogation: A fancy insurance word for "reimbursement." See *Sleeping Beauty.*

Sultana: Wife of the sultan, a civil ruler. Pronounced: sul-TAN-ah. See *The Shahzadi in the Suit of Leather.*

Supplement: Additional damages found after the initial inspection and once repairs are underway. Repairs should cease, the adjuster notified, so that another inspection and another agreed estimate of repairs obtained. See *Adjuster, Mend My Shoe.*

Sus: Gen Z slang for "suspicious"." Pronounced: SUH-ssss. Not to be confused with "sussed" (see below). See *The Princess and the Pea.*

Sussed: Past tense of "suss" which means "guess." Pronounced: SUH-ssed. See *Bearskin.*

TBH: Slang for "to be honest." See T*he Princess and the Pea.*

TYSM: Gen Z slang for "thank you so much." Don't worry. The author had to look it up, too. See *The Princess and the Pea.*

Temerity: Nerve. Pronounced: tah-MER-ah-tee. See *Bearskin.*

Third-Party Claimant: A person who is making a claim against the insured's policy. This person is the third party to the insurance policy. The first person being the policyholder; the second is the carrier. See *Patty Cake, Patty Cake.*

Trigger: The event or occurrence which must happen for the insurance policy to respond. See *It's Raining, It's Pouring.*

Umbrella Policy: A policy that is in excess of the underlying policy, such as a homeowner or auto policy. It often has "drop down" coverage. See *It's Raining, It's Pouring.*

Vermilion: Scarlet red. Pronounced: VER-million. See *The Practical Bride.*

Void: Cancel as if something never existed. This is usually used where fraud and misrepresentation are present in a claim or insurance application. See *Snow White and the Huntsman* and *Pinocchio.*

About the Author

In a magical land not so far away, there is a wise and witty fairy godmother named Chantal M. Roberts, CPCU, AIC, RPA. She doesn't have a magic wand or a crystal ball, but she does have something even better: the power to make insurance and claims concepts understandable and enjoyable.

With more than 20 years' experience as a multi-lined claims adjuster, claims manager, and an adjunct professor of risk management and insurance at the mythical Borough of Manhattan Community College, City University of New York, Chantal is an expert in her field. But she was not content keep her knowledge to herself.

Chantal is an award-nominated author who has previously written two books: one for mid-career adjusters, *The Art of Adjusting: Writing Down the Unwritten Rules of Claims Handling*, and a creative nonfiction story about a 400-year-old French playwright, Molière, *A Love Story: How the Heartland Fell in Love With a 400-Year-Old French Comedic Playwright*. But it is this book that truly showcases her fairy magic, providing laypeople with a better understanding of property and casualty insurance and claims so they can become their own best advocates.

Chantal hoped for some help with her chores from the birds outside her window when she took the gig to be an insurance fairy godmother, but she begrudgingly admits they aren't much help at all. Fortunately this doesn't stop her from spreading the joy and wonder of insurance and claims concepts to all who seek her guidance. When she isn't busy typing away on her keyboard (or at least trying to train small woodland creatures to do her chores), Chantal can be found at her castle in Overland Park, Kansas, with her extremely tolerant husband, her loving dog, and a cat who ignores her, where they live happily ever after.

The End

www.ingramcontent.com/pod-product-compliance
Lightning Source LLC
Chambersburg PA
CBHW040142200326
41458CB00025B/6343

* 9 7 8 1 7 3 7 4 2 6 8 5 1 *